The Repair Rule

The Repair Rule

How to Fix a Bad Moment Before It Becomes a Bigger Problem

Kaia Solander

Mindful Pages

Published in 2026

ISBN: 9789309333552 (PB)
ISBN: 9789309333651 (eBook)

Published by

Mindful Pages
Imprint of Alpha Editions LLC
312 W. 2nd St #1834
Casper, WY 82601, USA

This book was developed using advanced writing tools to support the drafting and ideation process. All content has been thoughtfully curated, refined, and reviewed to ensure quality and relevance.

Content

Introduction

On 13 April 1970, above the Pacific and more than 200,000 miles from Houston, Apollo 13's service module cracked open with a sound astronaut Jim Lovell later described as a bang, followed by a shudder through the spacecraft. In Mission Control, men in white shirts listened to static, telemetry, clipped voices, the dry scratch of pencils on paper. Something had gone wrong; everyone knew it before they knew what it was. The first task was not heroism. It was not even a solution. It was repair: stabilise the moment enough to keep the next decision from becoming worse.

The famous line, "Houston, we've had a problem," has survived because it holds a discipline many intimate conversations lack. It names a break without panicking the room. It does not pretend the damage is minor, and it does not waste oxygen assigning moral failure. The room did not explode. That restraint mattered. Before engineers could improvise a carbon-dioxide filter, before flight controllers could recalculate power, before the crew could turn a damaged spacecraft into a lifeboat, they had to preserve a shared field of attention. One bad moment had to be kept from breeding a larger one.

Most human conflict is less dramatic than Apollo 13, but it follows a surprisingly similar law. A rupture rarely stays the size it was when it first appeared. The interrupted sentence, the sharp tone at the sink, the delayed reply to a message, the joke that lands with a sting: each can remain a small fracture or widen into a story about respect, care, loyalty, or safety. Conflict has its own weather. A room can cool quickly, but the air still carries the metallic smell of the storm. Two people may stop speaking about what happened and still organise themselves around it. They become careful in odd places, brittle in familiar ones. Then came the next one.

The paradox of conflict is that the faster people try to get past it, the longer it can last. A conversation ends, but the body keeps the minutes. One person remembers the volume; the other remembers being corrected. One remembers the accusation; the other remembers the absence of apology. The calendar moves on, yet the relationship does not quite move with it. The next disagreement arrives preloaded, already carrying evidence from the previous trial. What appears to be an argument about dishes, timing, money, sex, children, tone, or whose family is being prioritised may be animated by a smaller, older fact: last time, the hurt was left unnamed.

There is a kind of politeness that is really avoidance in formal dress. It says "fine" with a hard mouth. It changes the subject with impressive speed. It acts normal while quietly revising the other person's reliability downward. The injury is not always large enough to justify a confrontation, yet not small enough to disappear. So it goes into storage. The storage has a cost. It changes how generously people interpret one another. It makes neutral phrases sound loaded. It turns forgetfulness into evidence, fatigue into rejection, distraction into contempt. A relationship can become crowded with unprocessed moments that nobody meant to keep.

Repair is the art of preventing that accumulation. It is not the same as winning, explaining, forgiving, analysing, or solving the entire issue before bedtime. It is the smaller and more urgent skill of restoring enough safety for two people to stay human in each other's presence. Resolution asks, "What is the answer?" Repair asks, "What happened between us, and what must be tended before the answer is even reachable?" That distinction is not sentimental. It is practical. People think better when they do not feel dismissed. They listen more accurately when they are not preparing a defence. They negotiate more fairly when connection has not been left bleeding quietly in the corner.

John and Julie Gottman's long-running work on couples, developed from research beginning at the University of Washington in Seattle in the 1970s and 1980s, made one point especially difficult to ignore: the health of a relationship is not measured by the absence of conflict. The Gottman Institute has repeatedly argued, based on decades of observational research, that all couples disagree and that many recurring issues are never solved in any final, tidy sense. The more revealing question is what people do after strain enters the room. Do they soften? Do they make a repair attempt? Do they notice when the other person is trying? Or do they become skilled archivists of injury, filing away every slight for future use?

That research is often misread as reassurance that conflict is harmless if people love each other enough. It is not. Conflict becomes corrosive when it teaches the nervous system to expect humiliation, dismissal, pursuit, withdrawal, or punishment. A couple can argue every week and remain tender if they know how to come back; another couple can argue twice a year and leave lasting damage if those arguments are laced with contempt or silence. Frequency is not the whole measure. The more exact measure is whether rupture is followed by repair, and whether repair is followed by altered behaviour. A door slammed once may frighten. A door slammed repeatedly becomes architecture.

The repairable moment is often embarrassingly ordinary. Someone walks in after work, still carrying the day on their face, and the other person begins with a complaint instead of greeting them. A phone glows on the table during a conversation that was meant to matter. A text message receives a thumbs-up where warmth was expected. A partner makes a practical suggestion when the other was asking, indirectly but sincerely, to be understood. None of these moments is catastrophic by itself. That is precisely why they are dangerous. Because they seem too small to name, they are allowed to harden into private interpretations. "I am not important." "They always make it about them." "There is no point telling the truth here." The fracture is hairline at first; the pressure does the rest.

Repair begins where performance ends. It does not require theatrical vulnerability, a perfect script, or a prolonged emotional inquest after every awkward exchange. Many people resist repair because they imagine it as a heavy ritual: two chairs facing each other, a solemn tone, the entire relationship spread out like evidence. But the most useful repair is often brief. It can be a sentence at the doorway. It can be a return after ten minutes. It can be a correction of tone, a clean apology, a small agreement about what happens next time. Its power lies in proportion. Too little, and the hurt remains vague. Too much, and the relationship becomes a courtroom with cushions.

The essential movement is simple, though not always easy: acknowledge the impact, clarify the intent, and agree one small change that prevents the same collision next time. Each part protects against a common failure. Acknowledging impact prevents the injured person from having to prove that something landed badly. Clarifying intent prevents the moment from becoming a false biography of character. Agreeing one small change prevents repair from floating away as a mood rather than becoming visible in conduct. Without impact, repair becomes self-defence. Without intent, it becomes accusation. Without change, it becomes theatre.

A small example reveals the whole structure. At breakfast, one partner interrupts while the other is explaining a plan for the weekend. The interruption is not vicious; it is efficient, perhaps even well meant. But the speaker stops, folds the napkin, and becomes quieter. A poor response treats the silence as moodiness or insists, "I was only trying to help." A better repair notices the altered room. "I cut across you just then. I can see it made you pull back. I was trying to solve the timing, not shut you down. I'll let you finish before I jump in." Nothing grand has happened. That is the point. A repeat pattern has been interrupted before it becomes the evening's atmosphere.

The difficulty is that most people attempt repair while still inside the threat of being wrong. The human mind, when accused, becomes a barrister with astonishing speed. It corrects details, produces counter-examples, questions tone, demands context, and searches the past for acquittal. The body joins in: chest tight, voice faster, jaw set, politeness sharpened into a blade. A person may say, "I want to understand," while every muscle is preparing to win. In that state, even accurate words can become hostile instruments. The first repair is often not spoken to the other person at all. It is the internal shift from proving a case to protecting the connection.

There are moments when the wisest sentence is not explanatory but regulating. "I need a minute, and I am coming back." That line is different from disappearance. It contains both a boundary and a promise. It recognises that timing is not a decorative matter in conflict; it is part of the ethics of the exchange. Speak too soon and the repair becomes another injury. Wait too long and the story sets like plaster. One person may need words to feel safe; another may need space to think without being followed. The clash between those needs can become its own conflict unless the couple learns to repair the process as well as the subject.

Digital life has made this harder. In May 2023, the Pew Research Center reported that a large majority of American adults owned smartphones; in Britain, Ofcom's 2023 communications reports likewise described mobile devices as central to daily communication. The exact figures matter less than the visible behaviour: people now conduct delicate relational moments through rectangles that flatten tone, accelerate reply, and preserve every wounded phrase. A message sent from a bus queue in Manchester at 8.17 on a wet Tuesday can become an exhibit by dinner. The phone invites speed precisely when slowness would be kinder. Sarcasm travels badly in blue bubbles. Silence travels even worse.

Yet the limitation must be named honestly. Not every rupture should be met with a neat repair attempt. When a pattern includes intimidation, coercion, repeated contempt, deliberate humiliation, or fear of what might happen if one speaks plainly, the language of mutual repair can be misused to keep the more vulnerable person engaged in an unsafe cycle. A person cannot repair a relationship alone by becoming more skilful at absorbing harm. There are conflicts that require distance, outside support, firmer boundaries, or a refusal to keep negotiating the terms of basic dignity. Repair is not a demand to stay. It is a discipline for moments where both people are still capable of shared responsibility.

Still, most relationships do not fail only in the obvious catastrophes. They erode in the small, repeated places where people decide, often silently, that it is not worth bringing themselves fully into the room. The tragedy is not always that love disappears; sometimes it is that love becomes administratively efficient and emotionally undernourished. People co-ordinate calendars, pay bills, arrange childcare, answer messages, visit relatives, load dishwashers, and slowly stop risking the truth of their experience. They do not lack commitment. They lack a trustworthy method for dealing with the bad ten minutes before it becomes a bad month.

A repair habit changes the scale of conflict. It gives proportion back to moments that would otherwise swell beyond their original size. Instead of asking whether the relationship is broken, two people can ask what exactly cracked. Instead of debating who is the more injured party, they can identify the behaviour that made safety dip.

Instead of promising wholesale transformation, they can agree to one observable change: no problem-solving before the other person has finished speaking; no serious argument by text after a certain point; a return time after taking space; a check-in after a tense family visit; a phrase that signals the old loop is starting. These are not decorative niceties. They are load-bearing beams.

The deepest promise of repair is not that conflict will become pleasant. It will not. A repairable life still includes irritation, mismatched needs, badly timed sentences, fatigue, defensiveness, and the occasional astonishing stupidity of saying exactly the wrong thing when tenderness was available. But repair changes what happens next. It gives people a way to return without crawling, to apologise without collapsing, to explain without erasing impact, and to change without staging a moral performance. It also gives the injured person something more useful than a verdict: evidence that the other person can notice, care, and adjust.

The choice at the centre of every bad moment is smaller than pride wants it to be and larger than comfort admits. Will this become proof, or will it become information? Proof ends curiosity. It builds a case, recruits the past, and waits for repetition. Information asks what the moment reveals about timing, fear, expectation, habit, or need. The same incident can become either. A missed call can become proof of indifference or information about a fragile time of day. A sharp reply can become proof of disrespect or information about overload and a missing boundary. This distinction is not a trick for making harm harmless. It is a way of keeping harm from writing more of the future than it deserves.

The hairline crack returns whenever pressure returns. That is the nature of relationships, not evidence of failure. People meet each other at their unfinished edges: hunger, shame, loyalty to old family rules, terror of being controlled, terror of being left, the private arithmetic of who has carried more. The task is not to become frictionless. Frictionless people are usually not close; they are managed. The task is to make contact survivable enough that truth does not have to disguise itself as anger, and care does not have to arrive too late to be believed.

A bad moment asks for a decision before anyone feels noble enough to make it. The decision is whether to protect the self-image or protect the bond; whether to keep explaining, or to measure the impact; whether to demand perfect understanding now, or to make one small agreement that earns trust later. The Repair Rule begins in that narrow space. It treats conflict not as a verdict on love, but as a test of what people do after contact hurts. The future of a relationship is often hidden there: not in the rupture itself, but in the first honest attempt to mend it before the next pressure comes.

Chapter 1
What Repair Is Now

The argument does not begin as an argument. It begins with a small interruption over something ordinary: a plan, a bill, a message, a child's bedtime, the shape of the evening. One person is speaking, still trying to find the exact words, when the other steps across the sentence with a correction or a practical answer. Nothing breaks loudly. There is no shouting, no slammed door, no dramatic accusation. Only a pause. A glance away. A cup placed down a little too carefully.

The interrupted person says, "It's fine," but the room knows it is not fine. The words do not match the temperature. The conversation resumes, yet something has tilted. A few minutes later the injured person becomes less generous, the other becomes confused, and both begin to behave as if the problem is either too small to mention or too large to touch. By evening, what could have been named in one honest sentence has become a private file of evidence.

This is how many bad moments grow: not by malice, but by mismanagement. The first injury is often slight enough to dismiss. The second injury is the dismissal itself. When a rupture is not named, each person is left to complete the story alone. One fills the silence with hurt; the other fills it with innocence. One thinks, "They knew what they did." The other thinks, "I cannot do anything right." The original moment disappears beneath interpretation, and interpretation is rarely kind when it is forced to work without reassurance.

Repair matters because closeness is not maintained by the absence of strain. It is maintained by what happens after strain appears. People who care about each other will still speak sharply, miss cues, interrupt, withdraw, over-explain, defend, minimise, and get the timing wrong. Good intentions do not prevent all impact. Tenderness does not guarantee skill. A relationship can contain real love and still become unsafe in ordinary moments if neither person knows how to return without turning the return into another contest.

The central tension is deceptively simple: most people want the comfort of being close again, but they do not want the exposure required to repair. To repair is to admit that something landed badly, even if it was not meant badly. It asks a person to remain dignified while being corrected by another person's pain. It asks the injured person to speak with enough clarity that the other can respond, not merely suffer under accusation. It asks both to resist the tempting theatre of total innocence.

The stakes are immediate because unaddressed ruptures change the next conversation before it starts. A partner who felt brushed aside yesterday may hear efficiency as contempt today. Someone who felt blamed last night may hear a simple question as prosecution in the morning. The trouble is no longer only the topic being discussed. The trouble is the emotional residue attached to the topic: the tone that returns, the guarded face, the familiar sinking feeling that says, "Here we are again." A relationship does not need constant drama to become exhausting. It only needs enough unrepaired moments for ordinary contact to feel risky.

The stakes are also cumulative. When small injuries are left unnamed, people begin to protect themselves in subtle ways. They edit their needs before speaking. They become overly careful, or deliberately careless. They stop asking for reassurance because asking has begun to feel humiliating. They turn a simple disagreement into a test of character because the present moment is carrying the weight of old ones. The cup placed down too carefully becomes a signal. The silence after a joke becomes a warning. The relationship starts communicating through weather rather than words.

Repair is not the same as resolution, and this distinction is the doorway into a more intelligent way of handling conflict. Resolution tries to settle the issue; repair restores enough safety for the issue to be approached without further damage. One asks for an answer. The other makes an answer possible. The movement begins with recognising why small ruptures grow, then turns towards the difference between solving the problem and restoring the bond, before arriving at a practical sequence for bad moments: pause, name the impact, clarify intent, take responsibility where it belongs, and make one small agreement that can survive ordinary pressure.

There is a quiet discipline in learning not to inflate every hurt into a verdict, and not to shrink every hurt into nothing. Repair lives between those failures. It refuses the cruelty of "you are overreacting" and the hopelessness of "this always happens." It treats the bad moment as real, but not necessarily final. It asks for enough honesty to name the crack while it is still small, enough humility to hear how it landed, and enough restraint to avoid turning the repair itself into another wound.

The question, then, is not whether two people will have bad moments. They will. The sharper question is what happens in the first few seconds after the room changes: when the cup is set down too carefully, when "fine" does not sound like safety, when one person feels the old story starting to gather force. Does the moment get tended while it is still small, or does it begin its quiet work of becoming something larger?

Why Small Ruptures Grow

At the University of Washington in Seattle in the 1980s, John Gottman and Robert Levenson began doing something deceptively plain: they watched couples talk. Not in the abstract language of compatibility or romance, but in the visible grammar of ordinary strain: interrupted sentences, tightened mouths, humour that landed too hard, eyes that moved away at the exact second a partner needed them to stay. The outcome of that work, developed over years of observation and later associated with what became known as the "Love Lab", helped shift the serious study of relationships away from grand declarations and towards micro-moments. What damaged closeness was not always the spectacular argument. Often it was the small uncorrected injury that taught the next conversation how to begin.

A couple can leave the table believing nothing has happened because nobody raised a voice. Yet the room has already recorded a difference. One person has swallowed a sentence. The other has mistaken silence for peace. A plate is rinsed with unusual force. A message later receives a reply that is technically civil and emotionally cold. The small moment does stay. It waits, not as a clear memory at first, but as a change in posture, a shorter answer, a reluctance to reach first.

Small ruptures grow because human beings are meaning-making creatures before they are fair witnesses. When something hurts, the mind does not merely preserve the event; it begins to interpret it. An interruption is not only an interruption. It may become evidence of being dismissed. A delayed apology is not only poor timing. It may become evidence that the other person values comfort over care. A distracted glance at a phone is not only distraction. It may become a quiet vote on one's importance. The visible behaviour is brief, but the meaning attached to it can last for days. That is the first enlargement: pain becomes story.

The difficulty is that many small hurts occur precisely between people who are trying not to make trouble. Kindness, when frightened, often disguises itself as avoidance. Someone says "fine" because the alternative seems disproportionate. Someone changes the subject because raising the issue feels petty. Someone tells themselves they are being mature by letting it go, even though the body has not let it go at all. The face smooths over before the feeling has finished moving. This is not peace; it is compression. A folded grievance takes up less space in the moment, but it does not vanish. It becomes denser.

Avoidance creates a vacuum, and a vacuum invites guessing. If the hurt person does not say, "When you cut me off, I felt as if my point did not matter," the other person may invent a more flattering explanation: tiredness, mood, over-sensitivity, nothing at all. If the other person does not say, "I interrupted because I was anxious about time, not because I thought you were wrong," the injured person may invent a harsher one. Neither person may be lying. Both may be protecting themselves from exposure. Yet the absence of naming turns the relationship into a courtroom without testimony. The verdict still arrives.

This is why "fine" deserves suspicion in the aftermath of a rupture. Sometimes it means exactly what it says: the sting has passed, no further tending is required, the bond is steady. But often "fine" means "I cannot risk this conversation yet." It can mean "I do not trust that you will hear me without making me defend my hurt." It can mean "I am checking whether you notice." It can even mean "I am punishing you a little, because speaking plainly would make me feel too needy." The word is small, but its cargo can be heavy. The test is not the vocabulary; it is the behaviour that follows. If warmth returns, perhaps fine is fine. If the room stays altered, the word has become a curtain.

Research on emotion suppression helps explain why these moments do not simply dissolve because people behave politely. In a widely cited 1993 study, psychologists James J. Gross and Robert W. Levenson examined what happens when people suppress emotional expression while viewing evocative material. Their work helped establish that holding expression down can change what is visible without making the internal response disappear. The relational implication is plain enough without forcing the science beyond its purpose: a person can look composed while remaining physiologically stirred, mentally active, and socially less available. Suppression edits the display; it does not necessarily complete the feeling.

In close relationships, that edited display can mislead both parties. The person who hides the hurt may begin to feel virtuous and lonely at once. They have not "made a fuss", but they have also denied the other person access to useful information. The person who caused the hurt may accept the quiet as proof of innocence. They may even feel irritated later when the injury resurfaces, because from their point of view the matter was closed. Here the ledger begins. Not a literal ledger, usually; few people sit down and itemise each slight with deliberate cruelty. It is more subtle than that. The nervous system remembers patterns. The mind stores examples. The next time something similar happens, the old entry lights up.

A single interrupted sentence can become a week of distance by a chain so ordinary that nobody recognises it as escalation. On Monday evening, one partner starts describing a difficult exchange at work. The other, already tired and eager to help, cuts in with a solution. The speaker stops. "Forget it," they say, but softly enough to make the line seem deniable. On Tuesday, when asked about their day, they answer, "Nothing much." On Wednesday, they do not mention an invitation they might have discussed together. On Thursday, the other person senses the coolness and becomes defensive: "You have been off with me all week." By Friday, the original interruption has disappeared from view. The argument is now about attitude, distance, tone, and who is making life difficult.

The rupture has grown because it has changed categories. At first it was behavioural: one person interrupted. Then it became emotional: one person felt dismissed. Then it became interpretive: "They do not care what I think." Then it became strategic: "I will stop telling them things." By the time it becomes relational, the question has swollen into something like, "Can I trust you with my inner life?" This is how minor injuries become major evidence. The behaviour that began it may have lasted three seconds, but the meaning was given time to recruit history.

A second example appears in the work of the Harvard Negotiation Project, associated with Roger Fisher and William Ury's *Getting to Yes*, first published in 1981 in the United States. Although the book belongs to the field of negotiation rather than intimacy, one of its enduring distinctions is useful here: separate the people from the problem. In a workplace negotiation room, a badly phrased objection can become personal insult if it is not clarified quickly. In a kitchen, the same principle applies with higher emotional voltage. "That plan will not work" may be heard as "You are incompetent." "We need to leave by six" may land as "You are always the problem." When the people become the problem, repair becomes harder because every practical issue now carries identity threat.

This does not mean every slight deserves immediate examination. There is a credible limitation here, and it matters. Some moments truly are too small to pursue. People are tired. Speech is imperfect. A relationship that interrogates every clumsy phrase can become airless, more anxious than honest. Not every silence is a wound; not every distracted glance is abandonment; not every brusque answer contains a hidden truth. The aim is not microscopic grievance-hunting. That would turn repair into surveillance. The wiser distinction is between a moment that passes cleanly and a moment that leaves a residue. The residue is the clue.

Residue can be observed. It appears in behaviour. Someone becomes formal where they are usually relaxed. They withhold ordinary affection, not as a declared boundary but as a quiet retreat. They answer the surface question while refusing the emotional invitation underneath it. They perform helpfulness with a faint edge. They say "do what you want" while clearly hoping the other person will not. These are not reliable proof of wrongdoing, but they are evidence that something remains unprocessed. The ledger has not been cleared. A relationship that ignores such signals teaches both people to communicate indirectly, and indirect communication is expensive. It wastes time, attention, and goodwill.

The cost is especially high for thoughtful, competent people because they are often skilled at functioning while unsettled. They can attend meetings, meet deadlines, send careful messages, manage children, pay bills, and remain outwardly reasonable while inwardly accumulating disappointment. Efficiency masks drift. The calendar fills; the conversation waits. What looks like maturity may be a refined ability to postpone emotional truth until it becomes heavier than the original incident. This is why high-functioning relationships can still become brittle. They run smoothly at the level of tasks while starving at the level of repair.

Small ruptures also grow because memory is not a neutral archive. Once a person feels hurt in a repeated way, they search the past for supporting material. A partner who feels routinely interrupted may remember not only Monday evening but last month's dinner, the family gathering where their story was corrected, the meeting they once described where nobody listened. The current injury becomes a magnet. It pulls old fragments towards itself and arranges them into a pattern. Sometimes the pattern is accurate. Sometimes it is distorted by fear. Usually it contains some truth and some heat. Without repair, the other person meets the heat and misses the truth.

This is where good intentions often fail. The person who caused the hurt leans on motive: "I was trying to help." The injured person leans on impact: "You made me feel small." Both statements may be true, but placed badly they collide. Motive without impact sounds like evasion. Impact without room for motive can sound like character assassination. The rupture grows when either truth is used to cancel the other. It shrinks when both can stand in the same room: what happened, how it landed, what was meant, and what should happen differently next time.

The small ledger is not cleared by dramatic promises. In fact, drama may deepen mistrust if it is not followed by a visible alteration in conduct. A partner who says, "I never want to hurt you," but interrupts again at the next tense moment has offered emotion without evidence. A colleague who apologises warmly for excluding someone from a decision, then repeats the exclusion in the next email chain, has made the apology decorative. Trust is not rebuilt by intensity of feeling alone. It is measured in the next observable choice: waiting before responding, asking one clarifying question, returning at the promised time, naming the tension before it spreads.

There is another reason small ruptures grow: shame makes people clumsy. To hear that one has hurt someone, especially unintentionally, can produce a sudden urge to escape the image of being careless, selfish, or cruel. That escape often takes the form of correction. "That is not what happened." "You are taking it the wrong way." "I said sorry already." "You do this too." Each sentence attempts to reduce shame, but increases distance. The injured person now has two tasks: carrying the original hurt and proving that it exists. This is how conversations become exhausting. One person asks to be met; the other asks to be acquitted.

The most dangerous small rupture is therefore not the mistake itself, but the moment after the mistake when self-protection outruns contact. This is the hinge. A sharp tone can be repaired. A forgotten message can be repaired. An interruption can be repaired. But if the person who caused the impact refuses to recognise the altered room, the injury changes shape. It becomes not only "you interrupted me" but "you cannot bear to know when you have hurt me." That second wound is harder to mend because it threatens the future. It suggests the bad moment will recur and the repair will be unavailable.

To name a rupture while it is small is not to exaggerate it. It is to keep it proportionate. A simple naming can prevent the mind from manufacturing a larger accusation. "That landed badly" is often less damaging than three days of coldness. "I felt cut off" is often kinder than pretending nothing happened while quietly withdrawing affection. Naming gives the other person a chance to respond to reality rather than to weather. It turns the hidden ledger into a visible receipt: here is the moment, here is the cost, here is where repair might begin.

And yet the act of naming requires judgement. Too soon, and it may emerge as attack. Too late, and it may arrive carrying interest. The question is not whether every discomfort deserves a tribunal, but whether a particular moment has begun to alter the field between two people. Has the interruption become distance? Has the silence become a story? Has "fine" become a locked door with someone waiting behind it, hoping the other person will notice? The next test is whether the rupture can be named before guessing does its quiet work.

Repair versus Resolution

On 17 April 1970, Apollo 13 landed safely in the South Pacific after a damaged oxygen tank turned a planned Moon landing into a survival operation. NASA did not resolve the original mission. The astronauts did not walk on the lunar surface, the spacecraft did not become undamaged, and the intended scientific work was not completed as planned. Yet the flight was saved because the people involved made a crucial distinction under pressure: they restored enough function to keep the crew alive before they could attend to everything the crisis had broken.

That distinction is easy to admire in engineering and strangely difficult to practise in relationships. When a bad moment happens between two people, the mind often reaches for total settlement. Who was right? What exactly happened? What does this prove?

What must be agreed before closeness can return? The conversation becomes a demand for complete resolution when the more urgent task is repair. The capsule must hold first. The mission can be discussed later.

Repair and resolution answer different questions. Resolution asks, "How do we solve the issue?" Repair asks, "How do we become safe enough with each other to face the issue well?" The difference is not semantic. It changes the entire emotional architecture of a conversation. A couple arguing about money may not settle spending priorities in one evening, but they can repair the contempt in a phrase such as "You never think ahead." A pair of colleagues may not agree immediately on who should lead a project, but they can repair the interruption that made one person stop contributing. A parent and adult child may not resolve old family history in one sitting, but they can repair the moment when sarcasm turned pain into performance.

This distinction matters because many conflicts collapse under the weight of an impossible expectation: the belief that connection must wait until the whole dispute is settled. That belief sounds principled, even mature. Why pretend everything is all right when the problem remains? Yet closeness does not require pretending. It requires enough honesty to separate the relationship wound from the practical disagreement. Two people may still disagree about the budget, the calendar, the parenting decision, the holiday, or the distribution of labour, while also saying, "The way we spoke just now damaged trust, and that needs tending." The issue remains on the table. The knife comes off it.

The confusion between repair and resolution often appears as over-explaining. Someone says, "That hurt," and the other person tries to solve the entire surrounding topic. They explain why the timing was impossible, why the decision made sense, why the facts were more complicated, why their intention should be obvious. Some of this may be accurate. Much of it may even be relevant later. But if the first injury was being dismissed, a long explanation can repeat the dismissal in polished form. The injured person asked for recognition; they received a briefing. The visible behaviour is familiar: one person talks faster, the other grows still, and the conversation becomes more intelligent while becoming less humane.

Repair is deliberately narrower. It does not ask for a verdict on the whole conflict. It asks for contact with the moment of damage. "I spoke over you." "That sounded colder than I meant." "I can see why that felt like I had already decided." "I should not have brought that up in front of them." These statements do not settle everything. They clear the smoke. Once the smoke lifts, the actual problem may still be difficult, but it is no longer being handled through the additional burden of humiliation, defensiveness, or withdrawal. Good repair reduces the number of problems in the room.

Resolution, by contrast, often requires information that is unavailable in the heat of the rupture. It may require comparison, reflection, negotiation, testing, or time. A couple cannot resolve a recurring conflict about housework by trading accusations at midnight beside an overflowing bin. They may need to compare schedules, define what counts as completion, account for invisible labour, and decide what each can realistically commit to when tired. But they can repair the sentence "You do nothing around here" before the practical work begins. That repair does not lower the standard; it protects the possibility of meeting it.

The phrase "good enough for now" is easily misunderstood. It is not an invitation to accept chronic disappointment, flimsy apologies, or vague promises. It is not the emotional equivalent of pushing clutter into a cupboard before guests arrive. "Good enough for now" means the relationship has regained enough steadiness for people to pause without punishment, return without dread, and think without performing innocence. It is a temporary bridge, not a final settlement. A bridge has a modest purpose. It lets people cross.

Historical and public examples make the distinction visible because the scale is larger, though the principle remains recognisable. After the 1978 Camp David Accords, negotiated at Camp David in Maryland by Egypt's Anwar Sadat, Israel's Menachem Begin, and United States President Jimmy Carter, the parties did not resolve every regional conflict or every future grievance. The accords contributed to the Egypt-Israel Peace Treaty signed in 1979, a concrete outcome of immense importance, yet they did not settle the whole moral and political landscape of the Middle East. Their power lay partly in narrowing the field: establishing terms, recognition, and commitments that allowed one dangerous front to be altered. A repair in human relationships works with a similar modesty. It does not claim universal peace. It makes the next conversation less dangerous.

There is a danger in pressing this analogy too hard. States are not couples, treaties are not apologies, and geopolitical agreements involve power, territory, security, and law in ways that intimate life does not. The comparison is useful only at the level of sequence: stabilisation often precedes settlement. When people demand complete resolution before any warmth may return, they may inadvertently prolong the very insecurity that makes resolution impossible. They keep the room in emergency lighting and then wonder why nobody can read the map.

This is why unresolved issues are not always signs of relational failure. Some differences are structural. Partners may have different thresholds for risk, different needs for solitude, different relationships with money, different family loyalties, different speeds of emotional processing. Friends may differ over availability. Siblings may differ over responsibility for ageing parents. Colleagues may differ over standards of urgency. Many of these tensions cannot be solved once and retired. They must be managed, revisited, and softened by reliable repair. The presence of a recurring difference does not necessarily mean the bond is weak. The absence of repair around that difference is what makes it dangerous.

The work associated with John Gottman and his colleagues is relevant here because it placed emphasis not merely on whether couples fought, but on how they attempted to recover during conflict. The term "repair attempt" became one of the more memorable contributions of that tradition: a small bid to reduce tension, re-establish contact, or prevent escalation. The bid might be a gentle phrase, a softening of tone, a touch, a joke that genuinely eases rather than mocks, or an admission that the conversation has gone off course. The central idea is not that every repair attempt succeeds. It is that relationships need such attempts to prevent conflict from becoming pure momentum.

Momentum is one of conflict's most underestimated forces. Once people begin arguing from threat, they gather speed. They stop measuring the exact size of the current issue and start reaching for old files. They compare sacrifices, question motives, correct minor details, and punish tone. The practical matter recedes. The argument develops an appetite. Repair interrupts that appetite by reducing the emotional acceleration. A single sentence can apply the brakes: "I am getting defensive, and I do not want to turn this into a fight." The issue has not been resolved. Something more immediate has happened: the conversation has been prevented from becoming stupider than the people in it.

Resolution without repair can produce a strangely hollow result. Two people may reach an agreement and still feel less safe afterwards. The bill may be paid, the schedule arranged, the apology extracted, the task reassigned, yet the injured person remains guarded because the manner of getting there caused further damage. Anyone who has "won" an argument and then felt lonely will recognise this. The surface decision changed; the atmosphere did not. A household can run more efficiently while becoming colder. A workplace can settle responsibilities while leaving one person less willing to speak candidly next time. A family can agree on logistics while preserving the old hierarchy of whose feelings are treated as inconvenient.

Repair without eventual resolution has its own failure. Warmth can become a sedative. Two people may soothe the room, exchange affectionate words, and then avoid the practical change that would prevent the same harm from recurring. This is the credible counter-example that must be faced: some people use repair language to delay accountability. They become expert at softening the immediate discomfort without altering the behaviour. "We are okay now" becomes a way of not discussing what keeps happening. In such cases, repair is not repair at all; it is emotional laundering. It cleans the visible surface while leaving the pattern intact.

The reconciliation is precision. Repair comes before resolution when the relationship is too activated to think well; resolution must follow when the issue requires a decision, boundary, plan, or changed behaviour. The order matters, but so does the follow-through. A clean repair may say, "I dismissed you earlier, and I understand why that made you stop engaging." A responsible resolution may later ask, "How will we handle disagreement about plans so neither of us takes over?" The repair restores the bond; the resolution adjusts the system. One without the other is incomplete. Together, they reduce repetition.

The distinction also protects dignity. When people confuse repair with surrender, they resist it because they believe acknowledging impact means conceding the entire dispute. A person may fear that saying "I spoke harshly" will be heard as "You are right about everything." So they defend even the indefensible. They refuse to apologise for tone because they still believe their point was valid. But tone and point are separable. One may be right about the deadline and wrong in the contempt used to discuss it. One may have a legitimate concern and express it in a way that injures trust. Repair allows a person to own the damage without abandoning discernment.

This is especially important for thoughtful people who prize accuracy. Accuracy can become a refuge from humility. A person may argue, correctly, that the other has misremembered the sequence of events, exaggerated a phrase, or overlooked context. The facts matter. They should not be discarded. But factual correction, delivered too early, can become another form of refusal. If someone says, "I felt small when you laughed," and the response is "I did not laugh, I exhaled," the conversation has moved from repair into forensic evasion. There may be a time to clarify the record. There is also a time to notice that the other person experienced ridicule. The order determines whether truth becomes a bridge or a weapon.

The bridge matters because connection is not merely pleasant; it improves the quality of later thinking. When two people feel less threatened, they can compare realities rather than defend identities. They can ask, "What did you hear?" rather than "How dare you think that?" They can make distinctions between intent, impact, habit, and pattern. They can consider constraints: time, money, health, workload, family obligations, old fears. Problem-solving requires cognitive room. Contempt, shame, and panic occupy that room quickly. Repair gives some of it back.

There is also a moral discipline in refusing to make closeness conditional on perfect agreement. Many adult relationships suffer from a hidden absolutism: if you understood me fully, you would agree with me; if you loved me properly, you would feel as I feel; if you were fair, you would arrive at my conclusion. This is a heavy demand to place on another consciousness. Repair offers a less tyrannical standard. It allows two people to say, "We have not settled the matter, but we have recognised the hurt, corrected the course, and preserved enough regard to continue." That is not compromise in the weak sense. It is emotional civilisation at close range.

The practical sign that repair has occurred is not that everyone feels delighted. Relief may be quiet. The room may remain tender, even awkward. But certain visible changes appear: the voice lowers, interruptions decrease, eye contact becomes possible, the injured person no longer has to repeat the wound in stronger terms, the responsible person stops campaigning for innocence, and the subject can be paused without threat. These are not sentimental markers. They are behavioural evidence that the conversation has moved from danger to workable discomfort.

Resolution has its own evidence: a decision made, a boundary named, a responsibility assigned, a plan tested, a date to revisit the agreement. It may come minutes later or days later, depending on the size of the issue and the steadiness of the people involved. But when resolution grows out of repair, it carries less resentment. The agreement is less likely to be heard as defeat. The practical plan does not have to bear the whole burden of proving love. It can simply do its job.

The hard question is therefore not, "Are we finished with this issue?" Many important issues are not finished quickly. Some are never finished in the clean way people imagine. The harder and more useful question is, "Are we safe enough to continue dealing with it?"

If the answer is no, more arguing will usually deepen the damage. If the answer is yes, even partial agreement can become honest progress. The bridge does not solve the river. It decides whether people can cross without pushing each other in.

The Repair Rule Overview

In June 2008, the World Health Organization introduced its Surgical Safety Checklist in Geneva after a global effort led by clinicians including Atul Gawande to reduce avoidable harm in operating theatres. The checklist did not make surgery simple, nor did it remove the need for judgement. Its power lay elsewhere: it slowed a high-stakes room at the precise moments when confidence, hierarchy, haste, and assumption could become dangerous. Before incision, names were confirmed. Risks were spoken aloud. Roles were clarified. The pause did real work.

The later study published by Alex Haynes and colleagues in *The New England Journal of Medicine* in 2009 reported improved outcomes across hospitals that tested the checklist, not because surgeons suddenly became more intelligent, but because the system made essential truths harder to skip. That is the quiet genius of a good sequence. It does not replace skill; it protects skill from stress. It gives competent people a way to behave sensibly when the room is moving faster than their better judgement.

A bad relational moment also has its own operating theatre: the kitchen counter, the car, the edge of the bed, the email thread, the doorway after work. The stakes are different, of course, but the danger of haste is familiar. Something lands badly. One person stiffens. The other senses trouble and begins to explain. Within seconds, the conversation can move from repairable injury to defensive escalation. What is needed is not a script that makes people sound rehearsed, but a sequence that keeps the essentials from being skipped: pause, name the impact, clarify intent, take accountability, and make one small agreement.

The sequence matters because conflict has momentum. Left alone, it tends to accelerate towards the most self-protective version of each person. The injured person may enlarge the moment into a verdict. The person who caused the impact may shrink it into a misunderstanding. Both distortions have a logic. Hurt wants recognition; shame wants escape. The Repair Rule does not flatter either impulse. It asks each person to move one step slower than their reflex. That slight delay can change the moral weather of the room.

The pause is not a decorative breath before the real conversation begins. It is the first act of repair. A pause measures whether the next sentence will serve contact or merely discharge heat. Anyone can recognise the signs of a moment outrunning itself: the voice becomes faster, the face becomes harder, the hands begin tidying objects that do not need tidying, the mind starts building a closing argument. Pausing interrupts that machinery. It gives the body a chance to leave emergency mode before the mouth begins issuing policy. Without this interruption, sincerity may arrive wearing the armour of accusation.

The pause also protects against the common mistake of trying to repair while still secretly trying to win. A person can say "I understand" in a tone that means "you are being unreasonable." They can say "I am sorry" while waiting for the counter-apology. They can ask "what do you need?" while hoping the need will be small, convenient, and flattering. The pause exposes the hidden contract. Am I trying to make the other person stop feeling, or am I trying to understand what happened between us? The question is uncomfortable. It is also clarifying.

Naming impact comes next because unspoken injury breeds interpretation. If the effect of the moment is not put into words, the mind supplies a story. "You interrupted me" becomes "you think I am stupid." "You looked away" becomes "you do not care." "You made that joke" becomes "you enjoy embarrassing me." Some of these interpretations may contain truth; some may be sharpened by older wounds. Naming impact keeps the focus close to the observable event and its felt consequence. It turns a fog into a shape: "When you corrected me in front of them, I felt exposed and stopped wanting to speak."

Impact language is powerful because it gives pain a location. It does not require mind-reading, moral sentencing, or a full history of the relationship. It does not say, "You always need to dominate." It says, "That interruption made it hard for me to finish." The difference is not politeness for its own sake. It is precision. A precise impact statement gives the other person something they can meet. A global accusation gives them something to survive. The visible measure is simple: after precision, people may still feel uncomfortable, but they usually know where to place their attention.

Clarifying intent follows, but only after impact has had room to land. Intent is delicate material. Offered too early, it sounds like a shield. "I did not mean it that way" may be true and still useless if it arrives before "I understand how it landed." Human beings do not experience one another's private motives; they experience tone, timing, facial expression, words, absences, and follow-through. Intent matters because it can prevent false conclusions from hardening, but it cannot erase the bruise. The order is everything. Impact first. Intent second.

A clean intent statement is brief because motive becomes less trustworthy the more it campaigns for itself. "I was trying to solve the timing, not dismiss your idea." "I meant that as teasing, not as criticism." "I was anxious about being late, not angry with you." Such sentences do not argue with the other person's experience. They add context without demanding acquittal. The best intent statements have a certain modesty. They do not ask to be admired. They simply reduce needless ambiguity, which is one of the great accelerants of conflict.

The Repair Rule then moves towards accountability, where many conversations either mature or collapse. Accountability is not self-condemnation. It is the disciplined naming of one's contribution to the rupture. The distinction matters because self-attack can become another form of escape. "I am terrible, I ruin everything, you should not have to deal with me" may sound remorseful, but it often forces the injured person to provide comfort. That reverses the burden. A steadier form says, "I interrupted you, and I can see why that made you pull back." No theatre. No collapse. A named action, a recognised effect.

Accountability works best when it is proportionate. A person should not swallow the whole conflict simply to restore peace, nor should they slice responsibility so thinly that nothing meaningful remains. The question is not, "How can I become innocent?" It is, "What part of this moment belongs to me?" In a repeated conflict, that part may be small and still decisive. The sigh before answering. The sarcastic aside. The refusal to return after asking for space. The choice to bring up a sensitive subject in public. Accountability becomes trustworthy when it can be seen in behaviour, not merely heard in language.

The final movement is a small agreement, because repair without alteration is only atmosphere. Warmth may return for an hour, but if the same collision happens again in the same way, the old apology starts to lose value. A small agreement converts insight into evidence. It might be as modest as waiting until the other person finishes before responding, returning after a timed pause, moving difficult conversations out of text, or using one phrase to signal that the old pattern has begun. The agreement should be small enough to keep under pressure. Grand promises often fail precisely because they are made in the relief of reconciliation rather than the reality of stress.

The smallness is not a weakness. It is the discipline. A couple arguing about being ignored after work may be tempted to redesign their entire emotional life before dinner. A smaller agreement might do more: the first few minutes after coming through the door will not be used for requests, complaints, or logistics unless something is urgent. That change is observable. It can be tested. It gives the vulnerable point a practical guardrail. The checklist returns here, not as bureaucracy, but as protection against the human tendency to remember wisdom only when calm.

The work of John Gottman and colleagues on repair attempts in couple conflict offers a useful research anchor for this principle. Their observational studies drew attention to the importance of small bids that reduce tension and restore connection during disagreement. A repair attempt may be a softening phrase, a humorous turn that does not belittle, an admission of defensiveness, or a brief request to restart. The exact wording is less important than the function: the move interrupts escalation and makes continued contact possible. A perfect sentence said coldly will not do this. A slightly clumsy sentence said with real ownership often will.

The Harvard Negotiation Project provides a second useful example, particularly through Roger Fisher and William Ury's *Getting to Yes*, published in 1981. Its famous distinction between positions and interests belongs to negotiation theory, but the relational echo is clear. A position says, "You must apologise properly before I talk." An interest may be, "I need to know you understand why that humiliated me." A position says, "I need space." An interest may be, "I need enough calm not to say something cruel." The Repair Rule helps translate rigid positions into repairable information. It does not make disagreement vanish; it makes the underlying human need more visible.

There is, however, a serious limitation. A sequence can be misused when it becomes performance. Someone may learn the language of impact, intent, accountability, and agreement while using it to manage appearances rather than alter conduct. The words may sound polished, but the pattern remains untouched. This is not repair; it is the imitation of repair. The difference shows up later. Does the person interrupt less? Do they return when they said they would? Do they stop making jokes at the other's expense? Do they change the decision, the timing, the tone, the setting? Follow-through is the audit.

There are also moments when continuing to talk is the wrong form of repair. Once contempt has entered the room, once interruptions become relentless, once someone is using the process to corner or exhaust the other, more language can deepen the damage. Stopping can be the most responsible move, provided it is not used as punishment. "I want to repair this, and I cannot do it well while we are speaking over each other. I am going to pause and come back at a specific time" carries a different meaning from disappearance. The first protects the bond. The second abandons it to speculation.

Brevity serves the same purpose. Many people lengthen repair because they are anxious about being misunderstood. They explain, qualify, revisit, add context, bring in older examples, and then wonder why the conversation has become heavier. The Repair Rule favours compactness not because feelings are simple, but because overloaded moments cannot carry unlimited language. A repair attempt should be strong enough to hold the essential truth and light enough for the other person to receive it. The room does not need a speech when a clean sentence would restore contact.

Sincerity is therefore more important than elegance. People often delay repair because they are searching for the flawless wording that will offend nobody and settle everything. That sentence rarely exists. What matters is whether the attempt recognises the other person's experience without surrendering honesty, whether it clarifies without defending, whether it owns without collapsing, and whether it turns towards a practical next step. The human ear is remarkably good at detecting the difference between repair and management. A hesitant truth may land better than a polished evasion.

The sequence is not a cage. It is a handrail. In some moments, the pause will do most of the work. In others, naming impact will reveal that intent was badly misunderstood. Sometimes accountability must come before explanation because the harm is already obvious. Sometimes the small agreement is the only part that proves the repair was real. The order exists to reduce avoidable injury, not to turn living people into procedural machines. What matters is the movement away from reflex and towards responsibility.

A bad moment presents a narrow opening. Too much pride closes it. Too much analysis can miss it. Too much talking can trample it. The Repair Rule asks for something more exacting: the courage to slow down, the honesty to name what landed, the restraint to clarify without self-defence, the dignity to own one's part, and the discipline to change one repeatable behaviour. The test is not whether the next sentence sounds perfect. The test is whether the next moment becomes safer, or whether the old pattern is allowed to keep writing the script.

Chapter 2
Timing the Repair Attempt

The room has gone quiet, but not peacefully. One person is standing at the sink with their back turned, rinsing a glass that has already been rinsed. The other is near the doorway, still holding the last sentence in their face, wanting to fix it now because the silence feels intolerable. Nothing dramatic has happened, not from the outside. A tired comment landed badly. A reply came too quickly. Someone felt blamed; someone else felt unfairly accused. The problem is no longer only what was said. It is when to return to it.

The person at the sink says, "Not now." The person at the doorway hears rejection. The person at the sink hears pressure. The glass knocks lightly against the tap, a small hard sound in a room already too alert. If they talk immediately, the conversation may flare again. If they leave it too long, each will begin privately arranging the facts into a more useful story. The injury is still soft. That is precisely the danger.

Timing is the hidden architecture of repair. The right words can fail when spoken into the wrong nervous system. The wrong moment can make even a sincere apology sound like a tactic, a question sound like interrogation, and a pause sound like abandonment. Repair asks for enough calm that listening is possible, but not so much delay that the silence becomes a second injury. The task is not to obey urgency or avoid discomfort. It is to read the room honestly enough to know whether the next sentence will restore contact or merely continue the collision.

This creates one of the most common trade-offs in intimate conflict: one person often needs immediacy to feel safe, while the other needs space to stay kind. Neither need is automatically superior. The wish to talk now may come from care, anxiety, fear of distance, or a sincere desire not to let hurt harden overnight. The wish to wait may come from self-control, overwhelm, dignity, or a genuine attempt not to say something damaging. Trouble begins when each person treats their timing preference as moral truth. "If you cared, you would talk now." "If you respected me, you would leave me alone." Both sentences make a prison out of a need.

The stakes are immediate because a repair attempt is not only judged by its content; it is judged by its timing. A forced conversation can make the injured person feel handled rather than heard. A postponed conversation without a clear return can make the other person feel discarded. The visible signs are rarely subtle: clipped answers, busy hands, a face that refuses softness, a sudden retreat into tasks, the phone picked up too quickly, the door closed with careful quietness. These behaviours may not prove bad intent, but they show that the relational field has changed. Timing decides whether that change is tended or left to gather meaning.

The stakes extend beyond a single evening. Couples, families, friends, and colleagues develop timing habits, and those habits become part of the relationship's emotional contract. In some relationships, every difficult moment must be processed immediately, no matter how tired, hungry, late, or flooded someone feels. In others, discomfort is always postponed with a vague promise that never becomes a conversation. Both patterns leak trust. One teaches people that repair means pressure. The other teaches them that delay means disappearance. Over time, the conflict is no longer only about money, tone, chores, messages, decisions, or affection. It is about whether pain will be met at a human pace.

The work begins with recognising the difference between a postponement and a withdrawal. A postponement keeps the door open. A withdrawal quietly locks it. The distinction often lies in the smallest visible commitments: a gentler tone, a specific return, a sentence that acknowledges the other person is not foolish for wanting repair. "I want to talk about this, but I am too heated to do it well" carries a different emotional meaning from "Drop it." One protects the future conversation. The other makes the present person feel like a nuisance.

Some ruptures ask for a brief repair before the deeper conversation is possible. A sharp sentence at bedtime may not be the moment to settle a long-running disagreement, but it may still require enough care to prevent the night from becoming evidence. A hurried apology in a doorway may not resolve the fear underneath, but it can stop the fear from being abandoned. Later, when steadier minds are available, the larger pattern can be examined without the added injury of having been ignored. The rhythm matters: a small act of contact now, a clearer return later.

This is where the next part of the book's movement narrows the lens. The question becomes how to choose a moment that is neither too hot nor too stale, how to invite repair without cornering the other person, and how to delay without making delay feel like punishment. From there, the distinction between fast repair and later talk becomes essential, because not every bad moment deserves the same size of conversation. Some require an immediate stitch. Some require a scheduled return. Many require both.

The unresolved tension is simple enough to feel familiar and difficult enough to expose a pattern: when the room changes, whose clock governs the repair? The person who cannot bear the silence, or the person who cannot think inside pressure? The answer cannot be found in urgency alone, nor in distance alone. It begins in the charged interval after the bad sentence, when one person wants to step forward, the other wants to step back, and both must decide whether timing will become another wound.

Choosing the Right Moment

On 27 October 1962, at the height of the Cuban Missile Crisis, a message from Soviet leader Nikita Khrushchev reached Washington while President John F. Kennedy and his advisers were weighing how to respond to nuclear danger without turning fear into catastrophe. The details belonged to statecraft, not domestic life, yet the principle was painfully human: answer too fast and the reply could inflame the crisis; wait too long and the silence could become its own provocation. Timing was not etiquette. It was substance.

In the White House, the decision was not merely what to say, but which moment could hold the saying. The same question appears in a quieter form after a bad exchange at home, in a meeting, or across a message thread. One person wants to speak while the hurt is still fresh; the other needs distance before they can listen without striking back. The doorway is open, but only barely. Step through too sharply and it closes.

A repair attempt depends on timing because the body often reaches a conclusion before the mind can revise it. A partner hears a clipped tone and stiffens. A colleague receives a curt reply and stops offering detail. A friend senses sarcasm and becomes formally polite. The visible scene may be small: folded arms, a chair pushed back, a glass placed down with unnecessary care, a reply reduced to three words. The concept is readiness. Readiness is not agreement, forgiveness, or calm in the abstract; it is the minimum state in which a person can hear a sentence without immediately turning it into ammunition.

The wrong moment bends good words out of shape. "I am sorry" can sound like impatience if it is delivered while the other person is still shaking. "Can we talk?" can sound like pressure if it arrives before someone has found their footing. "I did not mean that" can sound like erasure if the impact has not yet been acknowledged. The implication is uncomfortable but liberating: sincerity is not enough. A repair attempt must be timed so that sincerity has somewhere to land.

The research tradition associated with John Gottman and Robert Levenson is useful here because it takes seriously the bodily dimension of conflict. Their observational work with couples, developed from studies in Seattle and Berkeley over several decades, drew attention to how conflict is carried not only in words but in facial expression, physiology, interruption, tone, and the speed with which people recover from distress. The practical lesson is not that partners must diagnose one another like laboratory subjects. It is that a conversation can become unworkable before anyone says anything obviously cruel. When someone's face has hardened, when their answers have shortened, when every sentence is being received as prosecution, the doorway has narrowed.

There is a strong temptation to treat urgency as moral clarity. The person who wants to talk now may feel they are protecting the relationship from avoidance. They may fear that if the moment is not repaired immediately, the other person will drift into distance and never return. This fear is not foolish. Many relationships do contain a history of unresolved moments being swept under the rug until the rug becomes the relationship. The wish to talk now can therefore be an attempt to keep the rupture from hardening into resentment. It may come from care, not control.

Yet the person who asks for space may also be protecting the relationship. They may know the signs of their own escalation: the sarcastic answer, the courtroom voice, the urge to correct every detail, the cold little sentence designed to win by wounding. Space, when it includes a return, is not abandonment. It is containment. The visible difference matters. A person who says, "I cannot do this well right now, but I do want to come back to it," has left the doorway open. A person who says, "Whatever," and disappears into silence has changed space into punishment.

The right moment usually sits between heat and frost. Too much heat, and both people are still defending themselves from the threat of being wrong, rejected, controlled, or humiliated. Too much frost, and each has had time to build a private explanation that protects them from curiosity. A fresh rupture is like wet cement: it can still be shaped, but it can also be spoiled by rough handling. Leave it entirely unattended, and it sets into a form nobody consciously chose. This is why repair timing is less about the clock than about the condition of the room.

One cue is whether the injured person can describe impact without having to amplify it to be taken seriously. If they must raise their voice, repeat themselves, bring in last year, or sharpen the accusation simply to feel heard, the moment is already sliding away from repair. Another cue is whether the responsible person can listen without entering immediate defence. If every phrase is met with correction, context, or counter-complaint, the conversation is still too hot. The implication is not that repair should be abandoned. It means the repair may need a smaller entry point: a pause, a promise to return, or a brief acknowledgement that prevents silence from becoming neglect.

The work of psychologist James Gross on emotion regulation, especially research published in the 1990s at Stanford University, offers a useful frame for this. His studies on suppression and reappraisal helped distinguish between merely pushing expression down and changing how an emotional moment is understood. Suppression can make a face look calmer while leaving the body and mind highly active. Reappraisal changes the meaning of the moment itself. Applied carefully to relational repair, the distinction matters. A person who looks quiet may not be ready; they may simply be holding themselves together. A person who asks for a few minutes may be trying to make reappraisal possible rather than performing withdrawal.

A low-pressure invitation respects this difference. It does not corner the other person, and it does not abandon the moment. Its emotional shape is simple: I noticed something changed; I care enough to return; I will not force the door. The words might be plain rather than elegant. "That landed badly between us. I want to repair it when we can do it properly." The effect is to reduce the two fears that often drive timing clashes: the fear of being trapped and the fear of being forgotten. The invitation gives the moment a place to go.

The most careful timing also separates availability from appetite. People often ask, "Do you want to talk?" when the more accurate question is, "Can you talk in a way that will not make this worse?" Wanting is unstable after hurt. Someone may not want to talk but may be able to offer a small repair. Someone may desperately want to talk and be entirely unable to do so well. The visible test is behavioural: can the person slow their voice, remain on the present issue, acknowledge one sentence from the other side, and resist the old performance? If not, the moment may need holding rather than expanding.

A brief example shows the hinge. After dinner, one partner explains a concern about money. The other interrupts with a correction about the figures. The speaker stops and becomes quiet. The interrupter notices the shift and says, too quickly, "What? I was only saying the number was wrong." The room tightens. A repair attempt made at that speed will probably become a defence. A better moment opens when the interrupter stops trying to win the arithmetic and recognises the altered atmosphere: "I think I cut across you. I do want to understand, but I can feel myself getting defensive. Can we pause for a little while and come back before we sleep?" The point is not the exact wording. The point is that the pause contains a return.

Postponing without stonewalling requires evidence. Stonewalling leaves the other person alone with uncertainty. A responsible postponement gives three forms of reassurance: the issue matters, the delay has a reason, and there will be a return. Without those elements, space becomes indistinguishable from disappearance. The person left behind begins to guess, and guessing is rarely neutral after pain. They may start measuring the closed door, the unanswered message, the length of silence, the sound of ordinary tasks continuing as if nothing happened. The repair attempt has not been delayed; it has been replaced by a new rupture.

There is a counter-example worth taking seriously. Some people overvalue timing until it becomes an elegant excuse never to speak. They wait for the ideal emotional weather: no tiredness, no stress, no work the next day, no children nearby, no risk of tears, no unfinished tasks, no possibility of discomfort. That moment does not come. The demand for perfect readiness can become avoidance with better manners. In such cases, the problem is not mistiming but refusal. The distinction is visible in behaviour over repeated occasions. A person who genuinely needs time returns. A person who uses time to escape keeps moving the doorway further away.

This is where the idea of "not now" must be handled with moral care. "Not now" can protect a conversation from heat, or it can protect a person from accountability. The difference lies in whether it creates a future. A healthy delay narrows uncertainty. An evasive delay enlarges it. When someone says, "Not now," and then names a realistic return, the relationship receives a signal that the rupture still matters. When they say, "Not now," with no path back, the other person is asked to absorb both the original hurt and the new burden of pursuit.

The right moment also depends on the size of the rupture. A brief sting may need only a brief correction while the room is still warm. A deeper wound may need more space, because the first conversation after impact is not always capable of holding the whole truth. A humiliating comment made in front of others, a repeated dismissal, or a broken agreement may require a staged return: enough immediate acknowledgement to prevent abandonment, followed by a steadier conversation when both can think. Timing is therefore an act of proportion. It matches the size of the repair attempt to the size and temperature of the wound.

The motif of the doorway matters because repair is rarely a single dramatic entrance. Often it is a threshold held open by small decisions: not following someone from room to room, not pretending nothing happened, not demanding instant absolution, not using silence as a weapon, not letting the night swallow the issue without trace. The doorway is kept open by conduct before language. A softened face. A sentence that does not accuse. A promise that is actually kept. These are not refinements. They are the architecture of trust when trust is under strain.

For time-conscious people, this may sound inefficient. It is the opposite. Poor timing wastes enormous attention. A conversation forced too early can consume an evening and leave the issue worse. A conversation delayed without care can consume several days through distance, interpretation, and tense politeness. Repair timing reduces waste by asking a sharper question at the outset: is this a moment for a full conversation, a brief acknowledgement, or a clear pause with return? The answer saves energy because it prevents people from using the wrong tool at the wrong temperature.

The hardest cases arise when the timing needs are opposite. One person's nervous system calms through contact; the other's calms through solitude. One experiences delay as abandonment; the other experiences immediacy as invasion. Neither is lying. Neither has the whole truth. The relationship becomes workable when the pair stops arguing about whose timing style is superior and starts building a shared threshold. A short contact now may make space bearable. A clear return may make waiting possible. The question shifts from "Whose need wins?" to "What timing protects both dignity and repair?"

The moment to repair is therefore not simply the earliest possible moment, nor the calmest possible moment, nor the moment one person demands. It is the moment when enough openness exists for the truth to be received without being weaponised, and enough nearness remains for the truth to matter. That moment may last only a breath before the old pattern rushes in. The forward test is whether, at the doorway between heat and distance, the next sentence keeps repair available or quietly teaches the hurt to harden.

Fast Repair versus Later Talk

On 15 January 2009, Captain Chesley Sullenberger landed US Airways Flight 1549 on the Hudson River after both engines lost thrust shortly after take-off from LaGuardia Airport in New York. The full investigation, led by the National Transportation Safety Board, came later. In the cockpit, there was no time for exhaustive analysis, no space for a complete account of every cause, no luxury of perfect certainty. The urgent task was immediate stabilisation: keep the aircraft controllable, communicate clearly, choose the least disastrous option, and preserve life before explanation.

That sequence matters far beyond aviation. Some moments are too urgent for a complete conversation and too important to leave untouched. A couple standing in a hallway before work cannot always examine the whole history of why one person feels disregarded. A parent cannot always unpack a sharp exchange while a child is waiting by the door. A colleague cannot always process a tense meeting while the next appointment has already begun. Yet if nothing is said, the gap begins to speak. Silence fills itself. Trust leaks quietly.

The mistake is to treat every conflict as if it must be handled in one sitting. Some ruptures need two forms of attention: a fast repair that stops the relational bleeding, and a later talk that deals with the deeper pattern. The fast repair is not the whole remedy. It is the bandage that keeps the wound from being exposed to the dirt of guessing, resentment, and emotional self-protection. The later conversation is where meaning, responsibility, and future conduct can be examined with greater care. Confusing the two creates predictable trouble. If the fast repair tries to carry the full weight of resolution, it becomes rushed and clumsy. If the later talk is promised but never happens, the fast repair becomes decorative.

A fast repair has one modest purpose: prevent the bad moment from becoming a bad story before there is time to understand it properly. It does not require polished language. It requires enough recognition for the other person not to feel abandoned inside the rupture. A sentence can do this when it names the altered room without pretending to settle it: "That came out badly, and I do not want to leave it like that." The visible effect is small but real. The shoulders may not drop entirely. The hurt may not disappear. But the injured person no longer has to wonder whether the other has noticed.

The word *noticed* carries more weight than it seems. Much relational pain grows not only from the original impact, but from the fear that the impact is invisible to the person who caused it. When someone interrupts, snaps, withdraws, mocks, or dismisses, the injury deepens if they behave afterwards as though nothing has happened. The injured person must then choose between raising the issue and carrying it alone. A fast repair removes part of that burden. It says, in conduct rather than performance, "You are not imagining the shift between us." That recognition can preserve enough goodwill for a fuller conversation later.

The later talk has a different purpose. It is not merely the longer version of the fast repair. It asks what the rupture revealed. Was the sharp reply a moment of fatigue, or part of a pattern in which one person feels spoken down to? Was the silence a needed pause, or a familiar disappearance? Was the argument about timing, or about feeling unconsidered? These questions require more steadiness than the immediate aftermath usually provides. They ask people to compare experiences, distinguish intent from impact, and translate pain into one or two practical changes. The later talk turns the bandage into treatment.

The two-stage approach protects against a common false choice: talk now or bury it. Many relationships swing between those extremes. One person wants everything addressed before sleep, before leaving the room, before the other can breathe. Another wants to wait until there is a better moment, but the better moment never receives a name. The result is a repeated injury around timing itself. The first person experiences postponement as abandonment. The second experiences immediacy as being cornered. The conflict is no longer only about the original remark, decision, or disappointment. It is about whether repair will arrive at all.

A useful fast repair contains several quiet commitments without turning into a list. It acknowledges that something happened, recognises that the other person was affected, signals care for the relationship, and creates a path back. If any of these is missing, the repair weakens. "Sorry" without impact can sound like a bid to end discomfort. "We will talk later" without a return point can sound like fog. "You know I did not mean it" without acknowledgement can feel like erasure. A fast repair does not need length, but it needs substance. It must hold enough truth to keep the door from closing.

Consider a simple evening scene. One partner makes a joke at dinner that touches a private insecurity. The other laughs weakly, then grows quiet on the way home. The person who made the joke notices the silence but also sees that they are both tired, the train is crowded, and a deeper conversation there would feel exposed. A poor response is to pretend not to notice and hope sleep erases the sting. Another poor response is to demand immediate reassurance: "Are you seriously still upset?" A fast repair might say, "I think that joke landed badly. I am sorry I put that on display. I want to talk about it properly when we are home and not doing this in public." The repair is brief. It is also protective.

The crucial element is the return. Without it, later becomes a soft word for never. Many people have been trained by experience to distrust postponement because postponement has often been the polite face of avoidance. "Can we talk later?" has meant "Please stop making me uncomfortable." "Not now" has meant "I will wait until your hurt loses force." "I need space" has meant "I will decide alone when this matters again." The two-stage approach only builds trust when the later talk is anchored in a specific, believable return. The person asking for delay must leave a traceable path back to the conversation.

Specificity changes the emotional meaning of waiting. "Later" is vague enough to breed suspicion. "After dinner" is clearer. "Tomorrow evening after work" is clearer still. The exact timing will vary with the relationship and the size of the rupture, but the principle is constant: uncertainty is costly after hurt. A person who has already felt dismissed should not also have to manage the administrative burden of chasing the repair. A named return says, "You will not have to hunt me for this." It converts delay from disappearance into a shared holding pattern.

The counter-example is important. Not every conflict benefits from delay. Some fast repairs are used to avoid the difficult talk altogether; some later conversations are scheduled so far away that the emotional truth has gone underground. There are moments when the issue is clear, the harm is contained, and both people have enough steadiness to repair and resolve in the same exchange. Stretching such a moment into a formal later talk may make the relationship feel bureaucratic, as if every bruise requires a committee. Timing must serve the bond, not decorate the process.

There are also moments when a fast repair is not safe or meaningful because the pattern is too severe. If the exchange involves intimidation, repeated contempt, threats, or a person feeling unable to speak freely, a neat two-stage structure may become a way to keep the more vulnerable person engaged in harm. Repair language should never require someone to remain available for mistreatment. The limitation does not weaken the principle; it clarifies it. Fast repair and later talk are useful where both people can participate in good faith and where the aim is restoration rather than control.

In ordinary conflicts, however, the absence of a fast repair often imposes a hidden tax. The injured person may become watchful. The responsible person may become defensive before being accused. The next ordinary exchange arrives carrying extra charge. A question about whether the bins went out sounds like a verdict on reliability. A quiet mood sounds like punishment. A request for help sounds like criticism. The relationship begins spending attention on monitoring rather than living. This is the overnight leak: not an explosion, but a steady loss of ease.

A fast repair stops the leak by giving the relationship a temporary container. The container is not a solution. It is a promise that the moment will not be abandoned. In practical terms, it lets two people continue with the evening, the school run, the meeting, the family visit, or the workday without forcing them to pretend the rupture did not occur. The person hurt does not have to perform normality as proof of maturity. The person who caused the hurt does not have to produce a complete account before they have thought clearly. Both are spared the false urgency of solving everything while flooded.

The later talk then tests whether the fast repair was sincere. It is easy to sound accountable in the first minute after seeing the other person's face change. It is harder to return when the heat has cooled and convenience argues for silence. The return is where trust is measured. Does the person bring it up without being chased? Do they remember what was promised? Do they remain willing to hear impact after the immediate discomfort has passed? These behaviours matter more than dramatic remorse. A kept appointment can repair more than a beautiful apology that evaporates.

The later talk also protects against the false peace that follows fatigue. Many conflicts appear to vanish because both people become too tired to continue. Morning arrives, responsibilities resume, and the household or workplace begins moving again. There may even be kindness. Tea is made. A message is sent. A task is done. Yet the unexamined moment remains in the background. If there is no return, the apparent peace depends on both people not touching the sore place. That is not repair; it is careful navigation around a bruise.

The two-stage approach requires restraint from both sides. The person who wants immediate discussion must accept that full processing under pressure can damage the very connection they are trying to protect. The person who wants delay must accept that space without reassurance can feel like emotional abandonment. Each has a responsibility to make the waiting survivable. A brief acknowledgement can calm the person who fears being forgotten. A clear boundary can calm the person who fears being overwhelmed. The negotiation is not over who gets their preferred timing. It is over what keeps the bond from taking further damage while the truth waits to be handled.

There is a familiar example in professional life. After a tense meeting, a manager realises they shut down a colleague's objection too sharply. The colleague says little afterwards, but their face has closed. The manager has another meeting in five minutes. A full conversation in the corridor would be rushed and public. Saying nothing would leave the colleague to interpret the moment alone. A fast repair might be brief: "I cut you off in there. I am sorry. I want to come back to your point properly this afternoon." The later talk is where the manager can ask what was missed, acknowledge the effect on participation, and change how dissent is handled in the next meeting. The first sentence prevents drift; the later conversation repairs the working pattern.

The motif is the holding stitch: small, temporary, and not meant to replace the deeper work. A holding stitch does not pretend the fabric is whole. It prevents the tear from widening before proper mending can happen. That is what a fast repair offers after a bad moment. It does not settle the old fear, redesign the agreement, or explain every cause. It keeps the relationship from ripping further while time, privacy, and steadier attention become available.

The danger comes when people admire the holding stitch and never mend the cloth. A relationship can become full of quick apologies that briefly reduce tension but never alter the repeated injury. "I know, I know, I should not have said that" loses force when the same sentence returns each week. "We will talk later" becomes insulting when later is always cancelled by tiredness, work, children, screens, or the convenient restoration of mood. The later talk is not a luxury attached to fast repair. It is what gives fast repair its credibility.

The forward test is therefore sharp: after the bad moment, what is needed now to stop trust leaking, and what must be returned to later so the leak does not become part of the design? Too much conversation too soon can flood the room. Too little recognition can leave the other person alone in the dark. Somewhere between those failures is the disciplined sentence that holds the tear, names the return, and refuses to let "we never came back to it" become the quiet anthem of the relationship.

Chapter 3
Regulating Before You Speak

What if the most important part of a repair attempt happens before a single sentence is spoken? The bad moment may have lasted only a breath: a raised eyebrow, a clipped answer, a correction delivered too sharply. Yet within that breath, the body has already begun making plans. The jaw tightens. The chest narrows. A hand reaches for the phone, a cup, a door handle, anything that offers motion. The mind starts assembling evidence with alarming efficiency. It is preparing to win, escape, or go cold.

This is where many repair attempts fail before they begin. The words may sound reasonable, but the body has taken sides. A person says, "I just want to understand," while their tone cross-examines. Another says, "I am calm," while every answer is polished into ice. Someone offers an apology, but only after explaining why they were mostly justified. The conversation appears to be about meaning, fairness, or respect. Beneath it, a quieter contest is already under way: who can stay regulated enough not to turn hurt into harm?

The body keeps score quickly. A look of blame can be enough to make an intelligent adult become astonishingly primitive in posture and speech. Some people speed up, pouring words over the silence before the other person can accuse them. Some narrow the issue into technical corrections, as if winning the sequence of events will erase the emotional bruise. Some become sarcastic, because contempt feels stronger than vulnerability. Others turn impeccably polite, which can be more punishing than a shout because it removes warmth while preserving deniability.

The central tension is not whether strong feelings should be allowed. They should be. Anger can carry information; fear can identify what matters; hurt can show where the relationship has lost safety. The problem begins when feeling takes the microphone and calls it truth. Repair requires enough self-command to notice the first surge without obeying it. That is not repression. It is stewardship. The aim is not to become less human, but to become less automatic.

The stakes are immediate because the first moments after impact set the direction of the whole exchange. A defensive correction can turn a vulnerable disclosure into a debate. A sarcastic aside can turn a repair attempt into another injury. A retreat without a return can make the other person feel abandoned inside the rupture. These behaviours are visible, measurable, and costly: interrupted sentences, shorter replies, backs turned, doors closed too firmly, messages left unanswered, apologies delayed until they have lost credibility. Regulation is not a private wellness project. It is the condition that allows the next sentence to land.

The stakes are also cumulative. Over time, people learn one another's threat signatures. One partner hears the change in breathing before the argument begins. A colleague recognises the precise kind of politeness that means disagreement has gone underground. A friend notices when humour becomes a blade. These patterns teach everyone what to expect, and expectation shapes response. If repair is repeatedly attempted from a state of threat, the relationship begins to distrust repair itself. The phrase "can we talk?" starts to sound like danger.

A repairable moment begins with recognising one's own early signs, especially in the narrow interval before speech becomes performance. From there, the work is to reduce heat without disappearing: a breath that interrupts acceleration, a sentence that names the need for steadiness, a boundary that protects both dignity and connection. Returning then becomes part of the repair rather than an afterthought, because a pause without a return can become another wound. At times, the most responsible act is to stop completely before repeated interruption, contempt, or threats turn the exchange into something neither person can mend cleanly.

The small household motif here is the kettle just before it boils. Nothing has spilled yet, but the sound has changed. The pressure is rising; the room has been warned. Many people wait until the water is already over the edge before they admit there is heat in the system. Regulation asks for earlier honesty. It asks a person to notice the hiss before the scald, the tightening before the sentence, the argument forming before it borrows the voice.

The unresolved question is whether a person can catch themselves soon enough to protect the repair they claim to want. Not after the speech has sharpened. Not after the doorway has closed. Not after the old pattern has already taken the wheel. The test begins in the first charged seconds, when the body says attack, flee, or freeze, and the relationship needs something more disciplined than instinct.

Noticing Your Threat Response

In 1915, Walter Cannon, working at Harvard Medical School in Boston, described the body's emergency mobilisation in language that later became associated with "fight or flight". The phrase endured because it caught something observable: when threat appears, the body does not wait for a philosophical consultation. It prepares. Muscles ready themselves. Attention narrows. The organism begins to organise around survival. The modern argument at a kitchen table is not a predator in the grass, but the body is not always careful with categories.

A person hears, "You never listen," and something happens before they choose a reply. The throat tightens. The face warms. The mind rushes towards the transcript: what was said, when it was said, who started it, which detail proves the accusation is unfair. Another person hears the same line and goes still, almost elegant in their withdrawal, as if politeness could conceal the fact that the door inside them has closed. The body moves first. Speech follows.

That early movement matters because repair cannot begin while a person is still proving a case. The words may be about understanding, but the system underneath is about threat. A blamed person often becomes either a lawyer, a runner, or a locked room. The lawyer corrects details, cross-examines tone, and demands fair procedure before acknowledging pain. The runner changes subject, leaves the room, reaches for work, sleep, errands, or the phone. The locked room remains physically present but emotionally unavailable, answering with polished restraint and a face that gives nothing away. Each strategy has a private logic. Each makes repair harder.

Threat response is not a character flaw. It is a protective pattern. The problem is not that the body reacts; the problem is that the reaction is mistaken for wisdom. A person who speeds up may believe they are clarifying. A person who goes silent may believe they are preventing escalation. A person who becomes sarcastic may believe they are defending dignity. In each case, the behaviour carries information but also risk. The information is, "I feel exposed." The risk is that the response creates the very damage it fears.

The first ten seconds after feeling blamed are often the hinge. In that brief interval, an ordinary conversation can split into two paths. One path leads towards contact: a pause, a softening, a sentence that admits the impact has been heard. The other path leads towards litigation: "That is not what happened," "You do this too," "Why are you making it sound like I am a monster?" The content may be partly accurate. The timing makes it combustible. A detail corrected too soon can sound like a heart refused.

The most common sign of threat is acceleration. Words arrive faster than thought can examine them. The person begins filling every gap because silence feels like losing. They explain the whole context, then explain the explanation, then correct the other person's response to the explanation. Speed creates an illusion of control. It also leaves the other person less room to exist. The visible metric is interruption: fewer completed sentences, shorter pauses, more overlapping speech. Trust does not usually break because one person has many words. It weakens when those words occupy all the available air.

Another sign is factual narrowing. The accused person retreats to the one detail they can prove. "It was not Tuesday; it was Wednesday." "I did not shout; I raised my voice." "I did not say always." Precision matters, and relationships suffer when facts are treated casually. Yet in the heat of repair, detail can become a hiding place. The injured person is pointing to impact; the threatened person is examining punctuation. The implication is not that accuracy should be abandoned, but that accuracy must be placed in service of repair rather than used to avoid it. A corrected date cannot mend a dismissed feeling.

Sarcasm is threat wearing clever shoes. It offers distance from vulnerability while giving injury a socially plausible costume. "Well, forgive me for breathing." "Apparently I am the villain again." "Right, because you are always perfect." Such lines feel momentarily strengthening because they reverse the shame. The blamed person stops feeling exposed and makes the other person seem unreasonable instead. But sarcasm taxes the relationship heavily. It turns a bid for recognition into a contest of contempt. The visible cost appears quickly: the other person's face closes, the voice changes, the original issue disappears beneath a new wound.

Icy politeness is more respectable and sometimes more destructive. It avoids vulgar escalation. It does not shout. It may even sound impeccably civil. "Of course." "As you wish." "I have nothing further to add." The surface is controlled, but the temperature in the room drops. This response often belongs to people who pride themselves on not being dramatic. They do not erupt; they withdraw heat. The implication is that regulation must not be confused with freezing. Calm that removes all human signal is not repair-ready calm. It is distance with good manners.

The work of psychologist Paul Ekman, especially his studies of facial expression from the 1960s onwards at the University of California, San Francisco and elsewhere, helped show that emotion often appears in small, rapid changes of the face before it is fully managed. One need not turn this into amateur diagnosis to find the relational lesson useful. People leak threat. A tightened mouth, a brief eye roll, a look away at the exact point of vulnerability, a laugh without warmth: such signals may be fleeting, but they shape whether the next sentence feels safe. The other person may not consciously catalogue the expression. They still respond to it.

The work of John Gottman and Robert Levenson also belongs here, because their observation of couples highlighted how conflict is carried in tone, timing, physiology, and the ability to recover from escalation. The important point is not that every couple should become a research project. It is that repair requires attention to the whole human system, not merely the words chosen after the fact. A person can say the correct sentence with a threatening face. They can apologise while still radiating accusation. They can ask for calm in a voice that punishes. The body edits the sentence before the listener receives it.

There is a counter-example that deserves respect. Sometimes a person is not "defensive" because they are threatened by accountability; they are defending themselves against a false or unfair accusation. Not every claim of hurt is accurate in its interpretation. Not every complaint is proportionate. Some people use emotional language to control, corner, or avoid their own responsibility. In such cases, a reflex to correct the record is not automatically immature. Truth matters. Boundaries matter. Repair cannot mean accepting a distorted story simply to keep the peace.

The reconciliation lies in sequence. A person can notice their threat response without surrendering their judgement. They can slow down before disagreeing. They can recognise impact before contesting interpretation. They can say, "I want to respond carefully, because I am feeling defensive," rather than launching into a counter-case. This does not concede every point. It prevents the defence from becoming a second injury. Mature repair makes room for both: the other person's experience and one's own reality. The skill is keeping the two from trampling each other at the doorway.

Naming one's own signs is therefore not self-absorption; it is relational responsibility. The useful question is concrete: what does blame make me do in the first few seconds? Some people talk faster. Some become exacting. Some smile in a way that contains no kindness. Some become numb. Some switch into professional language, as if an intimate moment could be managed by minutes and action points. Some reach for the nearest task and begin performing competence. The pattern is rarely mysterious when examined after the fact. The difficulty is catching it while it is happening.

The body offers clues before the mouth has caused damage. Heat in the neck. Pressure behind the eyes. A sudden need to stand up. An urge to prove one precise fact. A desire to end the conversation with a line that cannot be answered. A fantasy of walking away and making the other person regret speaking. These signals are not instructions. They are dashboard lights. Ignore them, and the next sentence may be chosen by threat rather than care. Notice them, and a narrow space opens between impulse and conduct.

That space is small, but it is enough to change direction. The person who notices acceleration may stop mid-explanation. The person who notices sarcasm forming may let the clever sentence die unsaid. The person who notices icy politeness may admit, "I am going cold because I feel accused." The person who notices factual narrowing may hold the correction for later and attend to the impact first. Nothing sentimental is required. The repair begins when the person stops treating their first reaction as the most reliable part of them.

There is a particular nobility in not using intelligence as a weapon when blamed. Intelligent people can be exceptionally skilled at defending badly. They can argue in layers, distinguish terms, question assumptions, expose inconsistencies, and emerge technically victorious from conversations that leave both people poorer. The sharper the mind, the greater the responsibility to notice when precision has become armour. A relationship does not thrive because the more articulate person can always make a case. It thrives when that person can choose contact over conquest at the crucial moment.

The first ten seconds are not always enough to repair, but they are often enough to prevent further harm. They are enough to notice the inner lawyer reaching for evidence. Enough to catch the runner looking for an exit. Enough to feel the locked room closing. This is where the next movement begins: not with a grand promise to be calmer, but with the accurate recognition of one's own early warning signs. The forward test is severe and practical: when blame brushes the skin, can the person notice the threat response before it borrows their voice?

Reducing Heat Quickly

On 28 January 1986, after the Space Shuttle Challenger broke apart over the Atlantic, investigators later returned again and again to the conditions inside the decision-making room before launch at Kennedy Space Center in Florida. The catastrophe belonged to engineering, weather, institutional pressure, and communication failure; it should not be flattened into a domestic metaphor. Yet one lesson travels carefully: when pressure rises, people can become less capable of hearing the warning that would save them. Heat does not only produce noise. It narrows attention.

The same narrowing happens on a smaller, private scale when a repair conversation begins to overheat. One person says, "That hurt me," and the other hears, "You are bad." The first person reaches for clarity, the second reaches for defence, and within seconds the room has too much voltage for either to handle well. The danger is not feeling. Feeling is already present. The danger is unmanaged acceleration: faster speech, sharper tone, tighter jaw, harder eyes, sentences that arrive armed.

Reducing heat quickly is not the same as escaping the conversation. That distinction is essential. Disappearing may reduce one person's discomfort while increasing the other's alarm. Staying without regulation may satisfy the demand for presence while damaging the bond through impatience, sarcasm, or contempt. The useful middle is brief, visible self-command: enough pause to lower intensity, enough language to signal continued care, enough boundary to prevent the exchange from becoming a second injury. The hand must leave the hot pan before anyone debates the recipe.

A single breath can interrupt the body's rush towards defence, but only if it is used as a turn towards responsibility rather than a theatrical display of patience. Everyone recognises the punitive inhale: the exaggerated breath that says, "I am enduring you." That is not regulation; it is contempt with better posture. A useful breath is quieter. It gives the speaker a beat to notice whether the next sentence is about repair or retaliation. The visible change is modest: the voice slows, the shoulders lower, the answer begins closer to the present moment. Small changes matter.

The research of James Gross at Stanford University on emotion regulation, particularly his work from the 1990s onwards, helps explain why timing and method matter. Suppressing emotion is not the same as regulating it. A person can push expression down while remaining internally activated, and the suppressed feeling may still leak through tone, facial expression, or rigid politeness. Reappraisal, by contrast, changes how the person understands the moment. In relational terms, this means that merely clenching the jaw and "staying calm" may not help much. The question is whether the person can shift from "I am under attack" to "something landed badly, and I need to respond without making it worse."

One sentence can do that work when it names the heat without dramatizing it. "I am getting defensive, and I want to slow down." "I heard that as blame, and I may be reacting too fast." "I want to answer, but I need to make sure I am not just protecting myself." Such sentences are not confessions of defeat. They are acts of orientation. They tell the other person that the speaker has noticed the dangerous turn and is trying to re-enter the conversation with more care. The sentence becomes a handrail. It gives both people something steadier to hold.

The wrong sentence can raise the temperature while pretending to lower it. "Calm down" is a classic example. It is rarely received as an invitation to steadiness, because it places the burden of emotional management entirely on the other person and often implies that their feeling is the problem. "You are overreacting" does even more damage; it converts impact into defect. "I cannot deal with this" may be honest, but without a return it often sounds like abandonment. The implication is precise: heat is not reduced by commanding the other person to become easier to handle. It is reduced when someone takes responsibility for their own contribution to the temperature.

A boundary is sometimes necessary because repair cannot survive every kind of exchange. The word boundary is often misused to mean preference, punishment, or control, but in this context it has a narrower function: it protects the conditions under which repair remains possible. "I want to keep talking, but not while we are interrupting each other" is a boundary. "I am done" is often a wall. "I need a minute, and I will come back" is a boundary with a door in it. "I am leaving because you are impossible" is a verdict. The difference can be felt in the room.

The example is ordinary because ordinary is where most repair either succeeds or fails. A couple is discussing a family visit, and one partner says, "You always make plans without asking me." The other feels the familiar surge: heat in the face, a fast inventory of all the times they did ask, a desire to produce proof. The first version comes out badly: "That is completely unfair. You never remember anything I do." Now the argument has doubled. The second version catches the surge before it speaks fully: "I am getting defensive because I do not think 'always' is fair. I still want to understand why this felt decided without you." The issue remains. The heat drops enough for the next sentence to have a chance.

The phrase "I need a minute" differs from "I am done" because it treats the pause as part of the conversation rather than an exit from it. "I need a minute" says the speaker is not currently fit for repair, but intends to become fit. "I am done" may sometimes be necessary in genuinely unsafe or degrading exchanges, but in ordinary conflict it often lands as a slammed internal door. One protects the bond by preventing further damage. The other may protect the self by removing the bond from consideration. The difference is not softness. It is accountability for the effect of leaving.

The work of John Gottman and Robert Levenson on couple conflict is again relevant here because their observations gave weight to the idea that physiological arousal can make constructive conversation much harder. When people become highly activated, they often lose access to the very qualities repair requires: humour without cruelty, curiosity without interrogation, specificity without accusation, and listening without immediate rebuttal. The relational evidence is easy to see. People repeat themselves louder. They mishear softer meanings. They treat a pause as strategy. They grab one flawed phrase and use it to dismiss the whole complaint.

Reducing heat quickly therefore means reducing the number of injuries created after the original injury. It does not require instant peace. It asks only that the conversation stop manufacturing fresh harm. A sharp exchange may already have occurred; the next task is to prevent the defensive explanation, the sarcastic aside, the disgusted look, the punishing silence, or the dramatic exit from becoming the real memory. In many conflicts, the aftermath causes more damage than the trigger. A small rupture becomes serious when the repair attempt becomes the second rupture.

There is a limitation worth naming. Some people use "regulation" language to silence legitimate anger. They ask for calm only because anger makes them uncomfortable, not because the exchange has become unsafe or unworkable. They praise softness in the person they hurt while refusing to examine the harm. This is not reducing heat; it is managing appearances. A relationship that permits only tidy pain will eventually drive honesty underground. Strong feeling has a place. A raised voice, a tearful sentence, or visible agitation does not automatically mean repair has failed.

The reconciliation lies in purpose and behaviour. Heat should be reduced when it prevents listening, distorts meaning, or creates new harm. It should not be reduced merely to make the injured person more convenient. The test is whether lowering intensity increases truth or suppresses it. A good pause allows a clearer sentence to emerge. A bad pause teaches the hurt person to edit themselves. A good boundary protects dignity on both sides. A bad boundary protects one person from accountability. The difference shows up in the return.

What not to do is as important as what to do. Do not use the pause to rehearse a defence until it becomes more polished and less permeable. Many people physically step away while mentally remaining in combat. They pace the hallway preparing their closing argument. They text a friend in a way that turns complexity into prosecution. They select the most flattering facts and delete the inconvenient ones. By the time they return, they are not regulated; they are better armed. The pan has been taken off the flame, but the oil is still smoking.

A useful pause does something different. It loosens the grip of the case. It asks what part of the other person's pain may be true, what part of one's own reaction is self-protection, and what sentence would make the room safer rather than more winnable. This is difficult because the mind enjoys rehearsing. Rehearsal feels productive. It produces coherence, momentum, and moral confidence. But coherence can be dangerous when built entirely from one side of the evidence. The goal is not to return with the perfect argument. It is to return with more capacity.

Another common mistake is outsourcing the heat to a third party too quickly. A person leaves the conversation, sends a dramatic message to a friend, and receives the comfort of being agreed with before the facts have been tested. Support can be valuable, especially when a pattern is confusing or distressing, but immediate recruitment often hardens the story. The friend hears a courtroom summary, not the full weather of the room. By the time the person returns, repair has to compete with the applause of an invisible jury. The relationship is no longer two people trying to understand a rupture; it is one person returning with witnesses.

Reducing heat also requires attention to physical setting. Not every repair attempt can survive an audience, a moving car, a crowded kitchen, or the edge of sleep. The body reads context. Standing over someone can make even gentle words feel like pressure. Following someone from room to room can turn care into pursuit. Continuing by text can multiply misreadings because tone disappears and speed increases. A change in posture, distance, or medium may lower the temperature before any elaborate language is needed. Sitting down rather than looming, speaking from the doorway rather than blocking it, choosing voice over a long message: these small decisions make dignity more likely.

The motif of the hot pan returns because it respects urgency without panic. When a pan is smoking, one does not write a lecture on cooking technique while the alarm screams. One lowers the heat, moves the pan, opens a window, and only then asks what went wrong. Relational heat asks for the same order. Lower the intensity. Preserve safety. Stop adding fuel. Then examine the pattern. People often reverse this sequence because they want understanding before restraint. But restraint may be what makes understanding possible.

A quick reduction in heat does not guarantee a good outcome. It creates an opening. The other person may still be hurt. The practical issue may still be unresolved. A deeper apology may still be required. But the conversation has been spared the kind of escalation that leaves both people ashamed of what they said after the point had already been made. The result is not neatness; it is preserved capacity. The next words can land because the room is no longer being asked to hold fire and meaning at the same time.

The forward test is simple and severe. When the temperature rises, will the person reach for the old tools: speed, correction, sarcasm, icy restraint, disappearance, rehearsal? Or will they do the more disciplined thing and lower the heat without abandoning the bond? A breath, a sentence, a boundary: small enough to seem inadequate, powerful enough to keep the next sentence from becoming the wound everyone remembers.

Returning with Intention

On 11 April 1970, Apollo 13 left Kennedy Space Center in Florida with a clear mission: land in the Fra Mauro highlands of the Moon. After the oxygen tank explosion two days later, the mission changed. When the crew and flight controllers returned to the problem, they could not return to the old plan as if nothing had happened. The question was no longer how to complete the lunar landing. It was how to bring three astronauts home alive. The return had to be governed by a new intention, or it would have been a rehearsal of the wrong mission.

A paused conflict requires the same kind of re-entry. Not the same stakes, not the same grandeur, but the same discipline: coming back must be guided by what is now needed, not by the emotional script that existed before the pause. If the first exchange ended in defensiveness, sarcasm, interruption, or retreat, returning without a stated purpose often restarts the very machinery that made the pause necessary. The bodies may be calmer; the argument may still be waiting in the chair.

This is the hidden failure of many pauses. People leave the room to reduce heat, but they return with no new aim. One comes back ready to explain. The other comes back ready to be disappointed. Someone says, "So," and the old rhythm reappears: the correction, the accusation, the wounded tone, the tightening face. The pause has changed the clock but not the direction. The door opens, yet no one has decided what kind of conversation should walk through it.

Returning with intention means naming the purpose of the next few minutes before the conflict has a chance to reclaim the room. The purpose may be small: understand the impact, clarify what was meant, apologise for one part, agree one next step, or decide when a longer conversation should happen. The power lies in focus. A re-entry line places a boundary around the conversation so it does not become a general trial of the relationship. "I want to come back to understand what landed badly, not to argue the whole evening again." That sentence does not solve the issue. It points the room in a safer direction.

The alternative is drift, and drift favours old patterns. If a couple usually cycles through criticism and defence, a vague return gives the cycle room to begin again. If colleagues usually bury tension under politeness, a vague return allows the real issue to remain untouched. If family members usually mix the present problem with old grievances, a vague return gives history permission to crowd the table. Intention acts like a marked path through a field where both people have previously got lost. Without it, they may walk in circles with greater composure and call that progress.

A stated goal also protects dignity. After a conflict pause, both people may feel exposed. The one who asked for space may fear being seen as avoidant. The one who waited may fear being made foolish for caring. A clear re-entry reduces that uncertainty. It says, "I am not coming back to punish you, overwhelm you, or perform innocence. I am coming back to do one piece of repair." That narrowing is not evasive. It is merciful. Most overheated conversations fail because they try to carry too many tasks at once: apology, analysis, history, reassurance, future planning, and moral judgement. No wonder they collapse.

The work of Roger Fisher and William Ury in *Getting to Yes*, published in 1981 through the Harvard Negotiation Project, offers a useful parallel from negotiation practice. Their distinction between positions and interests helped many readers see that a repeated argument often hides a more basic concern. In relational repair, returning with intention performs a similar clarifying function. "I want you to admit you were wrong" may be the position. "I need to know you understand why I felt dismissed" may be the interest. "I need space" may be the position. "I need enough calm to respond without being cruel" may be the interest. Re-entry works better when it names the human task beneath the argumentative demand.

The intention should be proportionate to the moment. If the rupture was a brief interruption, the return may need only a brief acknowledgement and a commitment to listen differently. If the rupture touched a repeated pattern, the return may need more structure: what happened, what it meant, what each person will do next time. If the rupture revealed a serious breach of trust, the intention may simply be to establish whether a fuller conversation can happen safely. The size of the purpose should match the size of the wound. A teaspoon cannot carry a storm, but a storm should not be summoned for a teaspoon.

The re-entry line matters because beginnings set tone. "Can we talk now?" is sometimes too vague. It may sound like a threat to someone who has just regained composure. "I have been thinking" can also raise alarm if it introduces a prepared prosecution. A better return begins with ownership and direction: "I want to try again, and my aim is to understand the impact before I explain." Or: "I do not want to restart the fight; I want to agree what happens next time we hit this point." Such openings reduce defensiveness because they tell the other person what kind of attention is being requested.

This is where the difference between intention and agenda becomes important. An intention keeps the conversation honest. An agenda tries to control the outcome. "I want to understand what happened for you" is an intention. "I want you to understand why you overreacted" is an agenda wearing borrowed clothes. "I want to own my part and then talk about the practical issue" is an intention. "I want to apologise so we can stop talking about it" is an agenda. The difference is visible in flexibility. A person with an intention can be affected by what they hear. A person with an agenda is waiting for the other to arrive at a pre-selected conclusion.

Research associated with John Gottman and his colleagues on couple conflict gives weight to the importance of repair attempts and softened re-entry. Their observational work showed that small bids to reduce tension, change tone, or reconnect can alter the direction of a difficult exchange when they are recognised and received. The relevance here is not that every return must be gentle in a decorative sense. It is that the emotional start-up of a return shapes what follows. A harsh return asks the other person to defend. A deliberate return invites them to participate.

A useful return also distinguishes between the topic and the process. The topic may be money, timing, household work, family obligations, sex, work pressure, or a broken promise. The process is how the two people are handling the topic: interrupting, withdrawing, mocking, flooding, explaining, or going silent. If the pause happened because the process became damaging, the return should not rush back into the topic as though process does not matter. It may begin with, "Before we talk about the plan, I want to repair how I spoke." This sequencing prevents a practical discussion from being built on relational injury.

There is a credible limitation. Some people over-structure the return until it loses human warmth. They come back with language so careful that it feels rehearsed, clinical, or manipulative. The other person may feel managed rather than met. Repair is not improved by sounding like a policy document. The intention must be clear, but the voice must remain alive. A stumbling sentence with real humility often carries more trust than a perfectly arranged statement that leaves no room for the other person's reality. Precision should serve contact, not replace it.

The same limitation applies when intention becomes a way to avoid emotional risk. A person may say, "My intention is only to discuss next steps," because they do not want to hear how deeply the moment hurt. Another may insist, "The purpose is understanding impact," while refusing to talk about any practical change. A stated goal should narrow the conversation enough to make it workable, not narrow it so much that the inconvenient truth is excluded. The return must be contained without being evasive. It must hold shape without becoming a cage.

Coming back is also an act of reliability. If someone said, "I need ten minutes," then the return is part of the promise. If they said, "I will talk after the meeting," the return is part of the repair. Time commitments after conflict are not administrative details; they are emotional evidence. Returning when promised tells the other person that space was not abandonment. Failing to return teaches the opposite, even if the intention was innocent. A person may become busy, tired, distracted, or embarrassed, but the effect is still visible: the other is left holding the unresolved moment alone.

The marked path appears again here. A relationship needs some sign that the pause has not become a wilderness. The sign may be a sentence, a time, a hand briefly on a shoulder, a message that says, "I have not forgotten." These gestures do not settle the matter. They prevent the waiting from becoming its own story. Where no path is marked, imagination goes to work. The waiting person begins to wonder whether the issue matters, whether their hurt was inconvenient, whether the other is hoping the whole thing will decay into silence. Return interrupts that speculation.

Intention also helps when the return must happen across different emotional speeds. One person may be ready to examine the impact; the other may only be ready to acknowledge that the impact exists. One may want reassurance; the other may be capable only of setting a time for a deeper talk. A stated purpose allows the pair to choose the next smallest honest step instead of pretending they are equally prepared. This matters because false readiness breeds resentment. People agree to conversations they cannot actually hold, then sabotage them through impatience, vagueness, or withdrawal.

The re-entry should not begin by rehearsing the defence created during the pause. This is one of the most common errors. A person leaves to calm down and spends the entire interval refining their argument. They return slower, but not softer. Their facts are better organised; their curiosity is worse. The pause has been used as a preparation room for prosecution. Returning with intention requires a different use of the interval. The question is not, "How do I prove my side more effectively?" It is, "What would make the next exchange less damaging and more truthful?"

There are moments when the stated intention must be to stop, not continue. If the previous exchange involved repeated interruption, contempt, threats of leaving used as punishment, or a level of escalation that made honest speech impossible, returning may mean naming that a fuller conversation cannot happen yet. This is not failure when done clearly. It may sound like, "I want to repair this, but we are not able to do it safely while we keep cutting each other off. I will come back at a specific time when we can speak without that pattern." The intention remains repair; the immediate method is containment.

A good return does not guarantee a generous reception. The other person may still be hurt, suspicious, tired, or angry. They may not trust the new tone because they remember the old pattern. That hesitation should not be treated as ingratitude. If the rupture mattered, the return may need to demonstrate itself over several sentences before trust re-enters the room. The person returning with intention must resist the temptation to say, "I am trying, so why are you still upset?" Trying is valuable. It is not a receipt that obliges immediate relief.

The best re-entry has a certain steadiness. It does not rush to erase discomfort. It does not arrive carrying a speech. It does not demand that the other person reward the return. It simply marks the path back and names the next piece of work: understand the impact, clarify the misunderstanding, own the behaviour, agree the next step, or pause more safely. That steadiness makes a calmer start more likely because it removes some of the uncertainty that feeds escalation. People can tolerate discomfort more easily when they know what kind of conversation they are in.

The unresolved test sits at the threshold of every return. After the pause, will the person come back to resume the old fight with better phrasing, or to begin a different kind of conversation? The answer is revealed quickly: in the opening sentence, in the willingness to hear impact before self-defence, in whether the promised return actually happens, and in whether the marked path leads towards repair or merely circles back to the place where both people got lost.

When to Pause Completely

On 27 October 1962, during the Cuban Missile Crisis, President John F. Kennedy and his advisers in Washington faced a message from Nikita Khrushchev that arrived amid fear, pressure, and competing interpretations. The danger was not only what the United States might say, but when and how it might say it. A reply made from panic could harden the crisis; a reply made with restraint could keep the channel from collapsing. The most serious room in the world had to learn a simple discipline: not every moment is made safer by continuing to speak.

The same principle appears, without the geopolitical stakes, in the private rooms where ordinary conflicts tip from difficult into damaging. Two people begin with a real issue. Then the conversation starts to fray. One interrupts before the other has finished. The other raises the volume to be heard. A phrase of contempt slips in. Someone threatens to leave, not as a truthful boundary but as a weapon. At that point, continuing may feel courageous, but it is often only momentum. The kettle is already boiling.

A complete pause is different from a brief slowing down. It is not a breath between sentences, not a gentler tone, not a moment to choose better wording. It is the decision that the present exchange can no longer carry repair without creating new injury. The visible signs are usually plain: repeated interruptions, escalating contempt, mocking imitation, a refusal to let the other finish, threats of abandonment, or the kind of coldness that makes honest speech feel unsafe. These are not small imperfections in style. They change the conditions of the conversation. When the conditions are hostile, the content cannot be handled cleanly.

Repeated interruption is one of the clearest signals. A single interruption may be clumsy, anxious, or habitual. Repeated interruption after being asked to stop is different. It tells the other person that their account will not be allowed to exist long enough to be understood. The injured person then has to fight for airtime before they can even speak about pain. The repair attempt becomes a struggle over the right to finish a sentence. Once that struggle begins, the original issue often disappears behind the procedural injury: "You will not even let me speak." A complete pause may be the only way to protect the conversation from becoming a contest of volume and endurance.

Contempt is even more serious because it attacks the person beneath the argument. The research tradition associated with John Gottman and his colleagues placed particular emphasis on contempt as a corrosive feature in couple conflict, not because every sharp sentence carries equal weight, but because contempt communicates disgust, superiority, and dismissal. It can appear as an eye roll, a sneer, a mocking voice, a character attack, or a sentence designed to make the other person feel small. Once contempt enters the room, repair becomes difficult because the injured person is no longer only responding to a disagreement. They are responding to degradation. The implication is severe: where contempt is active, continuing to talk may reward the very behaviour that needs to stop.

Threats of leaving must be handled with precision. Sometimes leaving is necessary. A person may need to remove themselves from a conversation that has become unsafe, degrading, or impossible to conduct with dignity. That is a boundary. But threats of leaving can also be used to control the other person: "If you keep saying that, I am done with us," "Maybe I should just go," "You clearly do not want this relationship." Such statements turn attachment into a weapon. They force the other person to abandon the issue and soothe the threat. The practical effect is visible: the conversation shifts from repair to panic management. The original hurt is buried under the urgent task of preventing abandonment.

A complete pause protects connection only when it is made cleanly. A punishing pause says, "You have lost access to me." A protective pause says, "This exchange is becoming harmful, and I intend to return when it can be handled differently." The difference may seem subtle in language, but it is immense in effect. A punishing pause leaves the other person guessing, chasing, or freezing. A protective pause reduces uncertainty. It names the problem with the process, not the worth of the person. It sets a return point. It refuses to use disappearance as discipline.

The work of psychologist James Gross on emotion regulation, developed at Stanford University from the 1990s onwards, helps clarify why merely staying in the room is not always virtuous. Suppression can make someone look composed while their internal activation remains high. The face may become still, the voice controlled, the words technically civil, yet the person may be preparing a sharper answer, rehearsing an accusation, or withdrawing beyond reach. Remaining physically present is not the same as remaining repair-capable. A complete pause may become necessary when the outward conversation continues but the inner conversation has already become hostile.

A simple example shows the turning point. Two partners are arguing about a family obligation. One feels plans were made without consultation; the other feels accused after trying to be helpful. The first says, "You never consider me." The second replies, "That is ridiculous," and begins listing examples. The first interrupts. The second raises their voice. The first says, "Maybe I should just stop expecting anything from you." The second says, "Fine, maybe we should not go at all." By now, the topic has become secondary. The argument is producing fresh injuries faster than either person can repair them. A complete pause is not avoidance here. It is containment.

The clean pause would not sound like a dramatic exit. It would identify the process and preserve the return. "We are interrupting and threatening the relationship now. I do not want to continue like this. I am going to stop, and I will come back when we can speak without those threats." The wording need not be perfect, but the structure matters: name the unsafe pattern, stop the harmful exchange, and create a path back. Without the path back, the pause becomes a locked door. With the path back, it becomes a firebreak.

The term firebreak is useful because it does not romanticise the pause. A firebreak does not extinguish every flame. It prevents spread. In conflict, the spread is often more damaging than the spark. The original spark may be a missed message, a sharp tone, a thoughtless joke, or a disagreement about time. The spread is the contempt, threat, interruption, character attack, and punishing silence that follow. A complete pause creates distance between the initial rupture and the larger damage that is trying to attach itself.

There is a credible limitation. Some people call a pause whenever accountability approaches. They hear impact, feel discomfort, and immediately declare the conversation unsafe. They leave not because harm is escalating, but because truth is inconvenient. This misuse matters. If every difficult feeling is labelled "too much", repair becomes impossible. The other person learns that any honest complaint will be treated as an attack. The result is not safety; it is emotional censorship. A pause is justified by the condition of the exchange, not by the mere presence of discomfort.

The reconciliation lies in observable behaviour. A complete pause is warranted when the process itself is causing damage: repeated interruption, contemptuous delivery, intimidation, threats used to control, or an inability to stop escalating after attempts to slow down. It is less warranted when one person is simply uncomfortable hearing how their behaviour landed. Discomfort belongs in repair. Degradation does not. The distinction requires honesty because self-protection is clever. It can disguise avoidance as wisdom and punishment as a boundary.

Clear timing for reconnection is what keeps the pause from becoming abandonment. "Later" is often too vague after a rupture. It gives anxiety room to invent its own timetable. A more reliable pause names a return point that both can understand. The exact timing depends on context, but the promise must be believable. A person who says they will return must return, or at least update the other if circumstances genuinely change. Reliability is not a minor courtesy here. It is the proof that the pause was meant to protect repair, not evade it.

The return point also changes what happens during the break. Without a return, the pause becomes open-ended, and both people may use the space badly. One rehearses a defence. The other writes a harsher story. One seeks an ally who will confirm their innocence. The other reviews every previous slight. A clear return discourages this drift because the mind knows the issue has not vanished into fog. The firebreak has a boundary. There will be a place to meet again.

What one does during the complete pause matters as much as the pause itself. If the time away is spent polishing accusations, gathering evidence, composing cruel phrases, or imagining the other person's worst motives, the pause has lowered volume without lowering heat. The body may have left the room, but the conflict has continued in private. A protective pause asks a different use of the interval. It asks the person to notice their own contribution, separate impact from intent, consider what would make the return safer, and resist the pleasures of self-righteousness. This is not passivity. It is preparation for repair rather than preparation for battle.

The distinction between stopping and stonewalling is crucial. Stonewalling withholds presence to punish, control, or avoid. It often has no clear return and no stated care for the conversation. Stopping to protect repair is different. It remains relational even while it creates distance. It says, in effect, "I am not willing to keep injuring us in order to prove that I am still here." That sentence may be silent in the mind, but it should shape the behaviour. The door closes gently. The return is named. The bond is not made to beg.

A workplace example makes the principle visible in another setting. During a tense project review, a senior colleague repeatedly interrupts a junior colleague's explanation. The junior colleague grows shorter, then stops contributing. A second colleague notices the pattern and says, "We are not going to get a useful decision if one person cannot finish their point. Let us pause this discussion and come back with each person heard properly." The pause is not a retreat from the project. It protects the quality of the decision. If the meeting continues under the same interruption pattern, the practical outcome may look efficient while the relational cost shows up later as silence, resentment, or reduced candour.

Families need the same discipline, though the emotional stakes are often older. In family conflict, pausing completely may be necessary when the present disagreement has been swallowed by inherited roles. Someone becomes "the selfish one", "the sensitive one", "the difficult one", "the one who always leaves". Once labels replace listening, the conversation cannot repair the immediate rupture because it is no longer addressing the immediate rupture. It is reenacting a family script. A complete pause interrupts the script long enough for people to decide whether they are returning to the current issue or to an old courtroom.

The hardest part of pausing completely is tolerating the unfinished feeling. Human beings often want emotional closure before they have earned the conditions for it. They want the last word, the correction, the reassurance, the apology, the visible sign that they were not wrong to care. A pause denies that immediate satisfaction. It leaves the sentence unfinished on purpose. That can feel unbearable, especially for someone who associates distance with abandonment. This is why the return promise is not decorative. It is the thread that allows the unfinished moment to remain survivable.

A complete pause should never be used to create fear. If someone knows the other person is vulnerable to abandonment panic and deliberately withdraws without clarity, the pause has become a weapon. If someone knows the other needs time to regulate and deliberately follows them from room to room, urgency has become coercive. Both failures treat the other person's nervous system as territory to occupy. Protective pausing respects limits without exploiting them. It asks for enough distance to prevent harm and enough connection to prevent dread.

The firebreak returns at the end because it captures the necessary modesty of the act. Pausing completely does not solve the conflict. It does not prove maturity. It does not guarantee that the later conversation will be generous. It simply stops the spread. It refuses to let interruption become humiliation, let contempt become memory, let threats become the new centre of the argument. The deeper repair still waits on the other side: impact, intent, accountability, and the small agreement that changes the next collision.

The forward test is not whether a person can keep talking through anything. Endurance is not always wisdom. The harder test is whether they can recognise the moment when continuing would become a form of damage, and whether they can stop without punishing, leave without abandoning, and name the return without making it another bargaining chip. When the kettle is boiling and the room is losing its human shape, the repair may begin with the sentence that refuses to let one more word become one more wound.

Chapter 4
Naming Impact Without Blame

What changes in the room when a person says, "You do not care," instead of "When you looked at your phone while I was speaking, I felt unimportant"? The event may be the same. The hurt may be equally real. Yet one sentence puts the other person on trial, while the other places the injury on the table where both people can see it. The difference is not softness. It is accuracy.

A bad moment often arrives with more feeling than language can hold. Someone is wounded, but what comes out is a verdict. Someone feels dismissed, but what comes out is an accusation. Someone feels alone, but what comes out is a sentence sharp enough to make the other person defend rather than listen. The plate is not broken; the atmosphere is. A chair scrapes back. A face closes. The injury that needed recognition becomes a contest over character.

The tragedy is that many accusations begin as sincere attempts to be understood. "You never listen" may contain the real hurt of being interrupted again. "You only think about yourself" may be carrying the loneliness of handling too much unseen labour. "You are controlling" may be the frightened protest of someone who feels watched, corrected, or managed. The language is blunt because the feeling is urgent. But urgency does not guarantee precision. When pain speaks in verdicts, it often makes the listener less capable of hearing the pain.

The central tension is that impact must be named clearly enough to matter, but not so globally that it becomes an attack on the other person's entire moral identity. Too little force, and the hurt disappears into politeness. Too much blame, and the conversation becomes a defence hearing. The work is not to make pain tidy, charming, or convenient. It is to make it usable. A usable impact statement gives the other person something specific to recognise, repair, and change.

The stakes are immediate because accusation alters posture. A person accused of not caring will usually search for evidence that they do care. They may list sacrifices, correct the record, attack the tone, or withdraw into injured innocence. A person told that their phone use during a vulnerable sentence made the speaker feel unimportant has a different task. They may still feel uncomfortable. They may still need to clarify intent. But the point of contact is visible: a behaviour, an effect, and a need that was missed. The room has fewer shadows.

The stakes grow over time because relationships develop habits of translation. If one person often speaks pain as blame, the other learns to listen defensively before the sentence is finished. If one person often responds to impact as though it were prosecution, the injured person learns to intensify their language just to be taken seriously. Soon both are speaking through armour. One exaggerates to be heard; the other minimises to survive. The original hurt becomes harder to find, like a set of keys buried under papers that everyone keeps adding to.

The way forward begins with clean impact: what happened, what it landed like, and what was needed instead. From there, the harder discipline is separating what was seen or heard from the story that formed around it, without pretending the story is meaningless. Then comes the quieter test of listening for the tender centre beneath the complaint, because a well-shaped impact statement is only half the repair; the other half is whether someone can receive it without immediately adding their own defence. The path moves from expression to discernment to reception.

A receipt is a useful motif here: plain, specific, and harder to argue with than a cloud of suspicion. "You do not care" is a weather system. "You answered three messages while I was telling you something painful, and I felt alone in the conversation" is a receipt. It does not contain the whole relationship. It does not prove permanent neglect. It records a moment clearly enough that repair can begin. The receipt is not the final judgement; it is the evidence of impact.

The unresolved question is whether anger can become more exact without becoming less honest. Many people fear that if they remove blame, they will weaken the truth. Yet the opposite is often the case.

Blame scatters the truth across character, history, motive, and moral complaint. Impact gathers it back into the moment where something can actually be repaired. When the next rupture appears, the choice will be waiting: turn the hurt into a verdict, or name the impact clearly enough that the other person has a real chance to meet it.

Clear Impact Statements

In 1981, at the Harvard Negotiation Project in Cambridge, Massachusetts, Roger Fisher and William Ury gave public language to a distinction that had long mattered in difficult conversations: separate the people from the problem. Their book, *Getting to Yes*, was written for negotiation, not marriage, friendship, family life, or the small bruises of ordinary intimacy. Yet its central insight travels well. A sentence can either make another person the problem, or it can place the problem between two people where both may examine it.

That distinction becomes vivid in a kitchen after a missed cue. One person has been speaking about something tender. The other glances at a phone, replies to a message, and looks back as though nothing has happened. The speaker says, "You do not care." The sentence is understandable. It is also too large. It tries to carry hurt, interpretation, protest, history, and moral judgement in four words. The other person hears an accusation of character and begins searching for evidence of care. The original wound slips out of reach.

A clear impact statement does something more disciplined. It narrows the lens without shrinking the feeling. It says what happened, how it landed, and what was needed instead. "When you looked at your phone while I was telling you about my meeting, I felt alone in the conversation. I needed your attention for a minute before we moved on." The hurt remains. The dignity remains. What disappears is the mind-reading. The sentence no longer claims to know the other person's inner life; it describes the contact point where behaviour met experience.

This is why impact differs from accusation even when anger is present. Anger does not disqualify a person from speaking clearly. In fact, anger often becomes more useful when it is given an accurate address. "You never listen" is a flare sent into the sky. "You interrupted twice while I was trying to finish the point, and I felt dismissed" is a marked location. A flare may get attention, but it may also frighten the room into defence. A marked location gives repair somewhere to go. Specificity is not emotional dilution. It is emotional intelligence under pressure.

The structure is simple because complicated structures tend to fail when people are hurt. There is the event: what could have been seen, heard, or recorded by another observer. There is the landing: the effect it had inside the person who received it. There is the need: what would have protected connection in that moment. These parts do not have to appear in elegant order, and they need not sound polished. They simply have to keep the speaker close to reality. "When the joke was made in front of your friends, I felt exposed. I needed that to stay private." That is enough to begin.

The event matters because it anchors the conversation. Without an event, impact becomes mist. "You make me feel small" may be emotionally true, but the other person may not know where to look. Was it a tone, a phrase, an interruption, a comparison, a decision, a silence? The absence of an event forces them either to guess or defend against a global charge. "When you corrected my story twice at dinner" gives the listener a handle. They may still disagree with part of the interpretation, but they are no longer fighting a cloud.

The landing matters because behaviour alone does not reveal effect. Two people can experience the same act differently. One person may hear teasing as warmth; another may hear it as exposure. One may experience a reminder as care; another may experience it as control. A clear impact statement does not pretend the effect is universal. It says, "This is how it landed here, in me, in that moment." That phrasing is not weakness. It is accuracy. It prevents the speaker from turning personal pain into universal law.

The need matters because repair requires direction. If the sentence stops at injury, the other person may understand the hurt but not know what would help. A need is not a demand dressed in softer clothes. It is the relational requirement that was missing: attention, privacy, patience, reassurance, a slower pace, a chance to finish, a direct answer, a return after space. "I needed you to ask before sharing that" is clearer than "You embarrassed me." It moves the conversation from moral heat towards practical repair.

Marshall Rosenberg's *Nonviolent Communication*, first published in 1999 in the United States, offers a useful second anchor because it emphasised the difference between observation, feeling, need, and request. Its language has sometimes been copied so mechanically that it can sound artificial, but the underlying distinction remains valuable. Observations keep the conversation near what happened. Feelings name the human cost. Needs reveal what mattered. Requests point towards future conduct. The aim is not to speak like a manual. The aim is to stop smuggling accusation into sentences that are supposed to repair.

A receipt is a good image for impact language. It does not contain the whole moral history of the relationship. It records a transaction clearly enough that the cost can be understood. "You do not care" is not a receipt; it is a verdict. "You answered three messages while I was describing something painful, and I felt unimportant" is a receipt. It does not prove permanent neglect. It does not erase all the times the other person has been attentive. It records the moment that needs repair. The receipt keeps the conflict from expanding beyond the evidence.

This matters because the human mind often adds motive before it has checked impact. A person sees a partner arrive late and thinks, "They do not respect my time." A colleague receives a curt email and thinks, "They are trying to undermine me." A friend is not invited and thinks, "I am being pushed out." Sometimes those interpretations contain truth. Sometimes they are fuelled by fatigue, old wounds, fear, or incomplete information. Clear impact language allows the interpretation to be held without being presented as fact. "When I saw the plan had been made without me, I felt left out, and the story I told myself was that my view did not matter." That sentence is honest without becoming prosecutorial.

The phrase "the story I told myself" can be powerful when used sincerely. It does not mean the story is false. It means the speaker recognises the difference between observation and interpretation.

That recognition lowers defensiveness because it leaves room for information. The other person may be able to say, "I can see why it looked that way. I made the plan quickly because the booking was closing, not because I wanted to exclude you." The impact still matters. The intent may alter the meaning. Both can be true.

Accusation usually fuses event, interpretation, and character into one sentence. "You ignored me because you only care about work." The event may be that the person did not answer a message. The interpretation may be that the silence meant indifference. The character judgement is that work matters more than the relationship. Once fused, the sentence becomes difficult to repair because the listener must disentangle it before responding. They may want to acknowledge the missed message, clarify the reason, reject the character judgement, and soothe the hurt all at once. The conversation becomes crowded.

Clear impact statements uncrowd the room. "When I did not hear back after I sent that message, I felt anxious and unimportant. I needed a quick note that you had seen it." This sentence may still be uncomfortable to hear, especially if the listener was busy, overwhelmed, or acting without malice. But it gives them a clean task. They can acknowledge the effect, clarify the circumstance, and agree what is realistic next time. The issue has not been flattened into innocence or guilt. It has been made workable.

There is a credible limitation. Impact language can be misused. A person can say "I felt hurt" in a way that functions as a final verdict no one may question. They can wrap accusation in therapeutic grammar: "When you disagreed with me, I felt unsafe," when what they mean is "You are not allowed to challenge me." They can use the language of need to control another person's choices. This matters because precision should increase honesty, not make manipulation sound refined. Not every hurt interpretation is accurate. Not every need can or should be met in the way requested.

The reconciliation is to keep impact statements tethered to observable behaviour and open to clarification. "When you disagreed in front of the team, I felt undermined" may be a valid impact. It is not yet proof that the disagreement was wrong. The next question may reveal whether the setting was inappropriate, the tone was dismissive, or the speaker was interpreting any public disagreement as disloyalty. Clear impact language opens the inquiry; it does not end it. It gives pain a fair hearing without granting it absolute authority over the facts.

The difference between blame and impact also protects the person speaking. Blame often feels powerful in the instant because it pushes pain outward. "You are selfish" gives the speaker a hard surface to stand on. But it also gives the listener an obvious escape route: prove they are not selfish, attack the overstatement, or retreat from the verdict. Impact requires more courage because it stays closer to vulnerability. "I felt alone when you made the decision without me" exposes the softer truth beneath the accusation. It is less armoured. It is also harder to dismiss without revealing something.

The rewrite from "You do not care" shows the whole skill in miniature. The accusation says too much and too little. Too much, because it claims access to the other person's heart. Too little, because it does not say what happened. A clearer version might be: "When I was telling you about the hospital call and you kept scrolling, I felt as if I was carrying it by myself. I needed you to put the phone down and stay with me for a few minutes." The sentence is not timid. It is more exacting than the accusation because it names the behaviour, the wound, and the repairable need.

In professional settings, the same principle applies with different language. "You shut me down in that meeting" may be true in spirit, but it invites defence. "When I raised the risk about the deadline and the topic was moved on before I had finished, I felt my concern had been dismissed. I needed space to complete the point before the decision was made" gives the other person a specific moment to review. It also protects the speaker from sounding merely resentful. The receipt is clear: a point raised, a topic moved on, a concern left unfinished.

Clear impact statements do not guarantee a graceful response. The other person may still defend, minimise, correct, or counterattack. They may be unready to hear even well-shaped pain. But clarity changes what the speaker is contributing to the moment. Instead of adding fog, they add definition. Instead of throwing a verdict into the room, they place evidence of impact where repair can begin. This does not make the speaker responsible for the listener's maturity. It makes the speaker responsible for the accuracy of their own signal.

The skill becomes especially important when anger is justified. Many people associate clarity with calm, as though only mild feelings can be responsibly expressed. That is false. Strong feeling can be exact. A person can be furious and still say, "When you shared that private information, I felt exposed and betrayed. I needed you to ask me before telling anyone." The emotion gives the sentence force; the structure gives it direction. Without structure, anger may scatter into character attack. Without force, the impact may be politely ignored. Repair needs both truth and shape.

A relationship that learns clear impact language becomes less dependent on mind-reading. People do not have to infer everything from tone, silence, or withdrawal. They do not have to wait for resentment to become obvious before taking it seriously. The small rupture can be named while it is still small: the missed greeting, the cutting joke, the public correction, the decision made alone, the delayed return after space. Each receipt prevents the ledger from becoming a secret account of grievances that no one else can inspect.

The forward test is whether the next hurt can be spoken without becoming a trial. When the sentence "You do not care" rises to the tongue, can it be translated before it leaves the mouth? What happened? How did it land? What was needed instead? The answer may still be angry. It may still tremble. But if it brings a receipt rather than a verdict, the other person has a chance to repair the moment instead of defending their entire character.

Separating Facts from Stories

In 1944, psychologists Fritz Heider and Marianne Simmel published a short study at Smith College in Northampton, Massachusetts, using an animation of simple geometric shapes: a large triangle, a small triangle, a circle, and a box-like enclosure. Viewers did not merely describe shapes moving across a screen. Many gave the figures motives, personalities, conflicts, intentions. A triangle was bullying. A circle was escaping. A small shape was frightened. The experiment endured because it revealed something quietly radical about perception: people do not only see movement. They make meaning.

The same thing happens after a bad moment between two people. A message is left unanswered. A chair is pushed back. A tone changes. Someone looks away while the other is speaking. Those are the observable facts, the shapes moving on the screen. Then the story arrives: "They are ignoring me." "They think I am ridiculous." "They are trying to control me." "They do not care enough to ask." The story may be perceptive. It may be partly true. It may also be wrong, incomplete, or inflated by old pain. The mind fills gaps fast.

Arguments explode when facts and stories become fused. The factual event is usually small enough to discuss: the phone was on the table, the reply came late, the joke was made in front of others, the decision was taken without a conversation. The story is where the fire catches. "You wanted to embarrass me." "You were punishing me." "You never intended to include me." Once the story is presented as fact, the other person is no longer being asked to understand impact; they are being asked to accept a verdict about their inner life. Most people will defend themselves there, even when the hurt underneath deserves care.

Separating facts from stories does not mean abandoning the story. That is the common fear. People imagine that if they say, "The story I told myself was..." they are weakening their own case, surrendering moral force, or offering the other person a convenient escape. But a story can be labelled without being dismissed. It can be held up to the light rather than thrown across the room. "When you left before I finished, the story I told myself was that you did not want to hear me." That sentence preserves the impact while allowing room for information. It is both honest and unfinished.

The distinction matters because observable facts give the conversation common ground, while stories reveal the emotional meaning of those facts. If someone says, "You ignored me all evening," the other person may remember bringing a drink, asking about the day, or sitting nearby. The charge becomes easy to contest. If the sentence becomes, "When I told you about the call from my sister, you kept looking at the television, and I felt alone with it," the conversation has a clearer centre. The fact can be checked. The story can be understood. The impact can be repaired.

The legal philosopher and evidence scholar John Henry Wigmore, writing in the early twentieth century in the United States, treated evidence as something to be sorted, tested, and connected rather than swallowed whole. Intimate conflict is not a courtroom and should not become one; cross-examination is a poor model for love. Yet the underlying discipline is useful. Not every claim belongs in the same category. What was seen? What was heard? What was inferred? What was feared? What was remembered from earlier? A conversation becomes less explosive when these elements are not forced to wear the same uniform.

The receipt motif returns here because a receipt tells only what it can tell. It names the purchase, the time, the amount. It does not explain the buyer's soul. In repair, the receipt is the observable event: "You changed the plan after I had arranged my day." The story is the meaning: "I felt as if my time did not matter." The accusation is the overreach: "You only care about yourself." A receipt can open inquiry. A verdict closes it. When people confuse one with the other, they make the listener choose between self-defence and surrender, neither of which produces useful truth.

A story is not automatically false because it is a story. This point is crucial. Stories are how people organise lived experience. A person who has repeatedly been interrupted may accurately recognise dismissal in a new interruption. A partner who has often been left to carry invisible labour may correctly hear indifference in a casual "whatever you think". A colleague who has previously been excluded from decisions may reasonably feel alarm when a new plan appears without consultation. Patterns matter. The problem is not interpretation itself. The problem is treating interpretation as if it needs no testing.

Testing a story requires a different posture from proving it. Proof often arrives with a prosecutorial tone: "Admit it, you did that because you were angry." "So you just decided I did not matter?" "Were you even planning to tell me?" These questions may contain real hurt, but they are shaped to corner. Clarification asks for information without pretending not to have an emotional stake. "When you changed the plan without checking, I felt sidelined. What was happening for you then?" "When you went quiet after I spoke, I wondered if you were upset with me. Is that right?" The second form does not flatten the feeling. It makes room for reality to answer.

Cross-examination often fails because it seeks confession rather than understanding. The questioned person feels the trap and begins managing risk. They choose words more carefully, reveal less, and become more invested in avoiding liability than in repairing connection. The visible behaviours follow quickly: longer pauses before answers, defensive qualifications, irritation at the framing, a shift from warmth into procedure. Real information retreats. Clarification, by contrast, reduces the threat enough for more accurate material to emerge. The person may say, "I changed the plan because I thought you were too busy, but I can see how that left you out." That is useful. It contains both intent and impact.

The work of Chris Argyris, a scholar of organisational learning associated with Harvard, is relevant here because of the "ladder of inference", an idea developed in the field of organisational behaviour and later popularised through Peter Senge's *The Fifth Discipline* in 1990. The model describes how people move from observable data to selected data, interpretation, assumptions, conclusions, beliefs, and actions. Its vocabulary belongs to institutions and teams, but its domestic application is immediate. A person sees a partner glance away. They select that detail, interpret it as boredom, conclude they are not valued, and then withdraw. The withdrawal becomes new data for the other person, who builds a different ladder.

Two ladders can turn one small moment into a whole architecture of misunderstanding. One person tells a story of neglect; the other tells a story of being unfairly accused. One becomes cooler; the other becomes defensive. Each then uses the other's reaction as proof. "See, you are pulling away." "See, you are attacking me." The facts at the bottom of the ladder become almost irrelevant because the fight is now taking place near the top, where conclusions have hardened into identity claims. Separating facts from stories brings the conversation back down a few rungs, where repair is still possible.

This is not a call to become emotionally detached. Detachment can be another form of avoidance. The aim is not to speak as if one were filing a laboratory report on one's own hurt. The aim is to preserve the difference between "what happened" and "what it meant to me", because that difference allows two truths to stand together. "You arrived after the meal had started" can coexist with "I felt embarrassed sitting there alone." "I was delayed by a work call" can coexist with "I should have sent a message sooner." When facts and stories are separated, complexity does not have to become contradiction.

There is a credible limitation. Some people use the language of "that is just your story" to dismiss impact. This is a refined form of minimising. It sounds thoughtful, but it can be cruel. If a person names a pattern and the other replies, "That is only your interpretation," without engaging the behaviour, the distinction between fact and story has been weaponised. The injured person is pushed into defending their perception rather than being met in the effect. Labelling a story should never become a way to deny the receipt. The fact still matters. The impact still matters.

The reconciliation is to treat stories as hypotheses with emotional weight. A hypothesis is not a fantasy. It is a proposed explanation awaiting fuller evidence. "The story I told myself was that you were embarrassed by me" is not a final judgement, but neither is it trivial. It reveals the shape of the hurt. The other person's task is not to say, "Wrong." Nor is it necessarily to say, "Correct." A better response begins by recognising the impact: "I can see why it looked that way, and I hate that it landed like embarrassment. What was happening for me was different." Now the story can be revised without the hurt being erased.

This distinction becomes especially important when old injuries echo inside new ones. A person who grew up being mocked may hear playful teasing as danger faster than someone else would. A partner who has been lied to before may experience a delayed explanation as threat. A colleague who has been overlooked may read a missed email as exclusion. These interpretations are not random; they are shaped by history. But history is not always a reliable narrator of the present. It may warn accurately, or it may misfire. Repair requires respect for the history without making it the sole judge.

The practical cost of not separating facts from stories is that conversations become longer and less informative. Instead of examining the missed message, the two people debate whether one is selfish and the other is too sensitive. Instead of examining the public correction, they argue over whether humiliation was intended. Instead of examining the decision made alone, they litigate the entire distribution of care in the relationship. The more global the story, the less repairable the moment becomes. Precision saves time because it prevents the conversation from expanding beyond what can be responsibly handled.

Precision also protects dignity. If someone says, "When you went quiet, I told myself I had disgusted you," they reveal vulnerability without accusing the other person of cruelty. The other can respond with care rather than immediate defence. They might say, "I went quiet because I was overwhelmed, not because I was disgusted." This does not mean the silence had no impact. It means the meaning can be corrected. The injured person receives information; the silent person receives a chance to be known more accurately. Both benefit from the distinction.

The same discipline changes professional conflict. "You deliberately undermined me in the meeting" is a story presented as fact. It may be true, but stated that way it invites denial. "When I raised the concern about the deadline and you moved the discussion on before I had finished, I felt undermined. Were you trying to close the topic, or did you read the room differently?" This formulation keeps the receipt visible and asks for clarification rather than confession. It also makes future action easier to discuss. If the issue was haste, the remedy differs from the remedy for deliberate exclusion.

In close relationships, clarification must not sound like interrogation with softer punctuation. Tone carries the real question. "What did you mean by that?" can be curiosity or threat. "Help me understand" can be generous or condescending. The listener feels the difference in the face, the timing, the willingness to be surprised. A clarifying question should be open enough that the answer could genuinely change the story. If no answer could change it, the person is not asking; they are staging a trial.

Separating facts from stories becomes harder when the story has been right before. Repeated patterns give interpretation weight. If someone has often dismissed your concerns, a new dismissal may not require endless uncertainty. If someone regularly makes promises and fails to return, the story "they are avoiding this" may be a responsible reading of the evidence. The skill is not to pretend each incident is isolated. It is to name the pattern as a pattern while still identifying the current receipt. "This felt like the same pattern as last week: I raised something, you went quiet, and we never came back to it." That is stronger than a character attack because it gives both history and behaviour.

A relationship grows more repairable when both people become willing to be corrected about their stories. This humility is not self-doubt in the corrosive sense. It is intellectual honesty applied to emotional life. "I may be reading this through last time." "The story I am telling myself may not be the whole picture." "I want to check before I assume." Such sentences lower defensiveness because they do not require the other person to fight for the possibility of being misunderstood. They create a small corridor through which new information can enter.

The forward test is whether, at the moment interpretation begins to harden, the person can keep the receipt separate from the verdict. What was seen? What was heard? What did the mind add? What does the hurt fear is true? These questions do not weaken the impact; they refine it. The next argument will offer the old temptation: treat the story as certainty and demand that the other person plead against it. Repair asks for the harder movement, the one that keeps pain honest and reality open: name the fact, own the story, and ask before the story becomes the only room either person can stand in.

Listening for the Real Hurt

In 1951, Carl Rogers published *Client-Centred Therapy* in the United States and gave unusually serious attention to a deceptively simple act: listening in a way that lets another person recognise themselves more clearly. Rogers was not writing about household arguments, workplace friction, or the strained silence after a sharp exchange at dinner. Yet the principle travels with force. A person who feels accurately heard often becomes less frantic to prove the wound exists. The room changes when the hurt has a witness.

The same shift can happen in an ordinary conflict. Someone says, "You always take over." The surface complaint is blunt, perhaps unfair in its wording. The listener hears an attack and begins preparing a defence: examples of restraint, reminders of good intentions, evidence that the other person also dominates at times. But underneath the complaint there may be a more vulnerable sentence trying to survive: "I felt controlled." Or, "I felt as if my judgement did not matter." Or, "I was afraid there would be no room for me." The complaint is the wrapping. The hurt is inside.

Impact statements are only useful if they are received. A person may express the effect of a moment with care and still meet a wall of explanation. They may say, "When you looked away, I felt dismissed," and hear, "I was not looking away, I was thinking." They may say, "When you changed the plan, I felt excluded," and hear, "I had to decide quickly." Those responses may contain facts, but they miss the first task. Before intention is clarified, before context is supplied, before the listener adds their own case, the hurt needs to be located. Otherwise the injured person must intensify the signal simply to feel heard.

Listening for the real hurt means hearing beneath the accusation without rewarding distortion. It does not require agreement with every word. It does not require accepting exaggeration, blame, or an inaccurate interpretation of motive. It asks for a disciplined distinction: the complaint may be messy, but the pain beneath it may be precise. "You never care what I think" may not be fair as a total statement. The real hurt might be, "In that decision, I felt irrelevant."

To hear that is not to plead guilty to lifelong selfishness. It is to recognise the point where the other person felt the bond fail.

The visible sign of poor listening is escalation. The injured person repeats themselves, changes examples, raises volume, becomes more absolute, or withdraws into coldness. The listener, feeling accused, becomes more exacting. They correct the wording, challenge the sequence, demand fairness, or ask why the hurt was not phrased more calmly. Soon the conversation has moved away from impact and into procedure. The sentence "That hurt me" has become a debate about whether the speaker has presented their hurt in a sufficiently acceptable form. The real hurt goes underground.

A single reflection can alter that course. Reflection is not parroting. It is the act of naming what seems to have landed, in language the injured person can recognise. "You felt dismissed when I moved on before you had finished." "You felt alone when I did not respond to the message." "You felt controlled when I changed the plan without checking." These sentences do not add the listener's defence. They do not settle the facts in full. They tell the injured person that the impact has entered the room and has not been immediately rejected. That recognition can calm the room faster than explanation because it meets the emotional emergency before debating the surrounding evidence.

The work associated with Carl Rogers gives one strong anchor for this kind of listening because he emphasised accurate empathic understanding as a condition that helps people become less defended and more open. In relational repair, empathy is not theatrical warmth. It is disciplined accuracy. It listens for the human meaning of the event: dismissal, loneliness, exposure, powerlessness, humiliation, abandonment, being managed, being unseen. The listener's task is not to produce a beautiful response. It is to show that the hurt has been understood well enough that the injured person no longer has to shout it through the wall.

The complaint often points to one of several tender centres. Fear of being dismissed may hide beneath anger about interruption, correction, or a decision made too quickly. Loneliness may hide beneath resentment about household labour, unanswered messages, or a partner being physically present but emotionally elsewhere. Feeling controlled may hide beneath arguments about plans, money, family obligations, or advice that arrives before the person has asked for it. The content changes. The vulnerable point repeats. A person does not merely object to the calendar change; they fear they have become optional. They do not merely object to the suggestion; they fear their own judgement has been demoted.

The receipt motif still helps, but now the receipt must be read, not merely handed over. An impact statement says, "This is what the moment cost." Listening for the real hurt asks the receiver to identify the charge correctly. The cost may not be "the phone", but feeling alone during a difficult disclosure. It may not be "the joke", but being made visible in a way that felt unsafe. It may not be "the delay", but the old fear that promises do not hold. A person who argues about the price of the wrong item will never repair the actual debt.

This is why explanations so often fail when offered too early. Explanation addresses ambiguity; reflection addresses injury. If the injury has not been acknowledged, explanation sounds like refusal. "I was only trying to help" may be true, but if the hurt was feeling incompetent, the sentence may deepen the wound. "I was tired" may be true, but if the hurt was feeling unwanted, tiredness alone may sound like a reason the person should not have needed anything. The listener may believe they are providing context. The injured person may hear escape. The timing decides the meaning.

A well-formed reflection is brief because the listener is not meant to take over the emotional stage. "You felt shut out." "You felt exposed." "You felt as if your view did not count." Short sentences leave space for correction. The injured person may say, "Not shut out exactly; more like embarrassed." That correction is progress. It means the conversation is now working at the level of real impact rather than accusation. The listener can adjust: "Embarrassed because it happened in front of them." This is repair in motion. Not performance. Contact.

The work of John Gottman and colleagues on couple conflict gives another relevant anchor. Their research tradition placed importance on whether repair attempts are noticed and received, not merely whether they are made. That distinction matters here. A person may make a bid for understanding through an impact statement, but if the other cannot receive it, the bid fails. The problem is not always poor expression. Sometimes the injury is named clearly, and the listener still responds as though their innocence were the most urgent subject in the room. Listening for the real hurt reverses that priority. Innocence can wait a moment. Impact cannot.

There is, however, a serious limitation. Listening for the hurt beneath the complaint must not become a demand that one person absorb unfairness without reply. Some complaints are distorted. Some accusations are excessive. Some people use hurt as a shield against accountability. A listener may reflect impact and still need to challenge a false claim, set a boundary, or clarify facts later. Hearing the real hurt is not the same as surrendering the whole account. It is a sequencing decision. The hurt is acknowledged before the record is corrected, unless the exchange has become unsafe or degrading.

The reconciliation is to reflect without endorsing distortion. A person can say, "You felt dismissed when I moved the conversation on," without saying, "I never listen." They can say, "You felt controlled when I made the booking," without agreeing that they are controlling by nature. They can say, "You felt alone when I went quiet," without denying that they also felt overwhelmed. This is the elegance of a precise reflection: it recognises impact while leaving space for complexity. It does not collapse into confession. It does not harden into defence.

A workplace example shows the distinction. After a meeting, a colleague says, "You made me look stupid in there." The defensive response is ready: "That is unfair. I was challenging the timeline, not you." The real hurt may be public embarrassment. A reflective response might be, "You felt exposed when I questioned the timeline in front of everyone." That sentence does not decide whether the challenge was necessary. It identifies the impact of the setting and tone. The later conversation may still examine whether the risk needed to be raised, whether the meeting was the right place, and how to handle disagreement next time. But the first repair is to hear the embarrassment before arguing about the necessity.

In intimate life, the same skill can prevent a familiar spiral. One partner says, "You only care about work." The literal claim may be false. The listener may be able to produce many moments of affection, sacrifice, and attention. But the real hurt might be loneliness at a specific threshold: evenings where the laptop stays open, messages answered with half an ear, stories met with "mm" while the screen keeps glowing. A reflection such as, "You have been feeling alone with me even when I am in the room," may reach the centre faster than a defence of work ethic ever could. The sentence meets the wound rather than wrestling the exaggeration.

Listening for the real hurt requires the listener to tolerate being temporarily misunderstood. That is difficult. A person may hear an accusation that does not match their intent and feel an urgent need to correct the injustice. But if they correct too soon, they may confirm the other person's fear that impact is unwelcome. The skill lies in holding one's defence without letting it disappear. "I do want to explain what was happening for me, but I want to make sure I have understood the impact first." That sentence gives both truths a place in the queue. It is not passive. It is orderly.

The listener must also avoid improving the other person's statement into something more convenient. Sometimes reflection becomes sanitising. The injured person says, "I felt humiliated," and the listener responds, "So you were a bit uncomfortable." That is not reflection; it is dilution. At other times, the listener intensifies the hurt beyond what was said: "So you think I completely betrayed you." That is not reflection either; it is a defensive exaggeration disguised as empathy. Good reflection keeps close to the person's meaning and invites correction. It does not shrink or inflate.

The tone of reflection matters because the same words can soothe or mock. "You felt dismissed" can be spoken with care, or with the flat impatience of someone trying to complete a required step. The injured person hears the difference. A reflection delivered as a ticket to the speaker's own defence will not calm the room. It must carry a genuine willingness to be affected. Not overwhelmed, not self-punishing, but affected. The listener is allowing the other person's experience to matter before arranging their own explanation.

There is a quiet humility in admitting that the first complaint may not be the real complaint. Surface language is often shaped by fear. People complain about the dishes when the real hurt is feeling alone in the adult labour of the household. They complain about lateness when the real hurt is feeling unchosen. They complain about advice when the real hurt is feeling managed rather than trusted. To listen well is to ask, without saying it too bluntly, "What is the tender thing inside this hard sentence?" The answer may be softer than the accusation and more serious.

The skill changes the emotional economy of conflict. When people believe their hurt will be heard accurately, they have less need to overstate it. When they believe every impact statement will be cross-examined, they learn to arrive with stronger language, more examples, and a thicker case. Listening for the real hurt lowers the future volume by making exaggeration less necessary. The relationship no longer has to use pain as a loudspeaker. It can use language.

A useful reflection often contains three quiet elements: the event, the vulnerable meaning, and the emotional effect. "When I moved on before you finished, you felt dismissed and stopped wanting to speak." "When I did not answer, you felt alone and unsure whether the message mattered." "When I made the plan without asking, you felt controlled rather than included." These sentences are not elaborate. They are exact. They give the injured person evidence that the listener has not merely heard the words but understood the wound beneath them.

The next temptation is to add one's own case too quickly. "You felt dismissed, but I was under pressure." "You felt alone, but I had a deadline." "You felt controlled, but you never make decisions." The word *but* often cancels the reflection before it can do its work. Context may be needed, but it should not be smuggled into the first sentence of recognition. A cleaner order is possible: reflect, allow confirmation or correction, then clarify. The listener's case is not forbidden. It is simply not allowed to trample the first point of repair.

The forward test is whether, when faced with a complaint that feels unfairly phrased, the listener can hear past the wrapper without pretending the wrapper does not matter. What is the vulnerable point: dismissal, loneliness, control, exposure, abandonment, humiliation? Can it be reflected in one sentence before defence enters? The next conflict will offer the usual escape routes: correct the exaggeration, explain the intent, question the tone, produce the counter-example. Repair asks for the harder move, the one that often calms the room before any explanation can: hear the hurt accurately enough that it no longer has to fight for its existence.

Chapter 5
Clarifying Intent Without Defending

What happens when the sentence meant to repair a wound becomes the sentence that deepens it? Someone says, "That embarrassed me," and the reply comes quickly: "I did not mean it like that." The words may be true. The motive may be innocent. Yet the room tightens, because the injured person hears something colder beneath the explanation: *your experience is inconvenient to my self-image.* The speaker intended clarification. The listener received dismissal.

The scene is familiar because intent is one of the most delicate materials in repair. It can soften a false conclusion, but it can also harden a hurt if it arrives too early or too loudly. A person who feels exposed does not only need to know what was meant; they need to know that what happened to them has been registered. Until then, intent sounds like a shield. It gleams. It blocks.

This is the quiet paradox of motive: the more urgently people insist on their good intent, the less trustworthy they often sound. The insistence may come from panic, not dishonesty. Most people do not like seeing themselves as careless, selfish, cruel, dismissive, controlling, or cold. When accused of causing harm, they reach for the inner evidence first: what they meant, what they were trying to do, what they never would have chosen to cause. But the other person did not experience the private intention. They experienced the sentence, the timing, the facial expression, the absence, the decision, the joke, the silence.

The central tension is therefore not whether intent matters. It does. A misunderstood motive can become a lasting false story if it is never clarified. But intent must enter the repair as context, not as a verdict. It can say, "Here is what was happening in me," but it cannot say, "Therefore your hurt is wrong." It can reduce ambiguity, but it cannot cancel impact. Used well, it helps two people stop fighting ghosts. Used badly, it asks the injured person to comfort the person who caused the injury.

The stakes are immediate because defensive intent changes the task of the conversation. Instead of having their impact heard, the injured person is suddenly invited to reassure the other that they are not a bad person. The visible behaviour shifts quickly: the hurt person repeats the wound in stronger language, the other explains again, the tone sharpens, and soon the argument is no longer about the bad moment. It is about whether the injured person is being fair enough to the injurer's self understanding. That reversal breeds resentment because the wound has been displaced by the defence.

The stakes deepen when this becomes a pattern. If every impact statement is met with "I did not mean it," the relationship learns a bleak lesson: motive will always outrank effect. The hurt person begins to arrive with more evidence, harsher words, and less trust that their experience will be allowed to stand. The other person, feeling increasingly accused, becomes even more invested in proving innocence. Two people who may care deeply for each other begin speaking across a pane of glass. Each can see the other moving; neither feels reached.

The work now is to give intent its proper size. It begins with recognising what intent can and cannot repair, because a clean motive does not automatically create a clean impact. Then comes the discipline of saying intent simply, without turning it into a speech for the defence. The movement completes itself when both people check understanding both ways, so that impact is not exaggerated into character and intent is not used to erase consequence. The aim is not perfect agreement, but a shared enough account to prevent the same misread from returning.

A pane of glass is a useful image for misunderstood intent. From one side, the person sees their motive clearly: concern, efficiency, humour, fatigue, fear, care. From the other side, the injured person sees only what came through: interruption, coldness, exposure, pressure, absence. If each insists that their side is the whole truth, the glass stays between them. Repair begins when both become willing to describe what they can see without denying what the other side received.

The unresolved friction is whether a person can let their intent be known without making it the main character. Can they say, "I meant to help," after they have understood that help landed as control? Can they say, "I was trying to be funny," without asking laughter to excuse embarrassment? Can they ask, "Did I get that right?" and allow the answer to change them? The next bad moment will test not whether the motive was pure, but whether it can be offered humbly enough for the impact to remain real.

What Intent Can and Cannot Do

In 1986, philosopher Paul Grice's work on meaning and communication, developed earlier at Oxford and later widely discussed through his William James Lectures, had already shaped how scholars thought about what speakers intend and what hearers infer. His concern was not domestic repair, but the insight matters at the kitchen table as much as in the seminar room: meaning does not live only inside the speaker. It is created in the charged space between what is meant, what is said, what is heard, and what the moment makes believable.

A person says, "I was only joking," after a comment lands badly in front of friends. The private intent may genuinely have been playfulness. The public impact may still have been exposure. Another says, "I was trying to help," after taking over a task their partner wanted to handle. The intent may have been care. The impact may still have been control. Intent is real. So is impact. Trouble begins when one is used to cancel the other.

The sentence "I did not mean it" often inflames a repair attempt because it answers the wrong injury. The hurt person has usually not asked to inspect the speaker's private motive as the first order of business. They are trying to describe what happened to them when the words, tone, silence, timing, or decision reached them. If the response moves immediately to intent, it can sound like a refusal to hear the effect. The listener may say, "That embarrassed me," and the reply says, in effect, "But my innocence matters more." The pane of glass remains.

Intent can reduce confusion. It can prevent a bad moment from hardening into a false story about motive. It can stop "you wanted to humiliate me" from becoming the official record when the reality was clumsy humour, social anxiety, or poor judgement. It can explain why a message was short, why a decision was rushed, why a question sounded sharper than it was meant to sound. This is useful information. Relationships suffer when people are left to guess motives in the dark. But intent cannot erase the bruise. It cannot make embarrassment unembarrassing, loneliness unlonely, or dismissal undismissing simply because harm was not intended.

The distinction matters because people often treat good intent as a moral receipt that proves no payment is due. "I meant well" becomes the end of the conversation rather than the beginning of clarification. Yet in lived relationships, impact is measured through visible experience: the interrupted sentence, the unanswered message, the public correction, the flat tone, the changed plan, the missed return after a pause. The other person did not receive the intention directly. They received conduct. If the conduct landed badly, repair must meet that landing before intent can be trusted as context.

This is not an argument against motive. Motive matters deeply because human beings do not respond only to events; they respond to meanings. If a partner forgets to reply because they were in an urgent meeting, that carries a different meaning from ignoring the message as punishment. If a colleague challenges a point because the deadline is at risk, that differs from challenging it to embarrass someone. If a friend leaves a gathering early because they are unwell, that differs from leaving because they are resentful. Intent helps sort these meanings. It gives the story its proper shape. But it does not decide whether the effect needs care.

The work of legal philosopher H. L. A. Hart, particularly his mid-twentieth-century writing on responsibility and intention at Oxford, offers a useful parallel, though repair is not a courtroom. Law often distinguishes between what a person did, what they intended, what they could reasonably foresee, and what resulted. Intimate life requires a softer but equally important distinction. A person can lack malicious intent and still be responsible for repair. They can be innocent of cruelty and still accountable for clumsiness. They can mean affection and still cause embarrassment. The absence of malice is not the presence of repair.

The first error is using intent as a shield. The shield appears whenever a person places their motive between themselves and the other person's pain. "I was only trying to help." "I did not mean it that way." "You know I would never do that." Each sentence may be true. Each can also function as a barrier. The injured person is left outside the explanation, still holding the impact, while the speaker stands behind innocence. The shield protects self-image, but it also blocks contact. Repair asks the speaker to lower it long enough to see what actually happened.

The second error is over-explaining. Over-explaining often comes from fear, not arrogance. A person feels misunderstood and begins adding context: the earlier conversation, the pressure at work, the reason they were distracted, the memory they had in mind, the nuance of the phrase, the technical definition of the word, the fact that they did not mean "always" literally. The explanation becomes more detailed and less helpful. The injured person hears effort, but not necessarily recognition. The speaker is polishing the window from their side of the pane of glass while the other person is still saying, "Something hit me."

A cleaner alternative is brief and sequenced. "I can see that landed as criticism. I meant it as a question about timing, but I should have asked it more gently." The sentence does three things without becoming a speech. It acknowledges the impact, offers intent as context, and accepts responsibility for the form the message took. It does not demand that the other person stop feeling hurt. It does not ask for immediate acquittal. It does not make the repair depend on the purity of the motive. The intent is present, but it is not enthroned.

The order matters. Impact before intent is not a ritual of politeness; it is a recognition of how injury is experienced. When someone touches a hot pan, the first useful response is not a lecture on why the pan was left there. The burn must be recognised. Later, the reasons may matter: haste, distraction, poor placement, a misunderstanding about who was cooking. But if the first response is, "I did not mean for you to burn yourself," the burned person may feel strangely alone with the pain. The motive explains the event. It does not soothe the skin.

This is why "I did not mean it" can sound like "you should not feel it." The words do not logically say that, but emotional meaning is not governed by logic alone. Timing, tone, and sequence change the message. Said after impact has been heard, "I did not mean it that way" can reduce unnecessary fear. Said before impact has been acknowledged, it can sound like a correction of the injured person's reality. The same words pass through a different doorway and become a different act.

A second named example comes from the field of restorative justice, particularly the work of Howard Zehr, whose 1990 book *Changing Lenses* helped shape modern restorative thinking in the United States. Restorative practice is not the same as private relational repair, and it must not be romanticised or applied carelessly to serious harm. Yet one of its central insights is relevant: accountability begins by attending to harm and obligation, not by centring the offender's self-explanation. "Why I did it" may eventually matter. "What happened to you, and what is required now?" has to matter first. Intent is part of the context, not the court of final appeal.

There is a counter-example worth respecting. Sometimes intent must be clarified early because the assumed motive is so damaging that leaving it uncorrected would intensify the rupture. If someone says, "You were trying to humiliate me," and the speaker was not, a prompt clarification may be necessary. But even then, the form matters. "I was not trying to humiliate you, but I can see the comment did humiliate you" is very different from "I was not trying to humiliate you, so you are being unfair." The former corrects the motive while preserving the impact. The latter corrects the motive by erasing the impact.

The reconciliation lies in treating intent as one piece of evidence. It belongs in the conversation, but it does not own the conversation. The impact is evidence of how the moment landed. The intent is evidence of what the speaker meant to send. The behaviour is evidence of what actually crossed the space between them. The pattern is evidence of whether the same injury has happened before. Repair becomes possible when all of these are allowed to speak without any one of them becoming a tyrant.

Intent can also protect against the opposite danger: over-attribution. When hurt is intense, the mind may assign cruelty where there was haste, rejection where there was distraction, control where there was anxiety, indifference where there was exhaustion. Clarified intent can soften an interpretation that would otherwise become permanent. A partner who says, "I went quiet because I was overwhelmed, not because I stopped caring," gives the other person a chance to revise the story. But the sentence becomes repair only if it leaves room for the impact: "I can see that my silence still left you alone."

The word "only" deserves suspicion in these moments. "I was only joking." "I was only asking." "I was only trying to help." "Only" shrinks the other person's experience before it has been understood. It suggests that the speaker's category of the act should determine the receiver's category of the effect. But humour can humiliate. Questions can accuse. Help can control. Silence can punish even when punishment was not the purpose. Removing "only" often cleans the sentence. "I meant it as a joke, and I see it embarrassed you." The difference is small. The repair is larger.

Intent should also be offered in a size the moment can hold. A one-line statement is often enough. "I was anxious about time, not angry with you." "I meant to check the plan, not take it over." "I was distracted by the message, not uninterested in you." These lines reduce ambiguity without overwhelming the injured person. They do not require a footnoted defence. They do not wander into biography. Brevity signals that the speaker is not trying to win back innocence through volume.

Sometimes silence is kinder than intent. If the impact is fresh and obvious, explanation may add weight rather than clarity. A person who has mocked a partner in front of others may not need to begin with why they thought the joke would be harmless. A person who has broken a return promise after taking space may not need to lead with how busy the afternoon became. The first repair may be simpler: "That hurt you, and I understand why." Intent can wait until the other person has evidence that the impact matters. Not every true explanation is timely.

This restraint is difficult because people often experience misunderstood intent as an injury of its own. They feel mis-seen. They fear being cast as cruel. They worry that one bad moment will become a verdict on their character. That fear is human. It also needs discipline. If the speaker tries to repair their own mis-seeing before attending to the other person's hurt, the conversation reverses. The injured person is recruited into soothing the person who hurt them. The result may look like peace, but it is often resentment wearing good behaviour.

The pane of glass becomes thinner when the speaker can hold two realities at once: "That is not what I meant" and "That is how it landed." This double vision is one of the central competencies of repair. It prevents the common collapse into either self-condemnation or self-defence. Self-condemnation says, "I must be awful." Self-defence says, "You must be wrong." Repair says, "My intention was different from my impact, and I am responsible for taking that difference seriously." The sentence is sober. It leaves dignity intact.

Intent cannot decide whether another person should be hurt, but it can help decide what kind of repair is needed. If a sharp tone came from fatigue, the repair may involve apology and a plan for pausing before speaking at the end of a long day. If the same tone came from contempt, the repair required is deeper because the issue is not merely delivery. If a missed message came from an emergency, the repair differs from a missed message used to avoid discomfort. Intent does not erase impact; it helps diagnose the pattern. Diagnosis matters because a good repair matches the real cause, not the preferred explanation.

A professional example clarifies the point. A team leader gives abrupt feedback in a meeting. A colleague later says, "That made me feel foolish in front of everyone." A defensive reply says, "I did not mean to embarrass you; I was focused on the deadline." A cleaner response says, "I was focused on the deadline, but I can see my delivery embarrassed you. I should have raised that differently." The deadline remains relevant. The embarrassment is not dismissed. The responsibility is specific. The leader's intent becomes information, not immunity.

In intimate life, the same form carries warmth. "I was trying to protect us from being late, not control you. But I can hear that the way I pushed made you feel managed." This is stronger than a long speech about traffic, punctuality, family expectations, and past efforts. It gives the other person the essential context without making them argue their way back to the impact. The motive is no longer a shield. It is a window.

The forward test is whether the next misunderstood moment can hold this order: impact recognised, intent offered, responsibility kept. When the urge rises to say, "I did not mean it," can the speaker resist using innocence as a barricade? Can they let intent be true without letting it be final? The relationship will not be repaired by motive alone, nor by impact alone, but by the difficult honesty that allows both to stand in the same room without one being used to silence the other.

Saying Your Intent Simply

In 1975, philosopher H. Paul Grice's essay "Logic and Conversation" appeared in *Syntax and Semantics* and became one of the most influential accounts of how people rely on more than literal words to understand one another. Grice was concerned with implication, co-operation, and what speakers mean beyond the sentence itself. The relevance to repair is immediate. A listener does not receive intent as a sealed parcel. They infer it from timing, tone, context, history, facial expression, and what the speaker chooses to emphasise.

That is why a long explanation can make a simple motive less believable. Someone says, "I felt shut down when you moved on so quickly," and the response arrives in layers: the pressure of the meeting, the earlier email, the deadline, the fact that others were waiting, the speaker's general respect for the person, the reason the topic seemed less urgent at the time. The explanation may contain useful truth. Yet the injured person hears a stack of materials being built into a wall. Say less first.

A simple intent statement is not a slogan or an excuse. It is a small window. It lets the other person see what was happening inside the speaker without asking them to deny what happened inside themselves. "I was trying to keep us on time, not dismiss your point." "I meant that as concern, not criticism." "I went quiet because I was overwhelmed, not because I did not care." Each sentence reduces ambiguity without demanding acquittal. The impact remains standing. The intent simply takes its proper place beside it.

Simplicity matters because complicated intent often sounds like defence. The more words a person uses to prove innocence, the more the listener may suspect that innocence has become the central project. A repair conversation cannot carry endless context before the wound has been acknowledged. If the listener is still waiting for impact to be recognised, additional explanation feels like weight. The speaker may believe they are clarifying. The other person may experience being buried under the speaker's self-protection.

The one-line intent statement works because it respects the limits of the moment. It does not try to resolve every ambiguity, correct every assumption, or rescue the speaker's character from all possible misreadings. It names the motive that matters most. In doing so, it reduces the risk that the injured person will build a harsher story in the absence of information. "I was anxious about the cost, not angry with you" can prevent a financial conversation from becoming a referendum on affection. "I was trying to understand the plan, not challenge your competence" can keep a workplace exchange from turning into a status injury.

The tone of the intent statement determines whether it lands as information or rebuttal. The words may be identical, but the act can be entirely different. "I was trying to help" can be said with humility, after impact has been heard, and it may soften a false conclusion. The same sentence, said sharply, can mean, "Your hurt is unreasonable." The listener receives the whole delivery, not merely the grammar. A simple statement offered with impatience is not simple; it is compressed defence.

Timing carries equal force. Intent offered before impact often sounds like a correction. Intent offered after impact has been recognised can sound like orientation. "I can see that felt like I was taking over. My intent was to reduce the pressure, not to control the decision" is very different from "I was not controlling you; I was reducing pressure." The first sentence lets the hurt remain real. The second asks the hurt to make way for the speaker's account. The pane of glass either thins or thickens.

A useful intent statement usually contains a contrast, but the contrast must be handled carefully. "I meant X, not Y" can clarify without attacking the other person's interpretation. "I meant it as a question, not a criticism." "I was quiet because I was thinking, not because I was ignoring you." "I was worried about time, not trying to rush your feelings." The danger is using the "not" to scold the injured person for having heard Y. The cleaner posture says, "I understand why it may have landed that way; here is what I meant." The poorer posture says, "Because I meant X, you should never have felt Y."

This is where silence can be kinder than explanation. Some impacts are obvious enough that intent does not need immediate airtime. If a person publicly corrects a partner's private story, the first repair may not need a full account of why the correction seemed important. If someone snaps during a tense morning, the first repair may not need the entire history of poor sleep, work pressure, and traffic. Those things may be true. They may even matter later. But in the immediate repair, the cleaner act may be to say, "That was sharp. I am sorry." Silence around intent can show that the speaker is not trying to reduce the cost of what they did.

Silence is also kinder when the explanation would shift labour onto the injured person. "I was stressed" can be useful context, but it can also become an invitation to comfort the speaker. "I was triggered" can offer understanding, but it can also pull focus away from the impact. "I was only trying to make things easier" may be accurate, but it may make the hurt person feel obliged to appreciate an act that injured them. A mature speaker asks whether the intent will help the other person understand the moment, or merely help the speaker feel less accused.

The work of linguist Deborah Tannen, particularly *You Just Don't Understand* published in 1990 in the United States, offers a second useful anchor because it brought public attention to how conversational meaning is shaped by style, indirectness, interruption, pacing, and relational context. Tannen's work has sometimes been simplified in popular culture, but the enduring point remains valuable: what a speaker believes they are doing may not be what a listener experiences them as doing. One person's enthusiastic overlap may feel like interruption. One person's practical question may feel like doubt. One person's silence may feel like respect; to another it feels like abandonment. Intent must therefore be translated, not presumed.

A simple intent statement is a translation. It does not ask the other person to erase their experience. It says, "Here is the language of the sender; now let us compare it with what arrived." The comparison matters because repair often fails when people assume that the sent message and received message are identical. They are not. Between sending and receiving stand fatigue, history, setting, tone, timing, stress, old injuries, cultural habits, family scripts, and the particular tenderness of the subject. A short intent statement acknowledges that distance without dramatising it.

The sender-receiver motif is useful because it keeps responsibility distributed without making it vague. The speaker is responsible for what they send, including tone and timing. The listener is responsible for checking the story they build from what they receive. Both are responsible for repairing the gap when the message arrives damaged. But responsibility is not symmetrical in every moment. If one person's conduct has caused hurt, they do not get to rush into equal process talk before recognising the impact. Translation begins with the damaged message, not with the sender's wish to be seen as good.

There is a credible limitation. Sometimes a one-line intent statement is not enough because the misunderstanding involves context that genuinely changes the meaning of the event. A missed call during an emergency, a silence caused by bad news, a decision made under a deadline, or a phrase that has a particular cultural meaning may require fuller explanation. Brevity should not become obscurity. A person should not be so afraid of defending that they withhold information the other person needs to understand reality. The principle is not "never explain". It is "do not let explanation outrun recognition".

The reconciliation is sequencing and permission. A speaker can begin simply, then ask whether more context would help. "I was quiet because I was overwhelmed, not because I wanted to punish you. I can explain more, but I want to hear first how it landed." This keeps the intent available without making it dominant. It also gives the injured person some choice over how much information they can receive. Repair improves when context is offered as help, not deployed as evidence for acquittal.

A one-line intent statement must avoid the word "only" when "only" shrinks impact. "I was only joking" often sounds like "you should not be hurt." "I was only asking" often sounds like "you are making something out of nothing." "I was only trying to help" often sounds like "my motive should settle the matter." A cleaner sentence removes the minimiser: "I meant it as a joke, and I see it embarrassed you." "I meant it as a question, and I hear that it landed as doubt." "I was trying to help, and I can see it felt like I took over." These lines hold both sides of the glass.

The statement should also avoid biography unless biography is essential. "I have always been someone who..." usually pulls the conversation away from the moment. The injured person does not need a lecture on the speaker's personality before their impact is recognised. "I grew up in a family where..." may be important later, but used too early it can ask the hurt person to become compassionate before they have been met. Background can explain why a pattern exists. It does not repair the effect of the pattern. The first line should remain close to the present injury.

Consider a couple arguing about a plan for the weekend. One says, "You just decided everything without me." The other feels the defensive surge because, in their mind, they were trying to reduce stress. A poor response begins with a campaign: "That is not fair. I knew you were busy, and I was trying to be helpful, and last time you said you hated organising things, and I cannot read your mind." There may be truth in it. There is no repair in the shape of it. A cleaner response says, "I was trying to take pressure off you, not exclude you. I can see that making the plan without asking did feel excluding." The practical issue can still be discussed. The ambiguity has been reduced without erasing the impact.

In a workplace version, a manager gives direct feedback in a meeting and a colleague later says, "You made me look incompetent." The manager might be tempted to explain the project risk, the client deadline, the pressure from senior leadership, and the reason the question had to be asked. A one-line intent statement does better work at the start: "I was trying to test the timeline, not undermine you, and I can see the way I asked it put you on the spot." The sentence makes room for later context while acknowledging the immediate public effect. It does not confuse necessity with good delivery.

The one-line form is also useful when someone misreads silence. "I was quiet because I was trying not to react harshly, not because I stopped caring." That sentence may prevent silence from being interpreted as abandonment. But it should be paired with accountability if the silence had an effect: "I should have said I needed a minute." Without that addition, intent may still feel like a shield. The best simple statements often include a small ownership clause, because ownership shows that intent is not being used to escape the visible behaviour.

When silence is kinder, it is usually because the injured person is still absorbing the impact and the speaker's motive would only crowd the space. The discipline is to let the other person's sentence breathe. If they say, "That really embarrassed me," the repair may begin with, "I understand why." Not every gap needs to be filled by self-explanation. The urge to explain immediately is often a signal that shame has taken the microphone. A person can notice that urge without obeying it. They can let the first response be recognition.

The deeper maturity is being able to tolerate a temporary misread. That does not mean accepting a false story forever. It means not forcing correction into the first available second. The speaker may know, with complete sincerity, that they did not intend contempt, rejection, control, or humiliation. But the other person's nervous system has received something painful. If the speaker cannot wait long enough to recognise that, their intent statement will become another injury. Patience is part of clarity.

Saying intent simply also helps the speaker discover whether they believe their own account. Long explanations sometimes hide mixed motives. A person says they were "just helping", but beneath that was anxiety, impatience, and a need to control the outcome. A person says they were "just joking", but beneath that was irritation looking for a socially acceptable exit. Simplicity can expose the truth. If the one-line intent statement cannot be formed honestly, more words will not make it cleaner. The speaker may need to admit complexity: "Part of me was trying to help, and part of me was frustrated. I should not have let that come through as pressure."

This level of honesty protects against the false purity that damages repair. Motives are often mixed. Care and control can travel together. Humour and hostility can share a sentence. Efficiency and dismissal can wear the same coat. A simple intent statement should not polish the motive into innocence if innocence is not the truth. It should reduce ambiguity, not launder complexity. "I was worried about the timing, and I let that come out as criticism" may be more trustworthy than "I only meant to help." The former gives the other person reality. The latter asks them to accept a cleaner motive than the moment deserves.

The forward test is whether, under the pressure of being misunderstood, the speaker can offer intent as a window rather than a wall. One line. Plain tone. Right timing. Enough context to reduce a false conclusion, enough restraint to leave impact intact. The next rupture will invite the familiar flood of explanation, the biography, the minimising "only", the urge to rescue self-image before receiving pain. Repair asks for a leaner courage: say what was meant, do not argue with what was felt, and know when the kindest intent statement is the one left unsaid until the hurt has somewhere to stand.

Checking Understanding Both Ways

On 27 March 1977, at Los Rodeos Airport on Tenerife, two Boeing 747 aircraft collided on the runway in what remains one of aviation's most studied communication failures. The event involved fog, congestion, stress, hierarchy, and ambiguous language; it should not be reduced to a domestic lesson. Yet one principle travels carefully from cockpit to kitchen table: when the stakes are high and misunderstanding is possible, assuming that a message has been understood is not enough. The message must be checked.

In aviation, readback exists because a heard instruction is not necessarily a shared instruction. A clearance, altitude, heading, or runway instruction becomes safer when the receiver repeats it and the sender confirms or corrects it. Human beings are not machines, and intimate repair is not air traffic control. Still, the private equivalent is often missing at the very moment it is most needed. One person says, "I felt dismissed," the other replies, "I understand," but what they understand may be entirely different from what was meant. The word *understand* can become a fog of its own.

Repair improves when both people can summarise each other accurately enough to feel recognised rather than translated into something convenient. Accuracy here is not perfection. It is a behavioural test: can each person state the other's impact and intent in a way the other would recognise as fair? If not, the conversation may be proceeding on false ground. One person may think the issue is tone; the other may think it is timing. One may think the hurt is about a single comment; the other may be naming a pattern. One may think they have clarified intent; the other may have heard only a more polished defence.

The question "Did I get that right?" is small, but it changes the moral posture of the conversation. It says, "I am not treating my version of your experience as final." It gives the other person permission to correct without escalating. It also protects against the subtle arrogance of quick empathy, where someone responds with confident warmth but inaccurate content. "You felt ignored" may not be wrong, but perhaps the sharper truth is "You felt exposed."

"You thought I was angry" may not be the real issue; perhaps the fear was that the speaker had stopped caring. The check matters.

A useful loop begins with impact because impact is often the most misheard part of repair. The listener might say, "What I am hearing is that when I moved on before you finished, it felt like your point did not matter. Did I get that right?" The injured person then has a chance to refine the receipt. "Not exactly that my point did not matter; more that I felt embarrassed because it happened in front of the team." That correction is not failure. It is the repair becoming more accurate. The conversation has moved from accusation into calibration.

Calibration is a practical word for this work. A scale that is not calibrated gives readings with confidence and inaccuracy at the same time. Relationships do the same. People who know each other well often assume they can read each other without checking, but familiarity can make error more stubborn. A partner may think, "This is her abandonment fear again," and miss the fact that this time the issue is public disrespect. A colleague may think, "He always resists feedback," and miss the fact that the feedback was delivered in a meeting rather than privately. Calibration interrupts the arrogance of the familiar.

The loop must also include intent, because uncorrected assumptions about motive can harden into private doctrine. After impact has been reflected, the speaker's intent can be stated and checked. "What I meant was that I was worried about timing, not that your idea was unimportant. Is that what you heard me saying?" This is not a demand that the other person accept intent as innocence. It is an invitation to compare what was sent with what arrived. If the other person says, "No, I heard it as you shutting me down," the task is not to punish them for misunderstanding. The task is to locate where the message changed shape.

The work of Chris Argyris in organisational learning offers a useful anchor here, especially the "ladder of inference", later popularised through Peter Senge's *The Fifth Discipline* in 1990. The model describes how people move from observable data to selected meaning, assumptions, conclusions, and action, often without noticing the climb. In repair, the "Did I get that right?" loop brings both people down a few rungs. It asks what was observed, what was inferred, what was intended, and what was received. It slows the climb from one phrase to a fixed belief about character.

Correcting misunderstandings without punishing the attempt is a central discipline. Many people ask to be understood, then respond harshly when the first attempt is imperfect. "No, that is not what I said." "You always twist things." "How can you still not get it?" The frustration may be real, especially if the same misread has happened before. But punishment makes future attempts less likely. The listener learns that trying and failing is more dangerous than staying vague. Repair then loses the very feedback it needs to improve.

A cleaner correction preserves the effort while sharpening the meaning. "That is close, but the part I need you to understand is the embarrassment, not just the interruption." "Almost. I was not saying you meant to exclude me; I was saying the decision left me out." "Thank you for trying to say it back. What still feels missing is that it happened after I had already asked for more warning." These sentences do not flatter the listener falsely. They correct the map without tearing it up. The result is more information and less injury.

The second named example comes from medicine, where "teach-back" has long been used in patient communication. The Agency for Healthcare Research and Quality in the United States has promoted teach-back as a way for clinicians to check whether information has been explained clearly, asking patients to repeat the plan in their own words rather than merely asking, "Do you understand?" The purpose is not to test intelligence, but to test communication. The parallel to relational repair is direct but modest: "Do you understand?" often invites a polite yes. "Can I say back what I heard?" reveals whether understanding is shared.

The wording matters because checking can become patronising if it sounds like an exam. "Repeat back what I said" may feel controlling in a personal conflict. "I want to make sure I am getting you, not just reacting" lands differently. The emphasis is on the speaker's responsibility to understand, not the other person's duty to perform comprehension. This distinction protects dignity. Nobody wants to feel like a witness under instruction. People are more willing to clarify when the check feels like care rather than procedure.

There is a credible limitation. Some conflicts are not solved by better summarising because the problem is not misunderstanding. The other person may understand perfectly and still disagree, refuse accountability, or continue the behaviour. "Did I get that right?" is not magic. It can even become maddening when used to delay action. A person may summarise beautifully and change nothing. In such cases, shared language is not the same as repair. It is only the beginning of responsibility.

The reconciliation is to treat accurate understanding as necessary but insufficient. It reduces avoidable distortion, but it does not replace apology, agreement, boundary, or behaviour change. If someone says, "I understand that cancelling without notice made you feel unimportant," and then continues cancelling without notice, the loop has become theatre. The value of checking understanding is that it clarifies what must be repaired. It does not perform the repair by itself.

The loop works best when both sides submit to it. The injured person's impact deserves reflection, and the speaker's intent deserves accurate summary. One-sided checking can become another hierarchy: only one person's reality is examined while the other's is treated as either obvious or irrelevant. A balanced exchange might sound like this in substance: "You felt dismissed when I interrupted. I was trying to solve the timing, not shut you down. Did I get your impact right, and did you hear my intent accurately?" The goal is not symmetry for its own sake. It is a shared enough account of the rupture that the next step rests on reality.

Shared language prevents repeat misreads because it gives the relationship a reference point. After a repair, two people may discover that "helping" often lands as "taking over", or that "needing space" often lands as "leaving". Those phrases then become part of the couple's, family's, or team's repair vocabulary. "This is starting to feel like the helping-taking-over problem." "I am asking for space, not leaving." Such language is useful because it compresses learning. A whole pattern can be named before it fully unfolds.

The danger is that shared language can become shorthand for accusation. “You are doing the taking-over thing again” may be efficient, but it can also feel like a label slapped onto the other person before the moment has been understood. The language must remain alive enough to invite checking. “This is starting to land like taking over; is that what you mean to do?” gives the other person room to clarify. It also preserves the impact. The phrase becomes a doorway rather than a cage.

In intimate relationships, checking both ways often reveals that two people have been arguing with different versions of the same moment. One thought the sharp tone meant irritation; the other was frightened and trying not to show it. One thought the silence meant punishment; the other was trying to avoid saying something cruel. One thought the public correction meant humiliation; the other thought accuracy was being helpful. None of these clarifications automatically removes impact. But they change the shape of the problem. A hurt caused by misattuned care calls for a different repair from a hurt caused by contempt.

The practice also slows escalation because it makes caricature harder. It is more difficult to treat someone as selfish after you have accurately said, “You were trying to reduce my workload, but the way you did it left me out.” It is harder to treat someone as unreasonable after you have said, “You were not saying I never care; you were saying that in this moment you felt alone.” Accuracy softens the enemy image. It does not require admiration. It requires enough fairness to keep the other person human while still naming harm.

The most important correction may be tone. A person can use the “Did I get that right?” loop with a clipped voice that communicates impatience. The words check understanding; the delivery demands completion. A better tone carries genuine openness to being wrong. This does not mean becoming timid or apologising for having a perspective. It means allowing the other person’s correction to alter the next sentence. The listener who cannot be corrected is not checking understanding. They are waiting for validation.

A brief example shows the full movement. One partner says, "When you made that decision without asking me, I felt controlled." The other, feeling accused, wants to explain that they were trying to help. Instead they reflect: "You felt controlled because the decision was already made before you had a say. Did I get that right?" The answer comes: "Yes, and also embarrassed, because you told everyone before telling me." The first version was incomplete. The correction matters. The intent can then be offered simply: "I was trying to take pressure off you, not put you on display. But I can see that telling others first made it worse." Now the repair is dealing with the actual injury, not the guessed one.

In professional life, the same loop can save hours of strategic fog. A researcher tells a supervisor, "When you rewrote the abstract without talking to me, I felt as if my judgement did not count." The supervisor may intend efficiency. If they reply only with deadline pressure, the hurt remains. If they reflect first, the conversation changes: "You felt your intellectual contribution was overridden, not merely edited. Is that right?" The researcher may correct: "Yes, especially because the changes went to the group before I saw them." The intent and the process can then be clarified. The practical agreement becomes sharper because the impact has been understood accurately.

The loop should be brief. Over-processing can make repair feel heavy and artificial. The aim is not to turn every difficult exchange into a seminar on perception. It is to prevent the specific misread that would otherwise keep repeating. A single reflection, a correction, and a confirmation may be enough. If the conversation becomes circular, the loop is no longer clarifying; it is consuming the oxygen. The measure is whether the next sentence becomes more accurate. If not, the exchange may need a pause, not more paraphrase.

Checking understanding both ways asks for a rare combination: humility without self-erasure, clarity without prosecution, correction without contempt. It treats misunderstanding as common, not shameful. It assumes that even people who care can mishear impact, overstate intent, and carry old meanings into new moments. The sender-receiver gap does not close by wishing. It closes by testing the message.

The forward test is whether, after the next rupture, each person can resist the false comfort of being certain. Can the injured person allow their impact to be reflected imperfectly and then refine it without punishment? Can the responsible person offer intent without insisting it has already been understood? Can both ask, "Did I get that right?" and let the answer change the conversation? Repair becomes more durable when the people involved stop arguing with ghosts and start checking the message that actually arrived.

Chapter 6
Apology Language That Works

The apology arrives too quickly. One person has just named the hurt, still uncertain whether they have said too much or too little, and the other rushes in with, "I'm sorry, okay?" The words are there, but the room does not soften. A mug is turned in both hands. A chair shifts back a little. The injured person now faces a second task: deciding whether to accept an apology that has the shape of repair but not yet its substance.

There is another version, quieter and somehow worse. "I'm sorry you felt that way." The sentence seems civil. It contains the right ritual word. Yet it leaves the action unnamed, the impact half-recognised, and the injured person alone with the burden of interpretation. Sorry for what? Sorry because something was done, or sorry because the other person reacted? The apology has been placed on the table like an empty envelope. It suggests a message, but does not carry one.

Apology is one of the most overused and underdeveloped languages in close relationships. People learn the word early, but often not the discipline behind it. Some apologise to end discomfort. Some apologise to prove they are good. Some apologise so excessively that the injured person must abandon their own hurt and begin offering reassurance. Some refuse to apologise until every fact has been settled, as though accountability requires total agreement before any harm can be acknowledged. Each failure has a different surface. All of them make repair harder.

The central tension is that an apology must be humble enough to recognise harm and steady enough not to collapse under it. Regret alone is not enough. Feeling bad may be sincere, but it does not tell the other person what has been understood. A workable apology names the behaviour, recognises why it mattered, and leaves room for what is needed next. It does not grovel, because grovelling shifts attention to the apologiser's shame. It does not minimise, because minimising asks the injured person to shrink the wound so the apologiser can feel safer.

The stakes are immediate because a poor apology can become a new injury. A "but" smuggles in defence. An "if" questions whether the impact was real. A "you always" turns the apology into a counterattack wearing formal clothes. The injured person may then become louder, colder, or less willing to speak next time. The visible signs are familiar: the face hardens, the apology is rejected, the original issue becomes tangled with the apology itself, and both people leave the exchange feeling more misunderstood than before.

The stakes also accumulate. If apologies repeatedly arrive vague, pressured, self-punishing, or conditional, trust begins to reinterpret them before they are finished. "Sorry" stops sounding like repair and starts sounding like management. The injured person learns to wait for the hidden defence; the apologiser learns to expect suspicion and may offer even more explanation. A relationship can become fluent in apology while remaining poor at accountability. The stamp is on the envelope, but the address is wrong.

A better apology begins with the difference between regret and responsibility, because remorse without specificity leaves too much work for the other person. It then cleans away the common traps that turn apology into evasion, hidden blame, or emotional self-display. From there, the apology has to move towards the present need: space, reassurance, a redo, a plan, or a clearer return. And when a full apology would be dishonest because the person does not yet understand or agree with the whole interpretation, there is still a way to acknowledge impact without pretending certainty.

The envelope remains a useful image because apology is meant to deliver something. Not a performance. Not a demand for forgiveness. Not a speech about good intentions. It should carry recognition, ownership, and enough practical care to help the other person know what happens next. When the envelope is empty, the injured person must write the contents themselves. When it is overloaded with shame or explanation, the message becomes hard to find. A clean apology is neither empty nor overstuffed.

The unresolved question is not whether the word "sorry" will be spoken. Many people can say it. The sharper test is whether the apology will make the injured person feel less alone with the impact.

Will it name the action clearly enough to be trusted? Will it avoid recruiting the other person into comforting the apologiser? Will it open the door to what would help now, without forcing a bargain over the legitimacy of the hurt? The next repair may depend less on whether an apology appears than on whether it arrives carrying the truth.

The Difference Between Regret and Apology

In 1998, President Bill Clinton addressed the United States from the White House after months of public denial about his relationship with Monica Lewinsky. The speech was watched as an act of contrition, but much of the public debate that followed turned on a sharper question: had he apologised, or had he mainly expressed regret at the exposure and consequences of his conduct? Political life is not intimate life, and public apology is often crowded by strategy, law, reputation, and audience. Still, the distinction is useful because it exposes a common confusion. Feeling bad is not the same as taking responsibility.

A private apology fails in a similar way when it describes the apologiser's discomfort without naming the other person's wound. "I feel awful" may be true. "I hate that this happened" may be true. "I did not sleep last night" may be true. But none of those sentences yet tells the injured person what has been understood. The apologiser may be suffering from shame, fear of rejection, embarrassment, or loss of self-image. The injured person may still be waiting to hear the plain thing: what was done, why it mattered, and what responsibility is being accepted.

Regret is inward-facing. Apology is relational. Regret says, "I am distressed by this." Apology says, "I recognise what I did and how it affected you." This does not make regret worthless. Regret can be the first sign that conscience is awake. A person who feels nothing after causing harm is unlikely to repair well. But regret, left by itself, asks the other person to infer the missing pieces. They must decide whether the apologiser understands the action, the impact, the pattern, the cost, or only the awkwardness of being confronted. That burden is unfair. The envelope has arrived with no letter inside.

The sentence "Sorry you felt that" illustrates the problem with almost theatrical clarity. It contains the word sorry, but places the whole event inside the other person's feeling. The action disappears. The impact becomes a subjective inconvenience. The apologiser remains strangely untouched by responsibility. A cleaner apology would say, "I am sorry I made that joke in front of your friends. It put something private on display, and I can see why you felt exposed." The difference is not decorative. One sentence points at the injured person's reaction; the other names the behaviour and its meaning.

The research of Aaron Lazare, a psychiatrist and former chancellor of the University of Massachusetts Medical School, offers a useful anchor here. In his 2004 book *On Apology*, Lazare examined apology as a social and moral act involving acknowledgement, remorse, explanation where appropriate, and reparation. The relevance to daily repair is direct: an apology is not merely a feeling expressed aloud. It performs work. It identifies the offence, recognises the injured party's experience, and begins to restore dignity. Without that work, "sorry" can become a sound people make when they want the discomfort to end.

Vague remorse often leaves the injured person lonelier than silence would have done. At least silence makes its absence obvious. Vague remorse offers the appearance of repair while withholding its substance. The injured person may feel unreasonable for wanting more, because after all, an apology has been given. Yet something remains unsettled. They cannot tell whether the apologiser is sorry for interrupting, sorry for being caught, sorry that the evening went badly, sorry that the other person is upset, or sorry that accountability has become unavoidable. The apology floats. Nothing can attach to it.

A compact apology structure prevents this drift. It names the action, recognises the impact, and accepts responsibility without theatrical self-punishment. "I interrupted you twice while you were trying to explain the plan. That made it harder for you to feel heard, and I am sorry." The sentence is short, but it carries weight because it is addressed correctly. It does not require the injured person to extract the offence from a fog of emotion. It does not bury the point beneath a speech about motives. It does not ask for reassurance. It places responsibility where it belongs.

The action must be named because apology without behaviour is too slippery. "I am sorry for everything" may sound large, but it is often less useful than "I am sorry I left the conversation without saying when I would come back." The larger sentence can be emotionally dramatic while remaining practically vague. The smaller sentence gives the other person evidence that the apologiser has understood the actual point of rupture. Specificity is a form of respect. It tells the injured person they do not have to prove the wound all over again.

The impact must be recognised because naming the action alone can sound bureaucratic. "I am sorry I was late" may be adequate for a minor inconvenience, but when the lateness left someone waiting alone at an important moment, the apology needs to meet the emotional cost. "I am sorry I was late and did not update you. You were left waiting without knowing whether I had taken the evening seriously." That addition matters. It recognises not only the clock, but the meaning the delay carried. Repair attends to meaning.

Responsibility must be accepted because an apology that merely observes harm can feel evasive. "That must have been upsetting" may be empathic in some contexts, but after one's own conduct caused the upset it can sound detached, as though the harm appeared independently in the room. A responsible apology uses plain ownership: "I did that." "I said that." "I did not follow through." "I made the decision without checking." These statements are not self-condemnation. They are location markers. They tell the other person where accountability begins.

The envelope motif helps again: an apology should deliver recognition, not emotional packaging. Some apologies are empty envelopes, all form and no content. Some are overstuffed with explanation, shame, history, and self-defence until the essential message cannot be found. A compact apology is properly addressed and plainly filled. It does not need ornament. The injured person should not have to sort through paragraphs of distress to locate the one sentence that names the harm.

Public examples show the distinction because audiences often sense the difference even when they cannot name it. In 2017, after United Airlines passenger David Dao was forcibly removed from a flight in Chicago, the company's early public response drew criticism for language that many read as minimising and procedural. Later, United's chief executive Oscar Munoz issued a fuller apology, saying the passenger should never have been treated that way and accepting responsibility for making it right. Corporate statements are not private repair, and they operate under legal and reputational pressures. Yet the lesson is transferable: language that sounds like regret over an incident is weaker than language that names mistreatment and responsibility.

The limitation is equally important. Not every apology can or should contain full acceptance of every interpretation the injured person holds. A person may be genuinely sorry for impact while not agreeing with a broader accusation. They may apologise for speaking sharply without accepting the claim that they never respect the other person. They may apologise for making a unilateral decision without agreeing that they intended control. This is not avoidance when handled cleanly. It is precision. A good apology should not become a false confession simply to buy peace.

The reconciliation lies in apologising for what is clear while leaving room to discuss what is not. "I am sorry I raised my voice. That made the conversation feel unsafe, and I take responsibility for that. I do want to talk later about the part where you felt I was trying to intimidate you, because I need to understand it more fully." This kind of language avoids both collapse and denial. It repairs the known harm without pretending to have resolved every interpretation. It is more trustworthy than an apology that accepts everything in the moment and resents the acceptance later.

Grovelling is another way apology loses its usefulness. "I am terrible. I ruin everything. You should not have to deal with me." These sentences may sound remorseful, but they pull attention away from the injured person and towards the apologiser's shame. The other person is now pressured to comfort, contradict, or manage the collapse. The original wound is displaced by the apologiser's need for rescue. Grovelling may look like accountability from a distance;

up close it often functions as avoidance. It makes the repair about the apologiser's pain.

Minimising fails in the opposite direction. "I am sorry, but it was just a joke." "I am sorry if that upset you." "I am sorry, but you know I was tired." These sentences reduce responsibility by explaining before recognising. Context may be real. Tiredness may matter. Humour may have been intended. But minimising asks the injured person to shrink the impact so the apologiser can remain comfortable. An apology that cannot tolerate the size of the harm is not yet ready to repair it.

The compact form avoids both extremes. It is neither theatrical nor evasive. "I am sorry I shared that story at dinner. It was not mine to tell, and I can see why you felt exposed." This sentence does not beg for forgiveness. It does not defend the motive. It does not require the other person to soothe the apologiser. It gives the injured person the dignity of being understood. That is the first function of apology: not to erase pain, but to stop the injured person from carrying it alone.

An apology also differs from regret because it looks forward, even when it does not yet make a detailed plan. Regret may remain absorbed in the past: "I hate that I did that." Apology begins to imply future conduct: "I understand why that mattered, and I am responsible for not repeating it." The future does not need to be overpromised. In fact, overpromising can create fresh mistrust. But some sense of changed attention should be present. If the apology names the harm but offers no sign that the lesson will affect behaviour, it may feel emotionally sincere and practically thin.

The injured person often listens for that future signal. They want to know not only whether the apologiser feels bad, but whether the risk has changed. Will the private story be shared again? Will the interruption recur? Will the return after a pause be kept? Will the public correction happen in the same way next time? Trust is not restored by sorrow alone. It is restored when sorrow becomes attention, and attention becomes conduct. The apology begins that conversion.

The phrase "I am sorry you felt that" fails because it refuses the conversion. It does not name conduct. It does not recognise the reasonableness of impact. It does not indicate altered attention. It leaves the injured person holding the entire meaning of the event while the speaker stands at a safe distance. A stronger sentence takes a step closer: "I am sorry I dismissed your concern when you raised it. It made you feel alone with something that mattered, and I should have slowed down." The action is visible. The impact is named. The responsibility is not outsourced.

In close relationships, a workable apology also has to fit the scale of the wound. A small sting may need a simple correction: "I snapped. I am sorry." A repeated pattern may require fuller recognition: "I keep saying I will come back after taking space, and then I avoid it. That leaves you waiting and makes my pauses hard to trust." The second apology carries history because the injury carries history. A compact apology is not always brief in word count; it is brief in waste. Every sentence does work.

The same principle applies in professional life. "Sorry for the confusion" often obscures responsibility. Whose confusion? Created how? A clearer apology might say, "I am sorry I sent the revised brief without flagging the changes. That meant your team worked from the wrong version." The difference changes the repair. One sentence gestures vaguely towards inconvenience. The other identifies the behaviour and its practical effect. It also makes a next step easier because the problem has been named with enough precision to correct.

There is a kind of apology that sounds mature but remains strangely bloodless. It uses the correct components without any visible willingness to be affected. The words are accountable, but the tone is administrative. "I apologise for my role in the miscommunication." In certain formal settings, that may be the required language. In intimate repair, it often lands poorly because it lacks human recognition. A good apology does not need to be emotional in a dramatic way, but it must feel inhabited. The other person should be able to sense that the speaker is not merely completing a form.

The best apologies are often plain. "I am sorry I spoke over you. You were trying to tell me something important, and I made it feel as if my answer mattered more than your experience." That sentence does not solve the whole issue. It does something more immediate. It returns the injured person to moral visibility. It says, "The thing that happened to you has registered in me." Regret may feel bad in private. Apology lets the other person see that their pain has changed the speaker's understanding.

The forward test is whether the next "sorry" carries content or merely sound. Does it name the behaviour? Does it recognise why it mattered? Does it accept responsibility without collapsing into shame or sliding into defence? The word itself is not the repair. It is only the envelope. What matters is whether, when opened, it contains enough truth for the injured person to stop wondering whether the apologiser is sorry for the harm, or merely sorry to be standing in its consequences.

Avoiding Common Apology Traps

In 2017, after a passenger was forcibly removed from a United Airlines flight at Chicago O'Hare, the company's first public response became a case study in how apology language can fail under pressure. The initial wording referred to "re-accommodating" passengers, a phrase that sounded procedural where the public had seen distressing force. Later, United's chief executive, Oscar Munoz, issued a fuller apology that accepted responsibility more plainly. Corporate crisis statements are not the same as private repair, but the lesson is sharp: when language dodges the human reality of harm, people hear the dodge before they hear the apology.

The same failure happens at the edge of a bed, in a car park, after dinner, or at the end of a tense call. Someone says, "I am sorry, but you were pushing me." The word "sorry" appears, then disappears under the weight of defence. Someone says, "I am sorry if you were hurt," and the injury becomes hypothetical, as though the other person's face, silence, or withdrawal were not already evidence enough. Someone says, "I am sorry, but you always do this too," and the apology turns into a counterclaim. The envelope has been stamped, then filled with broken glass.

Apology traps are dangerous because they often sound close to accountability. They use familiar repair words while quietly redirecting blame, questioning impact, or asking the injured person to manage the apologiser's discomfort. A poor apology is not always crude. It may be polite, articulate, even emotionally intense. Yet the injured person feels something slide away from them: the action is blurred, the impact is softened, the responsibility is shared too soon, or the apologiser's shame becomes the main event. The apology becomes harder to accept because accepting it would require accepting the distortion inside it.

The word "but" is the most common trap because it cancels what came before. "I am sorry I snapped, but I was exhausted." Exhaustion may be true. It may matter later. But placed there, it competes with the apology for moral attention. The injured person hears that the snapping has already been explained before it has been fully owned. The same sentence can be cleaned by separating accountability from context: "I am sorry I snapped. I was exhausted, and I still should not have spoken to you that way." The difference is small in grammar and large in effect. Responsibility remains intact.

This does not mean context has no place. Human actions have conditions. Fatigue, pressure, fear, grief, confusion, urgency, and old sensitivities all shape behaviour. The problem is not context itself; the problem is context used as a shield. When "but" enters too early, it recruits the other person into judging whether the harm was understandable enough to stop hurting. A cleaner apology lets accountability stand on its own before explanation arrives. "I was under pressure" may help explain why the tone became sharp. It does not change the fact that the tone landed as contempt.

The word "if" causes a different injury. "I am sorry if I hurt you" sounds cautious, but often lands as doubt. It suggests that the harm is still under review, pending stronger evidence. There are situations where uncertainty is genuine, especially when the speaker is not yet sure what happened. But once impact has been named, "if" can feel like a refusal to recognise it. "I am sorry that hurt you" is better, though still incomplete if the action is missing. Stronger still: "I am sorry I dismissed your concern when you raised it. That hurt you, and I understand why."

There is a legitimate use of uncertainty, but it belongs in a different sentence. If someone is unsure about the interpretation, they can still apologise for the known behaviour. "I am sorry I left the room without saying when I would come back. I understand that affected you. I need to think more about whether I was avoiding the conversation, but I should not have left you guessing." This kind of wording refuses a fake confession while still repairing what is clear. The injured person receives accountability rather than a fog of caution.

"You always" is the trap that turns apology into litigation. "I am sorry I raised my voice, but you always push until I explode." The apology has barely begun before the other person is placed on trial. The speaker may be naming a real pattern, but the timing corrupts the repair. If a pattern needs to be discussed, it should not be smuggled into the apology as a counterattack. A cleaner version would say, "I am sorry I raised my voice. That is on me. I do want us to talk later about how these conversations escalate, but I should not have shouted." The apology keeps its lane.

Keeping the apology clean does not mean pretending the other person contributed nothing to the conflict. Mutual contribution is real in many arguments. One person may have pushed; the other may have snapped. One may have withdrawn; the other may have pursued. One may have accused; the other may have mocked. But a useful apology deals first with the part that belongs to the speaker. "My part was..." is stronger than "Yes, but your part was..." The former creates an opening. The latter creates a fight over sequencing.

The work of Aaron Lazare in *On Apology*, published in 2004, is useful here because it treats apology as an act that restores dignity through acknowledgement. An apology that contains hidden blame does the opposite. It asks the injured person to accept a partial restoration while absorbing a new diminishment. The person who was hurt must now decide whether to challenge the hidden blame and risk being seen as unforgiving, or accept the apology and swallow the distortion. That is why apology traps matter. They do not merely weaken repair. They make acceptance ethically awkward.

The envelope motif returns because a clean apology should deliver one message at a time. If the envelope contains apology, defence, accusation, self-pity, context, and negotiation all folded together, the receiver must sort the contents while still hurt. A clean apology is easier to accept because the message is legible. "I am sorry I made that comment in front of them. It put you on the spot, and I should have checked with you privately." The sentence does not ask the other person to handle the apologiser's shame, evaluate excuses, or defend their own reaction. It delivers what it promises.

Over-apologising is the trap that often hides behind sensitivity. It looks humble. It may even sound tender. "I am so sorry. I am awful. I cannot believe I did that. I always ruin everything. You must hate me." The injured person is then pulled away from their own experience and placed in the role of rescuer. They may feel pressure to say, "No, you are not awful," before their own hurt has been understood. The apology becomes a demand for comfort, even when the demand is unconscious. It reverses the direction of care.

This form of apology is especially difficult because the apologiser may genuinely feel distressed. Their shame is real. Their remorse may be sincere. Yet sincerity does not make the structure fair. When self-condemnation floods the room, the injured person becomes responsible for stabilising the person who caused the impact. A cleaner apology keeps shame in proportion. "I feel bad about how I handled that, and I am sorry I spoke to you with contempt." The feeling is present, but it does not take over. The injury remains the centre.

The research of psychologist June Price Tangney and colleagues on shame and guilt, developed through work published across the 1990s and 2000s, offers a useful distinction. Guilt tends to focus on behaviour: I did something wrong. Shame tends to focus on the whole self: I am wrong. In repair, guilt can support accountability because it points towards action. Shame can derail apology because it collapses the speaker into self-protection or self-attack. A person lost in shame may defend, disappear, or beg for reassurance. None of these reliably repairs the impact.

There is a credible limitation. Sometimes a stronger expression of remorse is appropriate because the harm was serious or repeated. A flat, compact apology may sound cold when the injury has been deep. The answer is not to forbid emotion, but to keep emotion in service of repair. "I am deeply sorry" can be appropriate when followed by clear ownership and changed conduct. The problem is not intensity; it is displacement. Emotion becomes a trap when it makes the injured person care for the apologiser before the apologiser has cared for the injury.

The same principle applies to under-apologising. Some people keep apologies so controlled that they become bloodless. "I regret the miscommunication" may work in a formal notice; in a close relationship, it can sound like a legal department wrote it. A clean apology should be neither collapsed nor sterile. It should be human enough to show that the impact matters and steady enough not to ask the injured person for emotional rescue. "I am sorry I missed what you were telling me. You needed my attention, and I gave you half of it." Plain language does more work than grand phrasing.

Another trap is the apology that arrives with an implied deadline for forgiveness. "I said I was sorry. What more do you want?" The sentence reveals that the apology was treated as a transaction: word given, discomfort should end. But apology is not a receipt that purchases immediate restoration. It is an opening act of repair. The injured person may need time, a practical question, a repeat of the changed behaviour, or simply the freedom not to be rushed. A clean apology does not demand instant relief as proof that it was accepted.

There is also the apology that asks the other person to declare the harm minor. "It was not a big deal, was it?" "We are okay now, right?" "You know I love you." These phrases may come from anxiety, but they pull the injured person into reassuring before they are ready. Love may be true and still not answer the injury. The person may know they are loved and still have been embarrassed, ignored, or frightened by the exchange. A clean apology tolerates the possibility that closeness has been dented and needs tending rather than reassurance by force.

Apology traps often appear when the speaker cannot bear the asymmetry of the moment. For a short time, attention must rest more heavily on the person harmed than on the person who caused the impact. That asymmetry can feel frightening to someone who fears being judged, abandoned, or misunderstood. So they rebalance too soon with context, counterclaim, shame, or pressure. The repair fails because the speaker tries to make the moment feel fair before making it truthful. Fairness matters, but it cannot be rushed in through the side door of an apology.

The cleanest apology is usually constructed from observable action, recognised impact, and owned responsibility. "I am sorry I interrupted you while you were explaining the decision. It made you feel dismissed, and I should have let you finish." There is no "but", no "if", no counter-history, no self-condemnation, no demand for comfort. The apology is easy to accept not because it is perfect, but because it does not ask the injured person to fight through hidden material to reach accountability.

In some cases, the apology should also include a boundary around future discussion. If there is another issue to raise, it can be named without contaminating the apology. "I am sorry I accused you in front of the children. That was wrong. I do still need to talk about the decision itself, but I should not have handled it that way." This protects both truths. The apology is not used to erase the underlying disagreement, and the disagreement is not used to dilute the apology. Each has its place.

Professional settings show the same pattern. "Sorry if the email was unclear, but you should have checked" is unlikely to repair trust. It questions the impact, defends the sender, and blames the receiver in a single movement. "I am sorry the instructions I sent were incomplete. That cost your team time, and I should have flagged the missing detail before the deadline" is cleaner. It names the behaviour and consequence. The later discussion may still include process, verification, or shared responsibility, but the apology itself is not polluted by countercharge.

The aim is to make the apology easy to accept, not easy for the apologiser to say. Those are different aims. Easy for the apologiser often means cushioned with excuses, diluted with uncertainty, padded with emotion, or protected by counterclaims. Easy to accept means the injured person can hear it without having to correct, soothe, argue, or translate. The clean apology reduces the labour placed on the person already carrying the impact.

A good test is to remove everything that is not apology and see whether the sentence becomes stronger. Delete the "but" and place context later. Replace "if" with the named impact when the impact is known. Move "you always" into a separate conversation about pattern. Reduce self-attack until it becomes responsibility. What remains may feel exposed because there is nowhere to hide. That exposure is part of the work. Apology asks for enough courage to stand beside the action without decorating it into innocence.

The forward test is whether the next apology can arrive clean. Not perfect. Clean. Can it resist the little hinge word that turns ownership into defence? Can it avoid making the hurt conditional? Can it leave the other person's faults out of the first repair sentence? Can it express remorse without requiring comfort? The traps are small because they enter through ordinary words. The damage is large because those words decide whether the apology delivers repair or hands the injured person another envelope full of glass.

Asking What Would Help Now

In 1979, after the accident at Three Mile Island in Pennsylvania, the public account of what went wrong did not end with regret. Investigations, including the report of the President's Commission chaired by John Kemeny, had to ask a harder practical question: what would reduce the risk now and in future? The context was technical, institutional, and far removed from the ordinary repairs of close relationships. Yet the sequence matters. Acknowledgement without a next step leaves people standing in the wreckage, waiting to discover whether anything has actually changed.

The same pause appears after a personal apology. Someone says, "I am sorry I spoke over you. That made you feel dismissed, and I should have let you finish." The sentence is clean. It names the action, recognises the impact, and accepts responsibility. But the injured person may still be sitting there with a tight face, unsure what to do with the apology. Do they need space? Do they need the sentence repeated with less defensiveness? Do they need the conversation restarted? Do they need a practical agreement about next time? A good apology opens the door. It does not always tell either person how to walk through it.

The question that follows apology is not decorative. It is the bridge between recognition and restored safety. "What would help now?" is different from "Are we fine?" and very different from "What else do you want from me?" The first makes room for repair. The second asks for premature closure. The third turns the injured person's need into an accusation of excess. The wording matters because, after hurt, even a practical question carries emotional weight. The same request can sound like care or impatience, depending on whether the apologiser is willing to hear the answer.

Asking what would help now keeps repair in the present. That is its power. A painful moment may connect to old patterns, and those patterns may deserve fuller attention later, but the nervous system often needs something smaller before it can face the larger material. A person may not yet know how to resolve the recurring issue, but they may know they need a few minutes alone, a direct reassurance, a chance to finish the interrupted sentence, or a commitment that the topic will not be dropped. Safety is often restored by something visible and modest. A chair moved closer. A phone placed face down. A promise to return kept. A sentence tried again.

The practical question also prevents the apology from becoming self-contained theatre. Some apologies are beautifully phrased and then left hanging in the air, as if the speaker has completed their moral task by saying the right thing. But repair is measured by what happens next. If the injured person needs a redo, the apology must make space for one. If they need not to be touched yet, the apology must respect distance. If they need reassurance that the issue will be revisited, the apology must help name a return. The next step is not an accessory to repair. It is where repair becomes embodied.

The work of Aaron Lazare in *On Apology*, published in 2004, helps clarify why this matters. Lazare treated apology as more than an expression of remorse; it is a social act that can restore dignity, acknowledge offence, and begin a process of reparation. Reparation need not be grand. In ordinary relationships, it often looks like one small act that matches the injury. If the harm was interruption, the repair may be letting the other person finish. If the harm was public exposure, the repair may be privacy and a promise not to repeat it. If the harm was disappearing after conflict, the repair may be a clear return time. The apology says, "I understand." The practical question asks, "What would help that understanding reach you?"

There are several forms the answer may take, though they need not be treated as a menu. Space is one of them. After a sharp exchange, the injured person may need distance not as punishment, but as recovery. The request might be, "I need a little time before we continue." The apologiser's task is not to bargain that need down because they feel anxious. If the apology was sincere, it must tolerate the possibility that closeness cannot be restored on demand. Space becomes repair when it is respected and bounded; it becomes abandonment when it is vague, punitive, or used to avoid return.

Reassurance is another possible need, and it is often more specific than people assume. A person may not need a long declaration of love. They may need to hear, "I do care what you think," after being dismissed in a decision. They may need, "I am not leaving this conversation; I just need to slow down," after a pause. They may need, "I understand that I embarrassed you, and I will not make that story public again," after exposure. Reassurance works when it answers the actual fear, not when it floods the room with generic affection. "You know I love you" may be true and still miss the wound.

Sometimes what helps now is a redo. A redo is not pretending the injury never happened; it is giving the moment a second pass with better care. If someone interrupted, the redo may be, "Start again. I will listen this time." If someone asked a question with a hard tone, the redo may be, "Let me ask that differently." If someone entered the room with a complaint instead of a greeting, the redo may be stepping back and beginning with warmth before addressing logistics. The redo is modest, almost ordinary, which is why it works. It gives the body a fresh piece of evidence.

A plan may also be needed, especially when the injury has happened before. The plan should be small enough to be kept. "I will never interrupt you again" sounds generous and is probably false. "When I notice myself jumping in, I will stop and ask you to finish" is more trustworthy. "We will communicate better" is too airy. "No serious conflict by text after one of us says we are getting heated" is more concrete. The practical question after apology should not demand a grand redesign of the relationship. It should ask what restores enough safety today and what prevents the most immediate repeat.

The second named anchor comes from restorative justice practice, particularly the work of Howard Zehr, whose 1990 book *Changing Lenses* helped shape modern restorative thinking. Restorative approaches vary widely and must be used carefully, especially where harm is serious or power is unequal. Still, one central question has relevance here: what needs arise from the harm, and whose obligations follow? The ordinary relational version is smaller, but the moral direction is similar. A good apology does not stop at the speaker's regret. It turns towards the affected person's need and the responsible person's next obligation.

There is a limitation. The question "What would help now?" can be misused to hand the entire repair back to the injured person. If asked too soon, or with a tone of impatience, it may sound like, "Tell me how to make this go away." The injured person may not know yet. They may still be too hurt to design the repair. They may resent being asked to manage the consequences of someone else's conduct. A responsible apologiser should therefore be willing to offer a small repair proposal when appropriate: "Would it help if I put my phone away and you finished what you were saying?" or "Would you prefer space now and a return after dinner?" The question should create care, not labour.

The reconciliation is to ask with humility and enough specificity to reduce burden. "What would help now?" is useful when the other person has capacity to answer. "Would you like space, a redo, or for me just to listen for a moment?" may be kinder when they seem overwhelmed. But even then, the options must not become pressure. The injured person should not be forced to choose from a list created for the apologiser's convenience. The aim is not to control the repair. It is to make the next kind action easier to find.

The tone of the question decides much of its meaning. "What do you want me to do?" can sound exasperated, as if the hurt person is making unreasonable demands. "What would help you feel a little safer with me right now?" carries a different posture. It does not assume the whole rupture can be fixed immediately. It asks for the next reachable step. The phrase "right now" is useful because it reduces the pressure to solve the entire pattern at once. It respects the scale of the moment.

Making the request without turning it into a negotiation requires discipline from both sides. If the injured person says, "I need you to let me finish what I was saying," the apologiser should not reply, "Fine, but only if you stop using that tone." That may be a valid later conversation, but inserted there it contaminates the repair. The need has just been named. The first response should meet it where possible. If the request is unrealistic or unfair, it can be adjusted without contempt. "I cannot talk for an hour right now, but I can listen for ten minutes and come back later" is different from "That is too much."

Not every need can be granted. This is important. A person may ask for immediate closeness when the other genuinely needs space. They may ask for total reassurance when the issue requires fuller discussion. They may ask for a promise that cannot honestly be made. Repair is not obedience. It is an attempt to restore safety with integrity. A good response to an impossible request should still protect the bond: "I cannot promise that I will never get defensive, but I can commit to pausing when I notice it and coming back." The refusal is not abandonment; it is truthful limitation.

The practical question can also reveal whether the apology has landed. If the injured person says, "I just need you to understand why it hurt," that may mean the apology did not yet reach the real impact. The next step is not to ask for a plan, but to reflect again. If they say, "I need a bit of space," the apology may have been received, but the body still needs time. If they say, "Please do not do that in front of other people again," the repair has moved into a clear boundary. Each answer gives information. The apologiser's willingness to be guided by that information is part of the repair.

The bridge motif matters because apology alone does not always cross the distance it identifies. It may reach the middle: "I see what happened." The practical question extends the bridge: "What would help you come back towards me, or help me come back towards you, without rushing the crossing?" Some bridges are short. A simple redo is enough. Some are longer. A repeated injury may need a plan and a later conversation. The bridge must fit the gap. Too small, and the person still feels stranded. Too grand, and nobody trusts it to hold.

In a domestic example, one partner snaps while leaving for work, then apologises by message: "I am sorry I spoke sharply this morning. You were trying to ask a simple question, and I made it feel like you were a burden." That apology is useful, but the next question matters: "Would it help if I called later and we reset, or would you rather have space until tonight?" The question gives the injured person a choice that is specific and manageable. It also prevents the apology from becoming a sealed event. The repair continues into conduct.

In a professional example, a colleague says after a meeting, "I am sorry I cut you off when you raised the concern about the timeline. That made it harder for your point to be heard." The practical question might be, "What would help now: should I reopen the point with the group, or would you prefer to raise it yourself with my support?" The apology acknowledges the injury; the question addresses the practical loss. The repair matches the harm because the harm was not only emotional. It affected participation and visibility.

There is a danger in asking too many questions. A flood of concern can overwhelm the injured person and make them feel responsible for directing the apologiser moment by moment. "Are you okay? What do you need? Should I leave? Should I stay? Are you still angry? Do you forgive me?" This may come from anxiety, but it places pressure on the person who was hurt. A better question is singular and calm. It offers steadiness. Repair is helped by enough curiosity, not by frantic caretaking of the apologiser's anxiety.

Asking what would help now also protects against the fantasy that apology alone restores safety. Sometimes it does, especially when the rupture is small and the apology is accurate. But often the injured person needs a visible sign that the speaker understands the specific nature of the wound. If the injury was being rushed, the repair may require slowing down. If the injury was being ignored, the repair may require attention. If the injury was being exposed, the repair may require privacy. Safety returns through matched action.

The phrase "restore safety" should be kept concrete. It does not mean making everyone feel perfectly comfortable. It means lowering the immediate risk of repeated hurt. Safety may look like stopping the joke, ending the text exchange, turning towards the person, asking before touching, setting a return time, or letting the interrupted sentence be finished. These actions are ordinary enough to be overlooked. They are also the evidence by which the apology is judged.

The next step should not become a contract extracted under emotional pressure. If the injured person is not ready to name what would help, that answer deserves respect. "I do not know yet" is information. It may mean the apology has opened a space but not filled it. The responsible person can hold that uncertainty without rushing to close it: "That makes sense. I will give you space, and I will check back later." This is not passivity. It is patience with the pace at which repair becomes possible.

The forward test is whether the apology can turn towards the next human need without becoming a negotiation, a performance, or a demand for immediate peace. What would help now: space, reassurance, a redo, a plan, or simply a moment in which the hurt does not have to explain itself again? The answer may be small. It may be inconvenient. It may be quieter than the apologiser hoped. But if the bridge is to hold, it must begin where the injured person is actually standing, not where the apologiser wishes they already were.

When You Are Not Ready to Apologise

On 1 February 2003, after Space Shuttle Columbia broke apart during re-entry over Texas, NASA did not begin with a completed explanation. The Columbia Accident Investigation Board, convened later, had to distinguish known facts from emerging interpretation, visible damage from deeper causes, and responsibility from premature certainty. The public grief was immediate. The full account was not. In serious failures, rushing to final language before the truth has been understood can distort responsibility rather than honour it.

Private repair has a smaller scale, but the same danger appears after a bad moment. Someone says, "You humiliated me." The other person feels the heat of the accusation and is not sure they agree. Perhaps they made a careless comment, but did not mean to expose anything private. Perhaps the impact was real, but the interpretation seems too large. Perhaps there is missing context. A full apology sticks in the throat because it would feel false, yet silence would be cruel. Something is needed between denial and surrender.

That middle ground is partial repair. It acknowledges impact before certainty has arrived. It says, "I can see that hurt you," without pretending, "I agree with every part of your interpretation." It recognises that a person may be harmed by a moment even while the full meaning of the moment still needs sorting. This is not evasive when spoken plainly. It is honest sequencing. The injured person's experience is not put on hold until the other person has completed their internal court case. The speaker's integrity is not sacrificed to a confession they do not yet believe.

Many people think apology has only two settings: full acceptance or refusal. This false choice causes damage. If they apologise before they are ready, resentment may gather behind the words. They may later feel trapped by a statement they made to end pressure rather than tell the truth. If they refuse to say anything, the injured person may feel abandoned inside the impact. The repairable path is narrower: acknowledge what is already clear, name what remains uncertain, and commit to returning with more understanding. The bridge may be temporary, but it must be real.

A partial repair begins with impact because impact is the part that can often be recognised before interpretation is settled. “I can see that what I said landed as dismissive.” “I understand that you felt exposed when I told that story.” “I hear that my silence after the argument made you feel alone.” These sentences do not yet decide the whole matter. They do not claim to understand every layer. They do not settle whether the other person’s broader conclusion is accurate. They say the essential first thing: the wound has been noticed. Stay with what is known.

The alternative is often a defensive refusal dressed as precision. “I am not apologising because that is not what I meant.” “I cannot say sorry for something I do not agree happened.” “You are making it sound worse than it was.” These sentences may contain a concern for truth, but they usually fail at care. They make the injured person wait outside recognition until the speaker is ready to approve the wording of the complaint. That waiting often becomes a second injury. The original hurt becomes joined to a harsher lesson: even naming impact will be treated as a threat.

Partial repair protects trust because it separates acknowledgement from total agreement. A person can say, “I am not ready to apologise for the whole interpretation, but I do want to acknowledge that my comment embarrassed you.” This is stronger than fake remorse and more relational than silence. It gives both people a place to stand. The injured person receives recognition that something painful happened. The speaker preserves honesty about what they still need to understand. Repair does not require pretending certainty. It requires refusing to use uncertainty as a shield.

The work of Aaron Lazare in *On Apology*, published in 2004, is useful here because he treated apology as a moral act that depends on accurate acknowledgement. An apology that is vague, coerced, or dishonest does not restore dignity reliably; it may merely produce a momentary ceasefire. Partial repair respects the moral seriousness of apology by not forcing it prematurely. It keeps the door open without handing over language the speaker cannot yet inhabit. A false apology may sound generous in the moment, but it often fails later when the promised ownership is not matched by conviction or conduct.

There is a familiar domestic example. One partner says during a tense evening, "You looked disgusted when I was talking about my family." The other feels startled. They were tired, perhaps overwhelmed, perhaps trying not to interrupt; disgust does not feel accurate. A defensive response would be, "That is ridiculous. I was not disgusted." A fake apology would be, "Fine, I am sorry I looked disgusted," delivered with a tone that poisons the words. A partial repair would sound different: "I do not think I felt disgust, but I can hear that my face landed that way and made you feel judged. I am sorry for the impact of that. I want to understand what you saw."

That sentence does not solve everything, and it should not pretend to. It keeps the interpretive question open while taking the impact seriously. The distinction matters. If the injured person truly experienced judgement, the repair must not begin by calling them unreasonable. If the speaker truly did not feel disgust, the repair should not require them to confess to contempt. Partial repair holds both realities in tension long enough for more accurate understanding to emerge. It is a temporary bridge, not a hiding place.

The second anchor comes from restorative justice, particularly the work of Howard Zehr, whose *Changing Lenses* was published in 1990. Restorative practice is not a simple template for intimate relationships, and it must be used with great caution where harm, fear, or power imbalance is serious. Still, one principle is relevant: repair begins by attending to harm, needs, and obligations rather than rushing only to the offender's explanation. Partial repair follows that order. It asks, "What harm can be acknowledged now?" before demanding a final narrative of motive, blame, and meaning.

The danger is that partial repair can be misused by people who never move beyond it. They become fluent in phrases such as "I hear that you feel hurt" while refusing to own any behaviour. They acknowledge impact as a performance, then avoid the harder question of responsibility. Over time, the injured person hears partial repair as emotional bureaucracy: polite, careful, and empty. This limitation must be taken seriously. Partial repair is trustworthy only when it includes a commitment to reflection, return, and, where warranted, fuller accountability.

The reconciliation lies in evidence. A sincere partial repair creates a clear next movement. "I need to think about the part where you felt I was trying to control you, but I do see that making the decision without asking left you out. I will come back to this after I have thought it through." That sentence offers a known piece, an uncertain piece, and a return. Without the return, partial repair becomes delay. With the return, it becomes honest pacing. The difference shows up in conduct, not tone alone.

Committing to reflection is more demanding than it sounds. It is not the same as waiting for the hurt person to calm down so the matter can disappear. It means genuinely examining the moment: what was said, what was done, what history surrounded it, what the other person felt, what part may belong to one's own defensiveness, and what kind of repair would match the harm. Reflection is not rumination in one's own favour. It is not building a better defence. It is allowing the other person's account to trouble the first version of the story.

The return must be specific enough to be believed. "I will think about it" is often too vague, especially in relationships where difficult subjects evaporate after the heat passes. A stronger commitment names the next contact. "I want to come back to this after dinner." "I need some time to think, and I will bring it up tomorrow morning." "I am not ready to give a full answer, but I will not drop it." These sentences prevent partial repair from becoming another form of disappearance. They keep the bridge visible.

There are moments when a partial apology is better than a full apology because the full apology would be dishonest. This can sound counterintuitive in a culture that often treats swift apology as the mark of maturity. But speed is not the same as accountability. A rushed apology may protect the apologiser from discomfort, or protect the relationship from temporary tension, while failing to protect truth. "I am sorry for everything" may soothe the room and damage trust later if the speaker does not actually know what "everything" contains. Better a smaller truthful apology than a large counterfeit one.

A professional example makes the point. A colleague says, "You undermined me in that meeting." The accused person genuinely does not know whether the disagreement was inappropriate, because the project risk did need to be raised. Yet they can recognise a public impact. A partial repair might be, "I do not yet agree that raising the issue was wrong, but I can see that the way I did it put you on the spot. I am sorry for that, and I want to talk about how to raise concerns without making you feel exposed." This preserves the legitimate issue while repairing the delivery.

Partial repair also helps when impact and intent are tangled. Someone may say, "You were trying to punish me by going quiet." The silent person may know they were overwhelmed, not punitive. But the silence still had an effect. A partial repair might say, "I was not trying to punish you, but I can see that going silent without telling you what was happening left you feeling shut out. I am sorry for leaving you to guess." The speaker corrects the motive without erasing the loneliness. This is the discipline of context without defence.

The bridge motif returns because partial repair is a crossing under construction. It cannot bear every weight yet. It can bear enough to prevent the relationship from falling into the river while fuller repair is built. The mistake is to either refuse the bridge because it is incomplete, or pretend it is a finished road. It is neither. It is a structure for honest movement when certainty has not caught up with impact. The person stepping onto it must do so carefully and keep building.

The injured person may still feel dissatisfied, and that does not mean partial repair has failed. Recognition without full apology may not be enough for the whole wound. It is not meant to be. It is meant to keep contact possible while preventing false speech. The injured person is entitled to say, "I need more than that later." The speaker is responsible for returning, listening, and deciding what further ownership is honest. Partial repair is not a discount version of apology. It is the first honest piece when the whole apology is not yet available.

A key phrase is, "I can acknowledge the impact before I understand everything." This posture is humble without being performative. It resists the arrogance of refusing all care until every fact is settled. It also resists the collapse of accepting every accusation to avoid tension. It tells the injured person, "You do not have to wait for my certainty to receive some recognition." That is often enough to lower the temperature. The person may still be hurt, but they are no longer entirely alone with the hurt.

The tone must be clean. "I am sorry you somehow felt hurt" is not partial repair; it is contempt in soft clothing. "I guess I can see how you might take it that way" may sound reluctant and superior. A trustworthy partial repair does not roll its eyes at the impact. It speaks with respect for the fact that another person's inner experience may contain truth the speaker has not yet understood. "I do not fully see it yet, but I believe that it hurt you, and I want to understand why" is far stronger than a grudging half-apology.

There is also a danger in using partial repair to avoid decisive apology when the harm is already obvious. If someone clearly broke a promise, revealed private information, mocked a vulnerability, or failed to return after saying they would, partial repair may be too little. "I hear that you felt hurt" becomes insulting when the action plainly calls for ownership. Uncertainty should be genuine, not convenient. The question is whether the speaker truly lacks clarity about responsibility, or simply dislikes the humility required to name it.

In repeated patterns, partial repair must become more accountable, not less. If the same issue has surfaced many times, "I need to think about it" may no longer be sufficient. The speaker may still be unsure about one interpretation, but the pattern itself is evidence. "I do not fully understand why this lands so strongly each time, but I can see that my interruptions keep making you shut down. I need to take that seriously now, not later." Here partial repair acknowledges that uncertainty about meaning does not erase certainty about repetition. A repeated impact deserves more weight.

The difference between partial repair and fake apology is honesty. Fake apology says what will end the discomfort. Partial repair says what is currently true and commits to the next truthful step. Fake apology may sound smoother. Partial repair may feel less satisfying at first because it leaves some tension unresolved. But trust is not built by smoothness. It is built by the experience that the other person will not lie to escape the moment, and will not abandon the moment because the truth is incomplete.

The forward test is whether, when a full apology is not yet honest, the person can still offer recognition without evasion. What impact can be acknowledged now? What interpretation remains uncertain? What return will prove that reflection is real? The next difficult repair may not permit a clean "I am sorry" at once. It may ask for something more exacting: the courage to say, "I see that I hurt you, I am not ready to claim certainty I do not have, and I will not use that uncertainty to leave you alone with the wound."

Chapter 7
Accountability in Small Steps

What if the apology is sincere, the impact has been named, and the room still does not trust the next time? The words may be right. The tone may be softer. Both people may even feel a brief relief, as if the worst of the rupture has passed. Then an ordinary moment returns: the same rushed morning, the same family pressure, the same tired conversation at the end of the day. One person speaks; the other interrupts. The old pattern reappears with a familiar click, like a drawer that never quite closes.

This is where accountability becomes visible or vanishes. It is easy to intend change in the clean air after an apology. It is harder to behave differently when the pressure that caused the rupture returns. A person may say, "I will do better," and mean it. But better is too soft a word to carry trust. It has no edges, no observable shape, no point at which the other person can tell whether anything has actually changed. "I will not interrupt when you are explaining something important" is different. It gives the promise a handle.

The hidden mistake is treating accountability as a large moral emotion rather than a small, repeatable practice. People often imagine that taking responsibility means accepting total blame, displaying enough remorse, or proving they are not defensive. That makes accountability feel humiliating, and humiliation rarely produces steadiness. The more useful question is narrower: what exactly belongs to me, and what will I do differently where the pattern tends to repeat? The answer does not need drama. It needs accuracy.

The central tension is between owning enough and swallowing too much. If a person owns too little, repair sounds evasive: "I am sorry you took it that way." If they own too much, repair becomes self-erasure: "Everything is my fault; I ruin every conversation." Neither builds trust. One leaves the injured person carrying the burden. The other pressures them to rescue the apologiser from collapse. Accountability works when it is proportionate, specific, and behavioural. It stands upright.

The stakes are immediate because vague accountability leaves the injured person uncertain about the future. They may accept the apology, but still scan for repetition. They listen for the same tone. They watch the same doorway. They wonder whether the promised change will survive tiredness, stress, embarrassment, or public pressure. Trust becomes easier to rebuild when the change can be seen: a pause before answering, a return at the agreed time, a message sent before plans change, a boundary kept with someone outside the relationship. These are not symbolic gestures. They are evidence.

The stakes deepen when the same rupture has happened before. Repetition changes the meaning of words. A first apology may be received as care; a fifth may be received as management. The injured person may not doubt sincerity, but they may doubt reliability. That distinction matters. Someone can genuinely feel sorry and still be untrustworthy in the repeated situation. Follow-through is where apology earns its future tense. Without it, remorse becomes a passing weather pattern: intense, visible, and soon gone.

The movement here is towards smallness with weight. Responsibility begins by naming one's contribution precisely, not claiming the entire conflict and not hiding inside intention. It then asks for a repair action that fits the actual impact: a check-in where absence caused uncertainty, a replacement plan where a promise failed, a clearer boundary where outside influence distorted the relationship. Finally, it requires a posture that is responsible without becoming collapsed, because self-punishment often looks humble while quietly pulling attention away from the person harmed.

A hinge is a useful image for this work. It is small, easily overlooked, and decisive. A door does not swing because someone delivers a speech about movement; it swings because the hinge holds under ordinary pressure. Accountability is the hinge between apology and trust. If it is vague, rusted, or ornamental, the relationship keeps sticking in the same place. If it is fitted carefully, the next difficult moment has a chance to move differently.

The unresolved question is whether responsibility can become practical before shame makes it theatrical. When the next repair is needed, will the person reach for the grand promise or the measurable change? Will they say, "I will do better," because the phrase feels generous, or will they name the behaviour that must change when the old pressure returns? The future of repair often rests there: not in the size of the remorse, but in the small hinge that proves whether the apology can carry weight.

Owning Your Part Precisely

In 1979, after the accident at Three Mile Island in Pennsylvania, public attention did not rest only on the damaged reactor. Investigators examined decisions, signals, training, communication, and the human reading of instruments under pressure. The lesson was not that one person could swallow the whole failure and make it simple. Serious accountability had to become specific before it could become useful. Which valve? Which indicator? Which assumption? Which procedure? A vague confession would have satisfied emotion for a moment and helped almost no one.

The same principle holds in a private rupture, though the scale is smaller and the room more familiar. One person says, "You cut me off again," and the other replies, "Fine, I will do better." The words appear responsible, but they do not yet name the behaviour that caused the hurt. Better how? Better when? Better under what pressure? The promise is broad enough to sound sincere and loose enough to escape measurement. The hinge is missing.

Owning your part precisely means locating the contribution that actually belongs to you and naming it without inflating or shrinking it. It is not an act of self-condemnation. It is not an attempt to become the sole villain so the conversation can end. It is a disciplined answer to a narrower question: what did I do, fail to do, say, imply, repeat, withhold, rush, or avoid that contributed to this rupture? The answer may be one sentence. It may be uncomfortable. It should be observable enough that both people could recognise whether it happens again.

The difficulty is that conflict tempts people towards extremes. One extreme is evasion: "I am sorry you felt that," "I was only trying to help," "That was not my intention." The other is collapse:

"Everything is my fault," "I always ruin things," "I cannot do anything right." Both can look like ways out of conflict, but neither produces reliable repair. Evasion leaves the injured person holding the impact alone. Collapse leaves the injured person managing the apologiser's shame. Precise ownership stays upright. It says, "Here is my part," without claiming every part.

Precision matters because it makes accountability measurable. "I will be more considerate" may be emotionally appealing, but it does not tell anyone what to look for next time. "I will ask before changing plans that affect your evening" gives the future a visible marker. "I will communicate better" sounds noble; "I will reply with a return time when I need space" can be tested. "I will do better" can mean anything. "I will not interrupt while you are explaining something important" means something. It creates evidence.

The language of behavioural specificity has a strong research echo in psychology. In 1968, Edwin Locke published work on goal-setting that later developed, with Gary Latham, into a substantial body of research showing that specific goals tend to guide action better than vague intentions. That research belongs to motivation and performance rather than intimate repair, and it should not be forced beyond its domain. Still, the practical implication travels well: an intention becomes more useful when it is translated into a concrete behaviour. A relationship cannot observe sincerity directly. It observes conduct.

The hinge motif captures this difference. A door does not swing on the builder's general commitment to architecture. It moves because a small piece of metal has been placed where movement actually occurs. Accountability works the same way. The pressure point must be found. If the rupture happens when one person is tired at the end of the day, the behavioural commitment must live there, not in a broad promise made on a calm Sunday morning. If the injury happens when plans are made around extended family, the change must live at that threshold. If the conflict begins when one person feels questioned and starts correcting details, the hinge is the first defensive correction.

Owning your part precisely begins with separating contribution from causation. You may not have caused the entire conflict. You may not agree with every interpretation. You may even have been responding to something real in the other person's behaviour. But you may still have contributed in a way that needs repair. "I did not create the deadline pressure, but I did speak sharply when you asked about it." "I do think we need to discuss the cost, but I raised it in a way that sounded like blame." "I was hurt too, but I left without saying when I would come back." These sentences refuse the false choice between innocence and total guilt.

This distinction is especially important for people who fear that owning any part will be used against them. They worry that saying "I interrupted" will be heard as "You were right about everything." They worry that acknowledging tone will erase the legitimacy of their concern. The fear is understandable, particularly in relationships where accountability has been turned into a weapon. But precision protects against overreach. "I interrupted when you were explaining the plan" is not the same as "I do not respect you." "I raised my voice" is not the same as "Your whole interpretation is correct." A precise admission defines its own borders.

The work of Chris Argyris in organisational learning is useful here because he examined how people protect themselves from embarrassment and threat while believing they are acting rationally. In conflict, self-protection often appears as abstraction. "The conversation got heated." "Mistakes were made." "Things escalated." These phrases may be grammatically tidy, but they remove agency. Who interrupted? Who left? Who made the joke? Who failed to return? Passive language can make a rupture sound like weather. Precise accountability gives the weather back its human hands.

A common repair failure is owning a trait instead of a behaviour. "I am impatient" may be true, but it is too broad to repair the immediate injury. It may even become an identity defence: this is just how I am. A more useful sentence is, "When I feel rushed, I start finishing your sentences." That names a condition, a behaviour, and a likely point of change. "I am bad at conflict" is similarly unhelpful if it becomes a fog. "When I feel blamed, I correct details before I acknowledge impact" gives the other person something real to recognise and the speaker something real to practise.

Another failure is owning intention instead of effect. "I should have meant better" is not the point. Many people already meant well. They meant to help, protect, clarify, save time, prevent embarrassment, reduce pressure, or keep the peace. But repair turns on what the intention became in contact with the other person. "I meant to help" is context. "I took over the task after you said you wanted to handle it" is ownership. The behaviour is where intention entered the room. The behaviour is where change must occur.

There is a credible limitation. Not every repair should become a narrow technical correction that ignores deeper meaning. Sometimes a behaviour represents a larger pattern: chronic dismissal, repeated secrecy, contempt, avoidance, or control. In those cases, "I will not interrupt" may be too small if interruption is only one expression of a broader unwillingness to listen. Precision should not be used to minimise. The task is to name the smallest behaviour that carries the real pattern, not to select the easiest fragment and call the matter settled.

The reconciliation is to connect the specific behaviour to the larger impact without overpromising transformation. "I keep interrupting when you disagree with me, and it makes you feel as if I cannot tolerate your view. I will stop myself from responding until you finish, and if I interrupt I will pause and ask you to continue." The sentence names the pattern, the impact, and the behavioural hinge. It does not claim instant personality reform. It gives repair something to hold. A large pattern becomes more changeable when its repeatable doorway is identified.

Precise ownership also protects the injured person from having to manage ambiguity. If the responsible person says, "I will be better," the other is left to watch everything, unsure which behaviour should change. They may monitor tone, timing, attention, follow-through, and mood all at once. This is exhausting. A precise commitment narrows the field: "I will not look at my phone when you are telling me something difficult." Now the repair has a visible test. The injured person does not have to police the whole relationship. They can notice whether the named behaviour changes.

A practical example shows the difference. During a conversation about household labour, one partner begins explaining how overwhelmed they feel. The other interrupts with a solution, then another, then a correction about what was done last week. The hurt person says, "You are not listening." A vague repair says, "I am sorry. I will do better." A precise repair says, "I interrupted you with solutions before you had finished. I can see that made you feel unheard. Next time I will ask whether you want listening or problem-solving before I suggest anything." The second statement does more than sound accountable. It changes the next decision point.

The phrase "my part" is useful when used honestly. "My part was raising the issue when we were both tired." "My part was making the joke after you had already looked uncomfortable." "My part was not telling you I needed space, then expecting you to know." These sentences do not decide the whole conflict. They prevent the speaker from hiding behind the complexity of the whole conflict. Complexity is real, but it can become a refuge. The more complicated the situation, the more important it is to name one clear contribution.

In professional life, precision changes accountability from reputation management into repair. A manager who says, "Sorry the meeting was difficult" has not owned much. A manager who says, "I dismissed your concern about the deadline before you finished explaining the risk" has begun. A colleague who says, "I should have been more collaborative" may mean well, but the team cannot measure it. "I sent the revised document without giving you a chance to review the section you own" names the conduct. The future change then becomes possible: review before circulation, not a general aspiration towards collegial warmth.

The second example also shows why precise ownership need not be emotionally dramatic. It may be calm and still serious. "I changed the plan without checking with you." "I used sarcasm when I felt criticised." "I promised to come back after a pause and did not." These sentences have a plainness that shame often dislikes. Shame prefers either hiding or spectacle. Precision offers neither. It asks the person to stand beside the behaviour without running from it or turning it into a performance.

There is a subtle trap in owning the other person's feelings rather than one's own conduct. "I made you feel unimportant" may be acceptable shorthand, but it can also sound as if the speaker has complete control over the other person's internal world. More precise language often works better: "When I kept checking my phone, you felt unimportant." The behaviour is named; the impact is recognised; the injured person's experience is not treated as a mechanical product. This protects both dignity and accuracy.

Similarly, precise ownership avoids moral inflation. "I betrayed you" may be accurate in some cases, but if the actual issue was a thoughtless interruption, the language may become too large and destabilising. Overlarge admissions can feel dramatic rather than trustworthy. "I did not protect your confidence when I told that story" is stronger than a vague "I betrayed you" if the repair requires privacy and future discretion. The right size of language matters. Too small, and it minimises. Too large, and it becomes theatre.

The bridge from ownership to changed behaviour should be short. After naming the contribution, the speaker should identify the specific behaviour that will change. Not a whole character renovation. Not a sweeping pledge. A repeatable action. "I will pause before responding when I feel blamed." "I will ask before giving advice." "I will tell you when I need space and when I will return." "I will not discuss private details with my family without checking with you." These commitments can be seen, remembered, and adjusted. They turn apology into evidence.

The injured person may still need time to trust the commitment. That is not cynicism; it may be wisdom. Repeated rupture changes the evidential standard. If the same apology has appeared before, words will carry less weight until behaviour follows. Precise ownership should not demand immediate restoration. It should accept that trust may need to observe the hinge under pressure. The next moment becomes the proof, not the intensity of the promise.

Owning your part precisely also helps prevent defensive counter-accounting. When one person owns a behaviour cleanly, the conversation is less likely to spiral into who did more wrong. "I raised my voice, and that was not okay" is harder to argue with than "I am sorry, but you pushed me." It may even invite reciprocal ownership later, because it lowers the threat in the room. But the point of owning one's part is not to manipulate the other into owning theirs. It is to clean up one's own contribution because the relationship deserves less mess.

The forward test is whether accountability can become small enough to be real. When the impulse rises to say, "I will do better," can the sentence be sharpened into a behaviour that can be observed? When shame urges collapse and pride urges defence, can the person name the hinge: the interruption, the sarcasm, the missed return, the public correction, the decision made alone? The future of trust depends not on the grandeur of remorse, but on whether the next ordinary pressure finds a different, measurable act waiting in the place where the old one used to be.

Repair Actions That Match Impact

In 1982, Johnson & Johnson faced a crisis after cyanide-laced Tylenol capsules were linked to deaths in the Chicago area. The company's response has often been discussed because it moved beyond words: products were pulled from shelves, warnings were issued, and tamper-resistant packaging later became part of the visible answer to a shattered sense of safety. Corporate crisis is not private relationship repair, and the scale of harm is entirely different. Yet the principle is clear enough to travel: when trust has been damaged, language alone rarely carries the whole repair.

A spoken apology may open the door, but action tells the injured person whether the door will stay open under pressure. "I am sorry I left you guessing" matters. Returning at the agreed time matters more. "I am sorry I shared something private" matters. Not sharing the next private detail with a friend, parent, colleague, or group chat matters more. "I am sorry I dismissed your concern" matters. Making room for that concern in the next decision matters more.

The apology names the injury; the action tests whether the lesson has entered conduct.

Words are often enough when the rupture is small, rare, and cleanly owned. A tired phrase, a brief interruption, a missed cue in an otherwise reliable relationship may be repaired by recognition, apology, and a return to warmth. But repetition changes the standard. Once the same hurt has appeared before, the injured person no longer listens only for remorse. They listen for evidence that the next similar moment will be handled differently. A repeated injury asks a practical question: what will interrupt the pattern when feeling bad is no longer enough?

A repair action should match the impact, not merely the apologiser's anxiety. This is where many sincere people fail. They respond to the discomfort of having hurt someone rather than to the particular shape of the hurt. They send a long message when the injury was being overwhelmed by words. They offer affection when the injury was a broken agreement. They make a dramatic promise when the injury was a small but repeated failure of follow-through. The action may be generous in intention and still poorly fitted. Repair is not measured by effort alone. It is measured by fit.

The fit begins with the impact. If the impact was uncertainty, the action may be a check-in. If someone took space after an argument and failed to return, the repair is not a speech about needing time to process. It is a clear return time next time, and a short message if that return time must change. The action answers the wound: "I was left waiting and guessing." A matched repair says, "You will not have to guess next time." That is different from "I care about you," though care may be true. The injured person needs the care translated into the place where trust leaked.

If the impact was disruption, the action may be a replacement plan. Someone cancels a commitment late, changes an arrangement without consultation, or fails to complete a task that another person relied on. A vague apology leaves the other person with extra work. A matched action absorbs some of that cost: reschedule with a specific time, take responsibility for the missed task, repair the logistical consequence, or create a clearer method for confirming plans. The repair is not punishment. It is the practical restoration of reliability where reliability was damaged.

If the impact was exposure, the action may be a boundary with a third party. A person shares private information with a parent, jokes about a partner's vulnerability in front of friends, or discusses a conflict with someone whose involvement makes the relationship feel crowded. "I am sorry I told them" may be necessary, but it may not be sufficient. A matched action might be to stop repeating the detail, correct the impression created, or agree which subjects are not shared outside the relationship without consent. The point is not secrecy for its own sake. The point is restoring control over what should not have been made public.

The idea has a strong parallel in restorative justice, particularly in the work of Howard Zehr, whose 1990 book *Changing Lenses* helped shift attention towards harm, needs, and obligations. Restorative justice cannot be casually imported into every private situation, especially where harm is serious, coercive, or unsafe. Still, one principle is useful: repair asks not only what rule was broken, but who was affected, what they need, and what obligation follows. In intimate life, that obligation may be modest: a return call, a corrected statement, a changed habit at a predictable pressure point, a boundary around a recurring intrusion.

The hinge motif remains useful because a matched action is usually small and placed at the exact point where the relationship keeps sticking. If the rupture happens during transitions after work, the action belongs there, not in a grand conversation at midnight. If the rupture happens in text messages, the action belongs in the decision to stop typing and speak later. If the rupture happens when one person feels embarrassed in public, the action belongs before the next public setting. The hinge is not impressive from a distance. It is decisive because it carries the weight where movement actually occurs.

The work of psychologist Edwin Locke and later Gary Latham on goal-setting, developed from the late 1960s onwards, again offers a useful analogy. Specific commitments guide behaviour better than vague aspirations because they identify what action is required. In repair, "I will be more thoughtful" sounds decent but gives little guidance under stress. "Before I confirm plans with my family, I will check whether they affect your time" has a practical edge. "I will stop being defensive" is too broad. "When you name impact, I will reflect it before explaining intent" is observable. The more specific the action, the less trust has to depend on mood.

Realistic actions matter because overpromising creates a second rupture. A person who says, "I will never do that again," may be trying to offer safety, but if the behaviour is a long-standing pattern, the promise may not be believable. When it fails, the injured person has to absorb not only the repeated behaviour but the broken promise attached to it. A more trustworthy action may be smaller: "If I interrupt, I will stop and ask you to finish," or "If I need space, I will name a return time before I leave the conversation." Realism is not a lowered standard. It is respect for the conditions under which change must actually occur.

Time-bound actions matter for the same reason. An open-ended promise can dissolve into intention. A time-bound action gives repair a visible frame. "I will check in after the meeting." "I will send the corrected version before the end of the day." "I will talk to my sister before the next visit about not making jokes about that subject." The precise timing should fit the situation, but some timing should exist. Without it, the injured person may become the monitor of the repair, waiting, asking, reminding, and gradually feeling as though the burden has returned to them. A repair action should reduce labour, not relocate it.

There is a credible limitation. Not every hurt can be repaired by an immediate action, and not every injured person will know what action would help. Some impacts require reflection, a fuller conversation, or outside support. Some requests made in pain may be unrealistic, punitive, or beyond what the other person can honestly provide. A matched repair is not obedience. It is an attempt to respond proportionately to the harm while remaining truthful about limits. If someone asks for constant reassurance after one missed message, that request may need care and clarification rather than automatic agreement.

The reconciliation is to choose the smallest action that meaningfully addresses the actual impact. Small does not mean trivial. It means repeatable, observable, and connected to the wound. If the impact was feeling ignored, the action might be undivided attention for the unfinished conversation. If the impact was feeling unsafe during escalation, the action might be a pause phrase and a return time. If the impact was feeling excluded from a decision, the action might be a check before finalising similar decisions. The action should be strong enough to register and modest enough to keep.

A domestic example shows the difference. One partner repeatedly agrees to come back after taking space, then lets the evening pass without returning. The apology after each instance may be sincere: "I am sorry; I got overwhelmed." But the injury is not simply the need for space. The injury is being left in uncertainty. A matched repair action would be to set a return time before taking space and, if that time becomes impossible, send a brief update. The repair is not "I will never need space again." That would be unrealistic and probably unkind. The repair is "My space will no longer leave you guessing."

A professional example works the same way. A team member presents a concern in a meeting, and a senior colleague brushes past it. Later, the senior colleague apologises. If the impact was that the concern lost visibility, the repair action should restore visibility. That may mean reopening the point in writing, inviting the person to present the risk at the next meeting, or explicitly crediting the concern when decisions are revisited. A private apology may help the relationship; it does not necessarily repair the practical loss. The action must match both emotional and functional impact.

Follow-through is the real apology when the pattern has history. This does not mean words are meaningless. Words name, soften, recognise, and orient. But where trust has been strained by repetition, the future listens louder than the present. The injured person watches whether the next family visit includes the agreed boundary, whether the next pause includes the promised return, whether the next conflict avoids the familiar public correction. They are not being unforgiving by watching. They are checking whether the hinge holds.

A repair action also protects the apologiser from the trap of endless verbal reassurance. Without action, the apologiser may feel compelled to keep explaining their sincerity, and the injured person may keep needing to hear it because nothing visible has changed. This becomes exhausting for both. A matched action reduces the need for repeated persuasion. The conduct says what the apology cannot keep proving. Over time, the argument does not need to be reopened because the new behaviour has begun to answer the old fear.

There is also a danger in choosing actions that are too dramatic. Grand gestures can overwhelm the injured person, especially if the harm was ordinary but repeated. A lavish gift after a dismissive argument may feel like avoidance. A public declaration after a private breach may create more exposure. A sweeping life overhaul after a small rupture may feel unstable rather than reassuring. The scale of the action should respect the scale and type of the impact. Repair is not theatre. It is fit.

The action must also avoid becoming a transaction. "I did the repair action, so you have to move on" turns accountability into a purchase of forgiveness. The injured person may appreciate the action and still need time. They may see the beginning of change and still not yet feel safe. Repair actions are evidence, not invoices. They support trust; they do not demand immediate emotional repayment. The responsible person should let the action stand without using it as pressure.

The injured person, too, has a role in keeping actions specific rather than symbolic when they can. "I need you to care more" is emotionally understandable, but difficult to act on directly. "I need you to check with me before accepting plans that change our evening" gives care a behavioural form. The point is not that the injured person must design the whole repair. The responsible person should carry much of that work. But when both can translate the wound into a clear action, the repair becomes less dependent on mind-reading.

Repair actions should be reviewed lightly, not audited obsessively. If the agreement was a check-in after difficult conversations, the question later may be, "Did that help?" rather than "Did you perform correctly?" If the action was a boundary with a third party, the later question may be whether the boundary reduced the feeling of exposure. The purpose is learning, not surveillance. A repair action that becomes a policing regime may create a new conflict around control. The hinge should move the door, not become the whole house.

The emotional posture matters. A repair action offered with resentment will not restore much. "Fine, I will text you every time so you do not panic" may technically resemble the requested action, but it adds contempt. A clean action carries respect for the impact: "I understand that not knowing when I will return makes the pause harder for you. I will send a time." Tone does not replace action, but it shapes whether the action feels like care or compliance under protest. The same behaviour can repair or injure depending on the meaning it carries.

Where third parties are involved, matching impact requires particular care. If a person has allowed a parent, friend, colleague, or former partner to become too influential in a shared decision, the repair action may require a boundary outside the immediate dyad. "I am sorry I let that conversation with my family decide our plans before speaking with you" is only the beginning. The matched action may be to speak to the family member, delay commitments until both partners have discussed them, or clarify that certain decisions are not made by committee. Trust is repaired not only between the two people, but at the point where the intrusion occurred.

A boundary with a third party should not be framed as punishment. It is a protection of the relationship's proper privacy or decision-making space. The action is not "I will cut everyone off because you are upset." It is "I will not discuss our conflict with someone who then treats you differently," or "I will not confirm plans that affect both of us before we have spoken." The distinction preserves dignity. It prevents repair from becoming another dramatic swing between exposure and isolation.

The most reliable repair action is often the one that can be performed under ordinary pressure. Anyone can make a careful promise in a quiet room. The test comes when the phone rings, the meeting overruns, the parent insists, the child interrupts, the train is late, the email arrives, the old defensiveness rises. A good repair action anticipates that pressure. It does not depend on ideal calm. It lives where the rupture usually begins. That is why smallness matters: small actions are more likely to survive real conditions.

The forward test is whether the next apology can become a matched act. What did the impact actually damage: certainty, privacy, voice, dignity, inclusion, reliability, calm? What small, visible action would speak directly to that damage without overpromising or turning repair into performance? The answer may be a check-in, a replacement plan, a boundary, a redo, a return time, or a changed behaviour at the hinge point. Words begin the repair, but follow-through decides whether the relationship learns to trust the words again.

Making Amends Without Self-Punishment

In 2004, psychiatrist Aaron Lazare published *On Apology*, a careful study of apology as a social act rather than a private feeling. His work distinguished the restoration of dignity from the display of remorse, a distinction many personal repairs miss. When someone has caused hurt, the crucial question is not whether they can suffer visibly enough to prove they care. It is whether they can recognise the harm, accept responsibility, and take the next honest step without making their shame the centre of the room.

A familiar scene shows the problem. One person says, "When you mocked that in front of everyone, I felt exposed." The other hears the impact, and instead of standing still inside responsibility, collapses into self-attack: "I am awful. I always ruin things. I do not know why you put up with me." The injured person is suddenly moved out of their own hurt and into the role of comforter. They may soften, but not because the repair has been completed. They soften because another distress has taken over.

Self-punishment often masquerades as accountability because it appears to accept blame with intensity. It uses the language of fault, but it does not remain focused on the injury. The subject changes from what happened to what kind of person the apologiser fears they are. That shift is subtle and costly. The injured person wanted recognition of the impact; they received a crisis of identity. The original wound is still there, now surrounded by the apologiser's need to be reassured. The repair bends under the weight of shame.

Accountability is not humiliation. It is steadiness. It says, "I did that, it mattered, and I will respond to it." Humiliation says, "I am bad, unbearable, beyond repair." The first posture keeps the other person's experience visible. The second pulls attention towards the apologiser's collapse. This distinction matters because people often mistake emotional intensity for moral seriousness. But the most trustworthy repair is rarely the most dramatic. It is the one that remains capable of listening.

The research of psychologist June Price Tangney and colleagues on shame and guilt, developed across the 1990s and 2000s, helps name the split. Guilt tends to focus on behaviour: I did something wrong. Shame tends to focus on the self: I am wrong. In repair, guilt can point towards amends because it keeps the action in view. Shame often triggers hiding, denial, anger, or self-attack because the whole self feels under threat. The relational result is visible: the speaker either defends fiercely or crumples completely. Neither posture gives the injured person a stable place to be met.

A steady apology is smaller and stronger. "I am sorry I made that joke in front of your friends. It put something private on display, and I should not have done that." No grovelling. No self-excusing. No theatrical despair. The action is named, the impact is recognised, and responsibility is accepted. This kind of sentence may feel less emotionally impressive than "I am terrible," but it does more repair. It leaves the injured person free to stay with their own experience rather than being recruited into rescuing the person who caused the hurt.

Self-punishment also creates a hidden bargain: if I suffer enough, perhaps I will not have to change as precisely. This is not usually conscious. A person may genuinely feel awful and believe that showing this awfulness proves accountability. Yet the relationship does not need proof that the apologiser can feel bad. It needs evidence that the behaviour has been understood and will be addressed. Feeling terrible after interrupting is not the same as learning to stop interrupting. Feeling ashamed after breaking a return promise is not the same as returning when promised next time. The hinge must still be repaired.

The hinge motif matters because amends require movement, not self-display. A door that sticks is not improved by the hinge apologising for its existence. It needs adjustment at the point of friction. Likewise, if the harm was a harsh tone, the amend is a different tone under pressure. If the harm was disappearing after conflict, the amend is a clear return time. If the harm was sharing private information, the amend is changed privacy behaviour. Self-punishment may produce a loud emotional scene, but the hinge remains untouched.

There is a second trap: self-punishment can provoke defensiveness after the collapse fails to bring relief. A person attacks themselves, the other does not immediately comfort them, and resentment appears. "I already said I was awful. What more do you want?" Now the self-attack becomes a form of pressure. The injured person is expected to treat the apologiser's shame as payment in full. This is not repair; it is a moral shortcut. The debt of attention has been moved away from the injury and towards the apologiser's distress.

A responsible posture sounds different. It keeps the focus on conduct and consequence. "I feel ashamed of how I spoke, but I do not want you to have to take care of that. I raised my voice, it made you feel unsafe, and I am going to pause before continuing when I feel myself escalating." This sentence allows shame to be present without letting it run the exchange. It is honest about feeling, but it refuses to make the feeling the other person's task. That refusal is an act of care.

The work of Kristin Neff on self-compassion, published from the early 2000s onwards, offers a useful, carefully bounded insight here. Self-compassion is often misunderstood as self-excusing softness, but her research tradition distinguishes it from self-indulgence. In the context of repair, a compassionate stance can help a person remain present enough to take responsibility. If the self is treated as entirely worthless, the person may defend or disappear. If the self is treated as human and accountable, the person can stay in the room and make amends. The point is not to feel better quickly. The point is to remain usable to the repair.

There is a credible limitation. Some people use "I should not beat myself up" as a way to avoid the appropriate discomfort of responsibility. They want to bypass shame so quickly that they also bypass remorse. This is not steadiness; it is evasion with therapeutic language. A person who has caused harm should expect some discomfort. The moral weight of impact should register. The question is what the discomfort produces. If it produces listening, ownership, and changed behaviour, it is useful. If it produces self-protection, collapse, or demands for reassurance, it has become another obstacle.

The reconciliation lies in distinguishing pain from punishment. Pain may be part of conscience. Punishment is the attempt to make pain itself the repair. A person can feel remorse without staging humiliation. They can say, "I hate that I hurt you," and still keep attention on the injured person. They can feel embarrassed without making embarrassment the central event. They can accept that the other person may not immediately soften. Steady accountability allows the injury to remain visible long enough for meaningful amends to form.

Making amends without self-punishment also protects the injured person's openness. When the responsible person collapses, the injured person may shut down, not because they no longer care, but because the repair has become too heavy. They may avoid naming future hurts to prevent another spiral of shame. They may minimise their own impact statements because they do not want to "make it worse". This creates a dangerous bargain: the more fragile the apologiser appears, the less honest the other person feels allowed to be. A relationship cannot repair well when one person's shame governs the truth.

A steadier posture gives the injured person room to stay real. If the responsible person can hear impact without falling apart, the injured person does not have to dilute it. They can say, "That embarrassed me," without being forced to add, "But you are not a bad person," before the first sentence has landed. They can request a change without fearing it will trigger despair. The repair becomes cleaner because each person is carrying the right part: the injured person names impact; the responsible person owns conduct; neither is required to manage the other's entire identity.

A domestic example clarifies the difference. During a family gathering, one partner tells a story the other considered private. Later, the injured partner says, "I felt exposed when you told that." A collapsed response says, "I am horrible. I can never get anything right with your family." A defensive response says, "I did not think it was private." A responsible response says, "I am sorry I told that story. I can see it put you on display, and I should have checked before sharing it. I will not repeat it, and I will ask before telling personal stories in front of others." The third response is not colder. It is kinder because it does not require rescue.

A professional example shows the same principle. A supervisor interrupts a junior colleague in a meeting, then hears later that the interruption made the colleague reluctant to contribute. Self-punishment might sound like, "I am such a terrible manager." That may extract reassurance: "No, you are not." It does not restore voice. A better amend says, "I interrupted you before you had finished. That reduced your chance to make the point clearly. At the next meeting I will return to your concern and give you the floor before we decide." The action matches the impact. The supervisor stays responsible, not collapsed.

Self-punishment often grows from the fantasy that a good person should never cause harm. Once harm occurs, the person must either deny it to preserve goodness or condemn themselves to prove morality. Both options are immature. Good people cause harm. Careful people miss cues. Loving people speak sharply. Competent people fail to return when they said they would. The issue is not whether one can maintain an unblemished self-image. The issue is whether one can respond to harm with enough honesty and steadiness to reduce the chance of repeating it.

This posture is especially important in repeated patterns. If the same rupture has happened before, shame may be intense because the person cannot hide behind surprise. They have evidence now. They know the impact. The temptation to collapse may be stronger: "I cannot believe I did it again." That sentence may be understandable, but the repair needs more. "I did it again" must become "I missed the cue when I felt rushed; next time I will stop when I hear myself start to correct you." The repeated pattern requires sharper accountability, not larger self-attack.

There is also a relational dignity in allowing consequences without self-punishment. The injured person may need space. They may not be ready to reassure, forgive, touch, laugh, or return to normal conversation. The responsible person can accept this without turning it into abandonment drama. "I understand you need space. I will not push for reassurance. I will check back at the time we agreed." That is accountable restraint. It does not demand that the injured person shorten their recovery in order to soothe the apologiser.

A common obstacle is the belief that self-forgiveness must wait until the other person has forgiven. But repair requires a form of self-possession before forgiveness is available. This is not absolution. It is the ability to remain morally present. A person who cannot bear themselves at all will struggle to bear the other person's pain. They will rush, defend, perform, plead, or vanish. The responsible posture is more sober: "I can face what I did without making it the whole of who I am." That stance makes amends possible.

The language of amends should therefore avoid global self-description. "I was careless with that information" is better than "I am careless." "I spoke contemptuously" is better than "I am disgusting." "I broke the return promise" is better than "I am impossible." Behavioural language keeps responsibility close to the repairable act. Global condemnation may feel morally intense, but it makes change harder because the problem becomes the whole self rather than the hinge point where action can differ.

This does not mean softening the seriousness of the harm. A precise sentence can be severe. "I used your vulnerability as a joke in front of other people" is sharper than "I am a terrible person." The first names the actual violation. The second dramatises the self and may avoid the specific truth. Precision is often more morally demanding than self-attack because it cannot hide in emotion. It stands in the light of what happened.

Making amends also requires refusing to turn repair into a performance of pain. Tears may come. A trembling voice may come. Remorse may be visible. None of that is wrong. The question is whether the emotion serves recognition or replaces it. If tears make the injured person stop speaking, the repair has shifted. If remorse leads to clearer ownership, it may help. Emotional expression is not the enemy. Emotional displacement is. The centre must remain the impact and the amend.

A useful inner test is whether the next sentence would help the injured person feel more understood or make them feel responsible for the apologiser. "I am so ashamed of myself" may be honest, but if it is the first sentence after impact, it may recruit care. "I am sorry I did that; I can see why it hurt" keeps the injured person at the centre. Shame can be spoken later if it helps transparency, but it should not be handed over as a burden.

The steadier posture also reduces the risk of withdrawal. Some people self-punish privately rather than aloud. They hear the impact, feel flooded with shame, and disappear. They tell themselves they are giving the other person space, but in fact they are avoiding the pain of being seen as harmful. The injured person then experiences abandonment after disclosure. A responsible response stays reachable: "I am feeling ashamed and I need a short pause, but I am not leaving this. I will come back." The distinction between space and disappearance matters as much here as anywhere.

The hinge returns because repair depends on staying connected to the point of movement. Self-punishment pulls the door off its frame. Defence wedges it shut. Steady accountability adjusts the hinge. It finds the behaviour, names the impact, makes the amend, and tolerates the other person's response without demanding immediate relief. That is less dramatic than collapse, but far more trustworthy. The relationship does not need the responsible person to bleed symbolically at the threshold. It needs them to hold the door differently next time.

The forward test is whether accountability can remain upright under shame. When the next impact is named, will the responsible person defend, collapse, or stand? Can they say what they did without making themselves the wound? Can they make amends without asking the injured person to comfort them? Can they feel remorse and still choose the small action that matches the harm? Repair becomes possible when responsibility is neither a courtroom nor a humiliation ritual, but a steady posture from which the truth can be faced and the next conduct changed.

Chapter 8
Making Small Agreements That Stick

The argument begins beside the front door, where bags are dropped, shoes are half-kicked off, and the day has not yet left anyone's face. One person comes in carrying fatigue like weather. The other has been waiting to speak about a practical problem that has grown heavier with each hour of being held alone. Before there is greeting, there is logistics. Before there is warmth, there is a question. The answer comes too sharply. A phone lights up on the table, and somehow the whole evening is already leaning in the wrong direction.

Nothing here requires a grand theory of love. The collision is repeatable because the situation is repeatable: the first minutes after work, the tired body, the waiting need, the small screen, the fragile hope of being received kindly. Later, both people may apologise. They may understand the impact. They may even agree that nobody was trying to hurt anyone. Yet the next evening arrives with the same doorway, the same fatigue, the same glowing phone, and the same risk. Insight has not yet become protection.

This is where repair must become an agreement. Not a sweeping promise to care more. Not a debate about whose needs are more reasonable. Not a declaration that everything will be different from now on. The useful move is smaller and more exacting: identify the next repeatable situation and place one workable guardrail there. "No phones in the first few minutes after work" is not a verdict on affection. It is a shared protection for a predictable vulnerable point. The plan does not prove love. It protects the conditions under which love can be felt.

The central tension is that people often want agreements to carry the emotional weight of the whole conflict. After feeling ignored, someone wants proof that they matter. After feeling controlled, someone wants proof that their autonomy is respected. After feeling abandoned, someone wants proof that the other person will return. Those longings are human, but an agreement cannot repair an entire history in one sentence. It must be modest enough to keep and specific enough to matter. A plan that tries to heal everything usually changes nothing.

The stakes are immediate because vague goodwill does not reliably survive pressure. People mean well in calm moments, then become hurried, hungry, embarrassed, defensive, distracted, or tired. The old pattern returns not because the apology was false, but because the environment that produced the rupture has not been redesigned. The visible evidence is plain: the same interruption, the same unanswered message, the same family conversation that overrides the couple's decision, the same late return after taking space. Trust does not ask only, "Were you sincere?" It asks, "What will be different when the same pressure comes back?"

The stakes accumulate because broken agreements are often more painful than the original rupture. An unrepaired hurt may wound once; a failed promise wounds twice. It says not only "this happened", but "we named it and still did not protect it." That is why overpromising is so dangerous. "I will never do that again" may sound comforting, but if the behaviour is tied to stress, habit, family pressure, or emotional flooding, the promise may be too large to carry. Consistency is quieter than intensity. It is also more trustworthy.

The work now is to turn conflict into a plan without making the plan a tool of control. The focus narrows to the next moment where the same hurt is likely to recur, then asks what small agreement would reduce the risk. From there, the agreement must be scaled to real life rather than ideal behaviour: one reminder phrase, one boundary, one pause, one return time, one protected window of attention. Because real agreements meet real conditions, they also need review, not as a reopening of the whole fight, but as a brief check on whether the guardrail is holding.

A guardrail is the right image because it does not accuse the driver of wanting to crash. It assumes that certain roads are sharp, dark, slippery, or too familiar for confidence alone. A couple who agrees not to begin difficult logistics in the doorway is not admitting failure. They are admitting that the doorway has become a risky bend. A family that agrees to pause before answering a provocative message is not avoiding honesty. It is preventing speed from doing the work of judgement. The guardrail is not the relationship. It protects the relationship from its known edges.

The unresolved question is whether two people can make an agreement small enough to keep without making it so small that it means nothing. Can they resist turning a painful moment into a constitution for the entire relationship? Can they choose one repeatable situation, one visible behaviour, one honest review, and let trust grow through evidence rather than drama? The next rupture will not ask whether their intentions were beautiful. It will ask whether the agreed guardrail is there when the road bends.

Turning Conflict into a Plan

In 1999, psychologist Peter Gollwitzer, working in the field of motivation and action at New York University and other institutions, published influential research on implementation intentions: the simple act of linking a future cue with a specific behaviour. The idea was not designed for intimate repair, but its usefulness is easy to recognise. A vague intention says, "I will handle that better." A planned response says, "When this situation appears, I will do this." The difference is the difference between hoping the old pattern will not return and placing a small guardrail where it usually does.

A couple argues every evening at the same threshold. One comes home tired and checks the phone while taking off shoes. The other has been waiting to discuss something practical: a school form, a bill, a family message, a decision that cannot wait forever. The first hears complaint before greeting. The second hears indifference before care. Within minutes, they are no longer discussing the bill or the form. They are debating who cares more, who carries more, who is more tired, who has been alone with more of the day. The phone on the table has become a witness.

The repair does not become stronger by making the argument larger. "You do not care about me when you come home" may contain real hurt, but it opens a trial too wide to settle. "I feel unimportant when the phone gets attention before I do in the first minutes after work" gives the injury a location. The plan can then be modest and precise: no phones in the first few minutes after coming through the door, unless something urgent is expected. The agreement does not decide who loves more. It protects the place where love has been hard to feel.

Turning conflict into a plan begins by asking where the next repeatable situation lives. Many repairs fail because they aim at the entire relationship rather than the next predictable doorway. A person promises to be more patient, more present, more respectful, more thoughtful. These are decent aspirations, but they do not tell the body what to do when the cue arrives: the tired arrival, the family call, the late message, the public correction, the money question, the moment one person gives advice before the other has finished. A plan needs a cue. Without a cue, the old habit often acts first.

The cue should be concrete enough to recognise before the conflict has fully formed. "When we talk about money" may be too broad. "When one of us opens the banking app after dinner and starts asking questions" is closer to the hinge. "When your mother calls" may be too loaded. "When a family request affects our weekend plans" is more workable. "When I feel ignored" is too internal to become a shared agreement by itself. "When one of us is on the phone during a serious conversation" gives both people a visible signal. A plan begins where observation is possible.

A good plan translates pain into protection without turning protection into control. This distinction matters. Control says, "You must behave this way so I never feel uncomfortable." Protection says, "We know this situation tends to hurt us, so let us place a boundary around the pattern." Control narrows the other person's freedom for the sake of one person's anxiety. Protection preserves both people's dignity by reducing a known risk. The same behaviour can carry either meaning depending on tone, flexibility, and mutuality. "You are not allowed to use your phone when you get home" lands differently from "Can we protect the first few minutes after work from phones so we actually greet each other?"

The guardrail motif helps because a guardrail is not an accusation. It does not say the driver is reckless by nature. It says the road has a bend. A couple who agrees not to discuss logistics in the first minutes after work is not declaring that one person is needy and the other careless. They are naming a dangerous bend: transition plus fatigue plus waiting need plus digital distraction. The guardrail is shared because both people are safer with it. One is less likely to feel ignored; the other is less likely to feel ambushed. The plan protects the bond from a situation that has repeatedly asked too much of goodwill alone.

The research of Edwin Locke and Gary Latham on goal-setting, developed over decades from Locke's earlier work in the late 1960s, offers a second useful anchor. Specific goals tend to guide performance more effectively than vague intentions, particularly when they are accepted and understood. In relational repair, the parallel is not mechanical, but it is powerful. "We should communicate better" has almost no behavioural force. "If one of us needs to pause during conflict, we will name a return time before leaving the room" has force because it tells people what action belongs to what moment. The agreement becomes visible.

The plan should be one clear agreement, not a constitution. Pain often tempts people to redesign the whole relationship at once. After an argument about being ignored, the injured person may want rules about phones, work, evenings, weekends, family visits, texting, and emotional availability. Some of those may eventually matter. But an overloaded agreement usually fails because it asks ordinary life to carry too many new requirements before any one of them has become habitual. A single agreement has a better chance of being remembered under pressure. It also allows success to build evidence rather than resentment.

The plan should also match the injury rather than the argument's most dramatic language. If the complaint is "You never care about me," the injury may be lack of greeting at the transition from work to home. If the complaint is "You are always controlling," the injury may be that decisions affecting both people are announced rather than discussed. If the complaint is "You shut me out," the injury may be that space is taken without a return time. The agreement should address the repeated behaviour, not the largest accusation. Otherwise the plan becomes too abstract to keep.

A simple example shows the conversion. The fight begins with a phone. One person says, "You care more about that screen than me." The other says, "That is unfair; I have been working all day." They could spend the evening debating devotion, fatigue, and fairness. Or they could identify the repeatable point: when one person comes home and the other needs connection, the phone becomes a symbol of absence. A workable agreement might be, "When we first get in after work, we put phones down for a short greeting before discussing tasks." The plan is not a moral verdict. It is a redesigned threshold.

The phrase "short greeting" matters because plans must be small enough to survive real conditions. A long debrief after work may be too much for someone depleted by the day. A complete ban on phones all evening may be unnecessary or unrealistic. The purpose is not to create an ideal household. It is to protect the vulnerable moment where the rupture keeps recurring. The agreement should be strong enough to change the pattern and light enough not to provoke rebellion. Consistency grows best in forms people can actually keep.

There is a credible limitation. Some conflicts cannot be reduced to a single small agreement without distortion. If the relationship contains intimidation, chronic contempt, coercion, repeated broken trust, or fear of speaking openly, a small plan may be inadequate or even misleading. "No phones after work" will not repair a relationship where one person is afraid of the other's anger. "Use a pause phrase" will not solve a pattern in which one person regularly uses silence to punish. Small agreements work where both people can participate in good faith and where the problem is a repeatable pattern, not a fundamental absence of safety.

The reconciliation is to treat the small agreement as a unit of repair, not as a substitute for all repair. It is one hinge, not the whole door. A good agreement can stabilise a recurring point of friction while larger questions remain open. Two people may still need to talk about work stress, family pressure, unequal labour, money, sex, trust, or emotional availability. But the small agreement prevents the same avoidable collision from consuming every conversation. It creates enough relief for deeper work to become possible without being constantly interrupted by the same preventable bruise.

The plan must be mutual in spirit even when the behaviours differ. Mutual does not mean identical. One person may agree to put the phone down at the door; the other may agree not to begin with a list of tasks before greeting. One may agree to name when they need space; the other may agree not to follow them from room to room during that space. Each action protects the same relational moment from a different side. This prevents the plan from becoming a one-person compliance order. Shared protection increases buy-in because both can see themselves as guardians of the agreement rather than subjects of it.

Language matters here. "From now on, you need to..." often invites resistance because it frames the plan as correction imposed by one person on another. "What could protect us at that moment?" opens a different kind of thinking. It shifts attention from blame to design. The bad moment becomes data. Not proof that one person is uncaring, but information about where the relationship needs a guardrail. This does not erase accountability for the original impact. It moves accountability into future form.

The most useful plans are often phrased as "when-then" agreements. When the situation appears, then the behaviour follows. When one person needs a pause, then they name a return time. When a family request affects both schedules, then the answer waits until both have checked it. When a conversation begins to happen by tense text, then it pauses and moves to voice or in person. When one person starts problem-solving too quickly, then the other can say the agreed reminder phrase. The "when" makes the cue visible. The "then" makes the repair actionable.

A plan should include the smallest signal that can be used before escalation. Waiting until the argument is already hot makes the agreement harder to remember. The signal might be a phrase both people understand: "This is the doorway moment," "Can we reset the first ten minutes?" "I need a return time," "This feels like taking over." The phrase should be neutral enough not to shame and clear enough not to be missed. It functions like a hand placed lightly on the guardrail before the bend becomes dangerous. The signal is not a weapon. It is a reminder of the agreement both chose.

The injured person may understandably want the plan to prove love, remorse, or seriousness. But a plan proves only what it can prove: that a specific behaviour can change in a specific situation. That is not nothing. In fact, it is often the first credible evidence that repair is more than language. But if the plan is asked to prove the entire relationship, it may collapse under emotional weight. "No phones after work" cannot prove permanent devotion. It can protect an important daily threshold where devotion has been hard to feel. That is its dignity.

The person who caused the impact may fear that agreeing to a plan means accepting an unfair character judgement. "If I agree to this, I am admitting I do not care." This fear can be reduced by keeping the plan behavioural. The agreement is not "I am careless and must be monitored." It is "This situation has been hurting us, and I will change this part of my conduct." Behavioural agreements protect dignity because they do not require identity labels. They ask for change where change can actually be made.

The plan also needs a light method of repair when it is missed. No agreement is perfectly kept. Someone will forget, misread the cue, be unusually stressed, or slip into the old pattern. If every miss becomes a moral collapse, the agreement will become frightening. A useful plan includes a way to recover: name the miss, reset the behaviour, return to the agreement. "I picked up the phone again. I am putting it down now." "I left without a return time; I will give one now." The recovery matters because it prevents one failure from becoming evidence that change is impossible.

There is a difference between a shared protection and a surveillance system. If one person begins monitoring every micro-deviation, the agreement may become another source of tension. "You looked at the phone for one second" may be technically true and relationally unhelpful if the spirit of the agreement is intact. Plans need enough precision to be useful and enough grace to remain human. The purpose is not compliance theatre. The purpose is to reduce repeat hurt. A plan that becomes a trap has lost its repair function.

A well-designed agreement also limits the burden of mind-reading. Instead of one person hoping the other will intuit what is needed after work, the plan states it. Instead of one person guessing whether space means abandonment, the plan includes a return time. Instead of one person silently resenting family influence, the plan establishes that shared decisions are checked before being promised elsewhere. The relationship becomes less dependent on emotional clairvoyance. This is not less romantic. It is less exhausting.

In professional settings, the same principle applies. After a meeting in which one colleague was repeatedly interrupted, the plan should not be "let us all be more respectful." It might be, "When someone raises a risk, they finish the point before responses begin." After confusion over a document, the plan should not be "communicate better." It might be, "When revisions are made after review, the owner of the section receives the updated version before it is circulated." These agreements are small, but they change the repeatable point of failure. They turn frustration into design.

The power of turning conflict into a plan is that it gives pain a job without making pain the ruler. The hurt is not ignored. It supplies information. But once the information has been understood, the relationship moves towards a practical guardrail. This prevents endless re-litigation of the same emotional claim. Instead of repeatedly debating who cares, two people can observe whether the protected greeting happens. Instead of repeatedly debating whether space is abandonment, they can observe whether return times are named and kept. Evidence begins to replace argument.

The forward test is whether the next painful moment can be translated before it expands into a verdict. What is the repeatable situation? What behaviour makes the hurt more likely? What small agreement would protect both people at that exact hinge? The plan should be neither a grand promise nor a control order. It should be a guardrail at the bend: modest, visible, shared, and strong enough that when the old road appears again, the relationship does not have to rely on hope alone.

Keeping Agreements Realistic

In 1977, Albert Bandura published *Social Learning Theory*, building on a body of work that helped establish self-efficacy as a serious psychological idea: people are more likely to act when they believe the action is within reach. The principle matters in repair because many agreements are made in the emotional afterglow of remorse, not in the actual conditions where they must later survive. A person promises patience while calm, presence while rested, tenderness while unthreatened. Then the ordinary pressures return: a late train, a hungry child, an urgent email, a family demand, a sharp tone from the person they love. The agreement meets real life and buckles.

Overpromising often looks generous at the moment it is made. "I will never speak to you like that again." "I will always tell you exactly what I am feeling." "I will stop getting defensive." "I will be fully present every evening." The injured person may want to believe it, because the promise sounds large enough to match the hurt. The speaker may want to offer it, because the promise relieves shame. But an agreement that cannot survive fatigue becomes a delayed disappointment. It comforts the room today and injures the relationship tomorrow. The guardrail was painted beautifully. It was never bolted down.

A realistic agreement is not a smaller love. It is a more honest design. It asks what a person can actually do when their better self is harder to reach. This is the correct standard because repair is tested under pressure, not during the calm conversation about repair. The promise must work when someone is tired, busy, embarrassed, overstimulated, hungry, late, or frightened of being wrong. An agreement that depends on ideal emotional weather is not an agreement; it is a wish with formal wording. A useful agreement anticipates the bend in the road.

The difference between intensity and consistency is crucial. Intensity says, "I mean this deeply." Consistency says, "You will be able to see this repeatedly." Many people trust intensity too much because it feels persuasive: the serious face, the long conversation, the emotional promise, the relief of being temporarily aligned. Consistency is less glamorous. It looks like putting the phone away at the same threshold, using the same pause phrase when heat rises, sending the return message when space is needed, or checking before accepting a plan that affects both people. It does not dazzle. It reassures.

The research tradition associated with Edwin Locke and Gary Latham on goal-setting is relevant again because it shows the value of specificity and attainability in guiding action. Their work belongs to performance psychology, not relationship repair, yet the application is plain. A goal that is too vague cannot direct behaviour, and a goal that is accepted but unrealistic invites failure. "I will be less reactive" may be emotionally sincere, but it offers little instruction when blame is felt in the body. "When I feel defensive, I will say, 'I need a minute to answer well,' before I explain" gives the person a usable move. The agreement becomes smaller, and therefore stronger.

A realistic agreement begins by stripping away moral theatre. The point is not to create the noblest possible sentence. The point is to create the behaviour most likely to occur when stress returns. If a person has a long habit of interrupting, "I will never interrupt again" may be too sweeping. "When I interrupt, I will stop myself and say, 'Finish your thought'" may be more reliable. If a person disappears after conflict, "I will always stay and talk" may be unwise, especially if staying leads to contempt or panic. "When I need space, I will name a return time before I leave" is more realistic and more protective.

Simple constraints help because they reduce the number of decisions required during heat. A reminder phrase is one such constraint. "This is the doorway moment." "We are moving into defence." "Return time." "Let me finish." The phrase should be short, neutral, and agreed in advance, because conflict is a poor time to invent language. A reminder phrase is not a verdict. It is a small bell rung before the old pattern takes over. Its purpose is to make the agreement easier to remember while the body is busy trying to survive the moment.

A boundary is another simple constraint. Not a dramatic wall, not a punishment, not a method of controlling another adult, but a clear limit that protects the repair conditions. "No serious conflict by text once either of us says the conversation is escalating." "No family commitments confirmed until both people affected have been asked." "No problem-solving until the person who raised the hurt has finished describing it." These boundaries are modest. They do not require constant emotional brilliance. They ask for one restraint at the point where the relationship has repeatedly suffered.

Complex rules usually fail because they demand too much executive capacity at the very moment people have the least. A couple may design an elaborate conflict protocol in a calm Sunday conversation, complete with stages, phrases, timing, emotional check-ins, and exceptions. Then Wednesday evening arrives, someone is late, dinner is burning, a message pings, and the whole system is forgotten. The failure is not proof that the couple does not care. It may be proof that the agreement was too complicated for the conditions it was meant to enter. Repair needs tools that fit the hand under stress.

The guardrail motif is useful here because a guardrail is simple by necessity. It does not explain the full theory of road safety as the car approaches the bend. It is just there, placed where the risk is known. A realistic agreement works the same way. If evenings are vulnerable, the agreement belongs in the evening. If family calls trigger unilateral decisions, the agreement belongs before the answer is given. If text arguments become cruel, the agreement belongs at the point where typing turns sharp. The guardrail cannot protect every road. It must protect the bend that keeps causing damage.

The work of Peter Gollwitzer on implementation intentions, particularly his research published in the 1990s, also helps explain why "when-then" agreements are useful. Linking a specific cue to a specific behaviour makes action easier to retrieve. "When I hear myself getting sarcastic, then I will pause and restart the sentence." "When I need space, then I will give a return time." "When one of us says 'phone down', then the screen goes away until the current point is finished." The cue carries the behaviour. The agreement becomes less dependent on willpower and more dependent on recognition.

There is a credible limitation. Some people use realism to lower the bar too far. They say, "I cannot promise anything," "This is just how I react," or "You know I am bad at this," and call that honesty. That is not realism; it is resignation. A realistic agreement should be demanding enough to change the repeated injury and modest enough to keep. If the agreement does not alter the risk at all, it is not a repair plan. If it requires a complete personality transplant by tomorrow, it is not a repair plan either. The discipline is finding the narrow action that changes the pattern without pretending humans become new under pressure.

The reconciliation lies in honest scaling. Scale down the promise, not the responsibility. If the rupture is repeated interruption, do not scale the responsibility down to "I will try to listen more." That is too vague. Scale it to the behaviour: "I will not answer until you finish the sentence, and if I jump in, I will stop and ask you to continue." If the rupture is failure to return after taking space, do not promise permanent emotional availability. Promise the hinge: "I will give a return time before I step away, and I will update you if I cannot meet it." The responsibility remains serious. The action becomes possible.

Realistic agreements also require attention to capacity. Some people make agreements from guilt, then discover that they lack the time, energy, skill, or emotional steadiness to enact them consistently. This does not make them bad; it means the agreement was poorly fitted. A person working a demanding shift may not be able to offer a full emotional debrief the moment they walk through the door. But they may be able to offer a greeting, a brief check-in, and a named time to talk later. A person who becomes flooded in conflict may not be able to continue a hard conversation indefinitely, but they may be able to pause without disappearing. Capacity should shape the form of the agreement, not excuse the absence of one.

A realistic agreement is also clear about exceptions. Exceptions are not loopholes when they are named honestly. If the "no phones after work" agreement has an urgent work exception, the exception should be visible: "I am expecting one urgent message; after I answer it, the phone goes away." Without named exceptions, practical life will keep breaking the agreement and each break will feel like betrayal. With named exceptions, flexibility does not become chaos.

The injured person does not have to guess whether the guardrail has been removed or temporarily opened for a reason.

The agreement must be small enough to recover when missed. This is often overlooked. If the promise is absolute, a single failure can feel catastrophic. "I said I would never interrupt, and I interrupted; therefore I have failed completely." A recoverable agreement builds in a repair move: "If I interrupt, I will stop and ask you to finish." The recovery does not excuse the interruption. It prevents the old pattern from taking the whole conversation hostage. A realistic agreement expects human slippage and designs a return path before shame or defensiveness takes over.

This matters because shame often turns a small miss into a large collapse. Someone forgets the agreement, sees the other person's face change, and feels the old self-attack rising: "I cannot do anything right." If the agreement has no recovery move, the person may defend or withdraw. If the agreement includes a recovery move, they can act quickly: "I missed it. I am putting the phone down now." The sentence is not grand. It restores the guardrail. The ability to recover may become as important as the ability not to miss.

A domestic example makes the scaling visible. The conflict is about evenings after work. The injured person wants attention before logistics. The other person feels overwhelmed by immediate demands. A too-large agreement says, "We will spend every evening reconnecting properly before doing anything else." It sounds warm and may fail within days. A realistic agreement says, "When we both get home, we put phones down and greet each other before raising tasks, unless something is urgent." The agreement is modest, clear, and tied to the repeated threshold. It protects the vulnerable moment without trying to redesign the whole evening.

A professional example shows the same principle. A research team keeps losing trust because changes to shared documents are circulated before all contributors have seen them. A vague agreement says, "We will communicate more carefully." A complicated agreement creates a long approval process nobody follows under deadline pressure. A realistic agreement says, "When a section owner's text is changed, that owner sees the revised section before it is circulated outside the team." The rule is simple, visible, and tied to the specific injury: people felt overridden and exposed by changes they had not seen.

Realistic agreements should not depend on one person becoming the permanent monitor. If the injured person must always remind, check, enforce, and interpret the agreement, resentment will grow. A good agreement distributes responsibility. The person whose behaviour caused harm should carry the cue where possible. If they are the one who needs space, they carry the return time. If they are the one who tends to invite family into decisions, they carry the check before committing. If they are the one who interrupts, they carry the pause. The injured person may name the pattern, but should not become its full-time manager.

Consistency over intensity also changes how progress is recognised. The most important evidence may be quiet. A person pauses before correcting. A phone stays face down. A return time is kept. A family request is delayed until both people have spoken. These acts may not feel emotionally dramatic, but they are the currency of trust. Trust grows by ordinary repetition. It does not require a ceremony each time. In fact, when repair actions become ordinary, the relationship becomes less dependent on crisis for proof of care.

The injured person may need to notice the difference without turning it into a scorecard. "I saw you pause then" can reinforce the new pattern without making the other person feel inspected. "That helped" may be enough. But constant evaluation can make the agreement feel like probation. The aim is evidence, not surveillance. The guardrail should reduce fear, not become a structure everyone stares at anxiously. Realistic agreements work best when they are remembered, used, and then allowed to become part of ordinary life.

There is also a temptation to add more rules after the first success. If one small agreement helps, why not build a whole system? Sometimes this is useful, but often it overloads the relationship. Add only where the next repeatable injury has been clearly identified. A repair culture grows by layering simple, tested agreements, not by legislating every possible hurt in advance. Too many rules can make closeness feel bureaucratic. Too few leave people guessing. The art is to protect the dangerous bends without fencing off the entire road.

A realistic agreement must be emotionally acceptable to both people. If one person experiences the agreement as humiliation, surveillance, or one-sided control, it will not hold well. That does not mean every discomfort invalidates the plan. Accountability is uncomfortable. But the agreement should be framed as shared protection, not a badge of guilt. "This helps us not repeat that fight" is different from "This is what you must do because you failed." The same behaviour can become either repair or resentment depending on the relational meaning attached to it.

The agreement should also be time-aware. Some plans are best treated as experiments rather than permanent decrees. "Let us try this for the next few evenings and see whether it helps" can reduce resistance because the agreement is allowed to be reviewed. An experiment is not less serious; it is more responsive. It recognises that people may not know in advance what will actually restore safety. The first version of the guardrail may need moving. What matters is not pride of design, but whether the bend becomes safer.

Realism is not cynicism. It does not say, "People do not change." It says, "People change more reliably when agreements fit the conditions in which they must be kept." A person can grow more patient, but patience often begins as one practised pause. A person can become more emotionally available, but availability may begin as one protected greeting or one kept return time. A person can become more respectful in conflict, but respect may begin as one boundary around sarcasm or interruption. Large qualities are built through small repeatable acts.

The forward test is whether an agreement can survive the ordinary day, not merely the earnest conversation. When stress returns, will the promise still know what to do? Is there one cue, one behaviour, one recovery move, one boundary where the old pattern usually bends? The agreement should be small enough to keep and real enough to matter. Intensity may soothe the room for an evening, but consistency is what teaches the relationship to trust the guardrail when the road is wet, visibility is poor, and everyone is tired.

Reviewing and Adjusting Agreements

In 1950, W. Edwards Deming gave lectures in Japan that helped shape a culture of quality improvement built around a simple discipline: do the work, study what happened, adjust the process. The industrial setting was far from the private world of conflict repair, and the comparison should not be overdrawn. Yet the principle is useful because it refuses two common failures: pretending a plan is sacred because it was carefully made, and abandoning it as useless because the first version did not work perfectly. A living system learns by review.

Relationships need the same humility. Two people make an agreement after a painful moment: no difficult logistics in the first minutes after work, a return time after taking space, no serious arguments by text, a check before sharing private information with a third party. The agreement helps for a while. Then ordinary life presses against it. One person forgets. The cue arrives at an inconvenient time. The wording feels awkward. The boundary works in one setting but not another. The guardrail is there, but the bend is sharper than expected.

A failed or imperfect agreement is not automatically proof that the repair was false. It may be proof that the plan was too broad, too complicated, too vague, too rigid, or placed at the wrong point in the pattern. Shame turns this discovery into accusation: "You said you would change." Defensiveness turns it into dismissal: "Nothing I do is enough." Review turns it into information. That difference matters because the way two people examine an agreement determines whether the agreement becomes stronger or the old fight simply returns in new clothing.

Reviewing an agreement is not the same as reopening the entire wound. Reopening drags the couple, family, friendship, or team back into the original trial: who cared, who failed, who suffered more, who has always been like this. Reviewing keeps the lens narrower. It asks whether the guardrail held where it was supposed to hold. Did the phone-free greeting actually reduce the feeling of being ignored? Did the return time make space feel less like abandonment? Did the boundary with a third party protect privacy, or did it create a different pressure? The purpose is adjustment, not prosecution.

A short debrief protects the agreement from becoming a battlefield. Its quiet structure is practical: what worked, what did not, what to try next. The first question prevents the conversation from becoming a failure inventory. Something may have worked, even if the whole agreement did not. The greeting may have softened the first few minutes but left the later logistics unresolved. The return time may have reduced panic but been too late in the evening for a useful conversation. The no-text boundary may have stopped escalation but left both people unsure how to restart. Naming what worked preserves evidence of progress.

The second question keeps the review honest. An agreement that technically exists but does not reduce the injury should not be defended out of pride. If the reminder phrase sounds patronising, it will not help. If the return time is too vague, waiting will still feel unsafe. If the boundary relies on one exhausted person remembering every step, it may fail under pressure. "What did not work?" is not an accusation when the tone remains curious. It is a diagnostic question. The plan is being tested against reality, not against someone's worth.

The third question moves the pair from judgement to design. "What should we try next?" is deliberately modest. It does not ask for a permanent solution to all future conflict. It asks for the next adjustment: a clearer cue, a shorter phrase, a more realistic time, a different setting, a smaller boundary, a more visible reminder. A plan might move from "no work talk after dinner" to "urgent work talk only after asking whether now is a good time." It might move from "come back later" to "come back before bed or send a message naming when we will talk." The revision is the repair continuing.

The guardrail motif remains useful because guardrails are not placed once for all eternity without inspection. If cars keep scraping the same bend, the issue may not be the drivers alone. The angle may be wrong. The sign may come too late. The road may be slick at a particular hour. In relationship terms, a missed agreement does not always mean lack of care. Sometimes the cue was not visible soon enough. Sometimes the boundary was too ambitious. Sometimes the recovery move was never specified. Review asks where the guardrail needs moving before blame takes over the whole road.

The work of Chris Argyris on organisational learning is relevant here because he distinguished between correcting an error within existing assumptions and examining the assumptions that keep producing the error. In private repair, a couple may keep saying, "We need to remember the agreement," when the real issue is that the agreement depends on memory at the worst possible moment. A team may keep saying, "We need to communicate better," when the real issue is that the communication step has no owner. Review improves when it tests the design, not merely the people. The question is not only "Who failed?" but "What made the agreed behaviour hard to do?"

There is a credible limitation. Review can become avoidance if people keep adjusting agreements instead of taking responsibility for repeatedly ignoring them. Some patterns do not fail because the plan is poorly designed; they fail because one person does not actually intend to honour the boundary when it becomes inconvenient. Endless revision can then become a polite substitute for accountability. The injured person is asked to keep co-designing a repair for behaviour the other person continues to choose. This is not flexibility. It is drift with better language.

The reconciliation lies in distinguishing design failure from commitment failure. A design failure sounds like, "We agreed to talk after dinner, but by then we were both too tired; perhaps we need a shorter check-in earlier." A commitment failure sounds like, "I agreed not to share that information, and I shared it again because I wanted support in the moment." The first calls for adjustment. The second calls for ownership. Many situations contain both. A responsible review has enough honesty to name the design problem without hiding the personal contribution.

The research of Peter Gollwitzer on implementation intentions, especially work published in the 1990s, supports the importance of linking cues to actions. Review is where those links are tested. Did the cue appear clearly enough? Was the action simple enough? Did both people recognise the moment in time? An agreement such as "when conflict escalates, we pause" may fail because escalation is recognised too late. A revised agreement might use an earlier cue: when one person starts correcting details before acknowledging impact, the agreed phrase is used. The revision does not abandon the aim. It sharpens the trigger.

Review also reduces shame by normalising iteration. If an agreement is treated as a moral exam, every miss becomes a verdict. People then defend, conceal, or collapse. If an agreement is treated as a working design, a miss becomes data to examine with care. This does not excuse harm. It keeps the conversation usable. "We missed the return time" can become, "What made it hard to return then, and what should the return plan be next time?" rather than, "You never meant it." The difference in tone can decide whether repair remains possible.

The debrief should be short because length can pull the original fight back into the room. A useful review does not require a full emotional excavation every time. It may take only a few sentences. "The phone-free greeting helped. The problem was that we still started logistics too abruptly. Next time, let us greet first, then ask whether it is a good moment for practical talk." This kind of exchange respects time and attention. It treats repair as part of ordinary relational maintenance, not a ceremony requiring perfect readiness.

Timing matters. Reviewing too soon may reopen the bruise before either person can think clearly. Reviewing too late may let the learning vanish or the story harden. The right moment is usually after the emotional heat has lowered but before the next repeatable situation arrives. If the agreement concerns evenings after work, the review should not wait until another doorway argument has already begun. If the agreement concerns family visits, it should be revisited before the next visit, not during the tense drive home. Review belongs upstream of the next collision.

The tone of review should be lighter than the tone of apology. That does not mean flippant. It means the purpose has changed. The question is no longer "Was there harm?" but "Did our protection work?" If every review carries the full emotional intensity of the original rupture, people will avoid review. They will associate it with dread. A steadier tone helps both people stay practical: curious, specific, and brief. The goal is to adjust the guardrail, not relive the crash.

A domestic example makes this clear. A couple agrees that when one person needs space during conflict, they will name a return time. The first attempt partly works: the person says they will return after a short break, but the conversation resumes too late and both are exhausted. A shame-driven review says, "You failed again." A useful review says, "The return time helped because I was not left guessing. What did not work was the timing; by then we were too tired. Next time, if it is late, let us do a brief repair before sleep and schedule the fuller conversation." The agreement evolves because the evidence has become clearer.

A professional example shows the same pattern. A team agrees that revised documents will be checked by section owners before circulation. The agreement works for ordinary revisions but fails under a tight deadline. The review should not dissolve into accusation or abandon the rule entirely. It might ask what worked: fewer surprises in normal circulation. What did not: no fast-track process for urgent changes. What to try next: if a deadline prevents full review, the sender marks the change clearly and alerts the section owner directly. The plan becomes more realistic because pressure has revealed a missing condition.

There is a danger in reviewing only failures. If the agreement is working, the relationship still benefits from noticing it. "That helped when you gave a return time earlier." "I noticed we avoided the text spiral." "The family check-in before answering made the weekend feel less pressured." These acknowledgements are not praise in a childish sense. They are evidence markers. They teach the relationship what to repeat. Trust grows not only from correcting misses, but from recognising the moments when the new pattern held.

At the same time, review should not become scorekeeping. A person who tracks every successful act as proof of virtue may later weaponise it: "I did the thing three times, so you cannot still be upset." That turns repair into accounting. The purpose of noticing progress is to strengthen the new pattern, not to purchase silence. Evidence should reassure, not pressure. A changed behaviour is meaningful because it reduces harm; it does not erase the past on command.

Flexible agreements are especially important because needs change as trust changes. Early on, an injured person may need more explicit reassurance, clearer return times, or stronger boundaries. As evidence accumulates, the agreement may loosen. A couple may begin with a strict no-text rule during conflict and later allow brief logistical messages while keeping emotional repair for voice or in person. A family may begin with careful boundaries around a sensitive topic and later need less formal protection. A good agreement can mature. Rigidity may be comforting at first, but it can become unnecessary or constricting if never reviewed.

Some agreements need strengthening rather than loosening. If the same miss keeps happening, the plan may require an earlier cue or a firmer boundary. "Please try not to bring this up with your friend" may need to become "I am not comfortable with our private conflict being discussed with someone who then treats me differently." "Let us avoid arguing by text" may need to become "If either of us says 'pause text', the conversation stops until we can speak." Adjustment is not failure. It is the relationship learning where the protection must be clearer.

Reviewing well also prevents the familiar spiral of mind-reading. Without review, one person may assume the agreement is working because the conflict has been quieter, while the other may feel they are suppressing hurt to avoid another discussion. One may think the boundary is too strict; the other may think it is barely sufficient. A brief debrief surfaces these differences before they become fresh resentment. The question "Is this still helping?" can save a relationship from months of quiet compliance that later erupts as "I never wanted this."

The best reviews keep interpretation close to behaviour. Instead of "You clearly did not care about the agreement," the review says, "The return time was missed." Instead of "You are controlling this process," it says, "The reminder phrase felt sharp when it was said in front of others." Instead of "This plan is pointless," it says, "The plan works when we are alone, but not when family is present." Behavioural language keeps the review repairable. Character language drags it back into the original fight.

A short debrief also allows both people to remain learners rather than defendants. "What worked?" invites acknowledgement. "What did not?" invites honesty. "What should we try next?" invites agency. None of these questions requires humiliation. None requires pretending the harm was insignificant. They keep the agreement flexible by making adjustment part of the design from the start. When people know an agreement can be refined, they are less likely to feel trapped by the first version or ashamed when it needs revision.

The forward test is whether two people can review the guardrail without re-enacting the crash. Did it help? Did it fail? Did it fail because the plan was badly placed, because the cue came too late, because the pressure was greater than expected, or because someone did not honour the commitment? The answer may be uncomfortable, but it need not be catastrophic. Agreements that stick are rarely perfect at birth. They become trustworthy through honest review, modest adjustment, and the shared willingness to learn what actually protects the relationship when the road bends again.

Chapter 9
Interrupting Repeat Fight Patterns

The argument begins with the calendar. One person asks whether the train tickets have been booked, and the other answers with a stiffness that seems larger than the question. A bag is still on the floor. A kettle clicks off in the kitchen. Someone says, "I was going to do it," and someone else hears, "Stop asking me." Within moments, the subject has moved from travel to trust, from timing to respect, from one task to the old familiar ache of feeling either chased or abandoned.

Both people know this argument. They could almost change parts and still speak the lines. One asks again, more urgently, because silence feels like neglect. The other withdraws further, because urgency feels like attack. The more one pursues, the more the other disappears; the more one disappears, the more the other pursues. Nobody planned the choreography. Still, it happens. The pattern has learned the room.

Repeat fights are rarely just repeated topics. They are repeated sequences. The same cue appears, the same protective move follows, and the same injury returns wearing different clothes. A logistics question becomes a bid for reassurance. A practical reminder becomes a threat to competence. A request for space becomes a fear of abandonment. A suggestion becomes evidence of control. The surface issue may change, but the emotional route is worn smooth by use. Once the route is entered, intelligence alone often cannot stop it.

The central tension is that people tend to personalise what they have not yet mapped. "You are impossible." "You always shut down." "You never let anything go." These accusations may contain fragments of observation, but they miss the larger mechanism. A loop is not an excuse; it is a pattern of mutual activation. Naming it reduces blame because it gives both people something to stand beside rather than something to throw. The question changes from "Which one of us is the problem?" to "What happens between us when the pattern starts?"

The stakes are immediate because a familiar loop steals choice. It makes people faster, narrower, and less curious. A partner who feels pursued stops explaining and starts escaping. A partner who feels abandoned stops asking plainly and starts protesting. A person who feels criticised begins defending facts that are not the real issue. A person who feels helpless begins fixing, advising, or smoothing until the other feels unseen. These behaviours are visible: quicker voices, shorter answers, repeated interruptions, phones picked up, doors left half-closed, apologies delayed until they no longer reach the original hurt. The fight is no longer being chosen. It is being run.

The stakes also deepen over time because repetition breeds despair. The first time a conflict repeats, people may feel frustrated. The tenth time, they may feel doomed. "Here we are again" becomes less a sentence than a climate. Despair is dangerous because it tempts people to make identities out of patterns: the pursuer, the withdrawer, the critic, the defender, the fixer, the avoider. Once the identity hardens, repair feels naive. But patterns, unlike fixed character, can be interrupted. The key is catching the loop early enough that the old choreography has not yet claimed every step.

The work begins by spotting the loop as a sequence rather than a personality flaw: who moves towards, who moves away, who corrects, who defends, who fixes, who avoids, and which cue begins the turn. From there, the task narrows to one pattern break that can be repeated under pressure: slowing down, asking one honest question, or taking a timed pause before the old role takes over. When the pattern repeats despite good intentions, the repair is not to declare failure, but to study the missed cue, name the trigger, and ask what support would make the next interruption more likely.

A train track is the right image for a repeat fight. Once the wheels are on it, the destination can feel inevitable. The point is not to argue with the track after the train is moving at full speed. The point is to notice the switch before the route is set. A neutral sentence can become that switch: "We are in the old loop." Not "you are doing it again." Not "this is your fault." The pattern is named as something shared, something active, something that can be interrupted before it carries both people to the same exhausted station.

The unresolved question is whether two people can recognise a repeat without surrendering to it. When the logistics question begins to sound like criticism, when the request for space begins to feel like disappearance, when the helpful suggestion begins to land as control, can the pattern be named before blame takes the microphone? The next fight may look like a familiar argument about time, money, chores, family, or plans. The deeper test is whether either person can hear the wheels catching the old track and reach for the switch before the journey becomes inevitable.

Spotting Your Conflict Loop

In 1988, psychologist Sue Johnson and psychiatrist Leslie Greenberg published early work that helped establish emotionally focused therapy as a serious model for understanding couple distress. Its central insight was not that couples fight because they lack enough information. Often, they fight because each person's protective move triggers the other person's protective move, and the relationship becomes caught in a negative cycle. The argument has content, but the content is not the whole engine. Underneath it, two people are trying to protect themselves from threat and accidentally becoming threatening to each other.

The scene is ordinary. A couple is planning a visit to relatives, and one person asks whether the train tickets have been booked. The other hears criticism, not logistics. "I said I would do it." The first hears defensiveness, not reassurance. "I was only asking." The other becomes shorter. The first becomes sharper. Within a few minutes, the tickets have become almost irrelevant. The real fight is about reliability, pressure, appreciation, and the old fear that one person is carrying the relationship while the other is being treated as incompetent. The train track is already under the wheels.

A conflict loop is a repeated sequence of protection. It is not simply a repeated subject. The subject may change from travel to money, from housework to family visits, from work stress to unanswered messages, but the movement is recognisable: one person reaches, the other withdraws; one criticises, the other defends; one fixes, the other avoids; one asks for reassurance through pressure, the other hears pressure and retreats. The loop becomes the real opponent. As long as each person sees only the other's latest move, both keep feeding the pattern they hate.

Pursue-withdraw is one of the most recognisable loops. One person experiences distance as danger and moves closer through questions, protest, repeated bids, or emotional urgency. The other experiences that closeness as pressure and creates distance through silence, delay, distraction, minimising, or physical retreat. The pursuer sees abandonment. The withdrawer sees attack. The more one pursues, the more the other withdraws; the more the other withdraws, the more desperate the pursuit becomes. Neither person is necessarily trying to harm the other. Both are trying to reduce their own alarm, and each method increases the other's.

Criticise-defend has a different rhythm. One person raises a concern through blame because softer language has begun to feel useless. The other hears the blame and prepares a defence because accountability feels like accusation. The critic says, "You never think ahead." The defender says, "That is not fair; I did three things this week." The critic feels the point has been dodged and sharpens the claim. The defender feels misrepresented and reaches for more evidence. Soon the conflict is no longer about the missed task. It is about whether one person is unreasonable and the other unappreciated. Accuracy becomes a weapon rather than a bridge.

Fix-avoid often appears in relationships where one person copes through action and the other copes through space. A hurt is named, and the fixer begins offering solutions: "We can change the schedule, send the message, make a plan, solve it now." The avoider experiences the speed as invasion and retreats, sometimes into silence, sometimes into vague agreement, sometimes into "I do not want to talk about this." The fixer then intensifies because the lack of response feels irresponsible. The avoider withdraws further because the intensifying feels controlling. The original need may have been simple: to be heard before being managed.

The early cues of a loop are usually bodily and behavioural before they are verbal. A voice becomes brisk. A face goes still. Someone starts correcting details that are not central. Someone asks the same question in a slightly tighter tone. Someone reaches for the phone.

Someone becomes suddenly busy with dishes, bags, papers, doors. The words may remain civil, but the pattern has begun. The train track is not dramatic at first. It is just the familiar direction under the conversation.

Spotting the loop requires looking for sequence rather than blame. Who tends to move towards? Who tends to move away? Who raises the stakes? Who narrows the argument into facts? Who tries to solve before hearing the hurt? Who gives in too quickly and resents it later? These questions are not labels for permanent identity. They are maps of movement. A person may pursue in one relationship and withdraw in another. A person may defend at work and fix at home. The aim is not to name a type. The aim is to recognise the recurring steps before they become a script.

The work of John Bowlby on attachment, developed from the mid-twentieth century onwards, offers one useful frame for why these loops become so powerful. Human beings organise around the availability of significant others. When connection feels threatened, people protest, cling, flee, appease, explain, shut down, or control. Adult conflict often carries this deeper alarm beneath practical content. A question about tickets may not be only about tickets. It may ask, "Can I rely on you?" A defensive answer may not be only irritation. It may say, "Do you see me as incapable?" The surface argument is the receipt; the loop is the payment system behind it.

The logistics argument that becomes a bid for reassurance is especially revealing. One person says, "Did you book the tickets?" The hidden fear may be, "I am worried I will be left holding this again." The other says, "I told you I would," and the hidden fear may be, "You do not trust me." If neither fear is named, each person responds to the other's armour. The first asks again, more sharply, to secure reassurance. The second pulls back, more stiffly, to protect dignity. The loop can then spend an evening proving the very fears that began it: one feels alone; the other feels judged.

A named pattern reduces personal blame because it places attention on the choreography rather than on a single villain. "We are in the ask-defend loop" is different from "You are being defensive again." "This is the chase-and-shut-down pattern" is different from "You never talk." The first phrasing gives both people a way to step beside the conflict and see it. The second phrasing pushes one person further into the role they are already trying to escape. Naming the pattern is not a soft way to avoid responsibility. It is a sharper way to locate responsibility where it can be used.

There is a danger, however, in naming loops too quickly or too smugly. Pattern language can become a weapon. "You are withdrawing" may be accurate, but if said with accusation it will probably produce more withdrawal. "Here comes your criticism again" may identify a sequence while humiliating the person who is trying, however clumsily, to name a hurt. When the label becomes another accusation, it joins the loop rather than interrupting it. A useful pattern name must be neutral enough that both people can stand inside it without feeling condemned.

The limitation is important for another reason: not every repeated conflict is merely a mutual loop. Some patterns contain unequal power, intimidation, contempt, coercion, or a repeated refusal to respect basic boundaries. In those situations, describing the problem only as "our cycle" can hide responsibility and pressure the injured person to co-own what is not equally theirs. A loop map should never flatten harm into symmetry. It should clarify the sequence while preserving moral accuracy. Sometimes both people are caught. Sometimes one person is repeatedly harmed. The difference matters.

The reconciliation is to map behaviour precisely and ethically. A loop map should describe observable moves, not excuse them. "When I raise a concern, you leave the room without a return time, and I follow with more messages" is useful. "We both have issues" may be too vague. "When you criticise, I defend" may be useful if both parts are truly present. "We trigger each other" can be lazy if it avoids naming that one person's contempt is doing most of the damage. The map is meant to increase choice, not dilute accountability.

A second checkable anchor comes from the field of family systems theory, especially Murray Bowen's work from the mid-twentieth century onwards. Bowen emphasised patterns of interaction within families rather than viewing distress only inside isolated individuals. The language differs from contemporary repair work, but the useful inheritance is clear: relational behaviour is often circular. One person's move becomes the other person's cue, and the response then becomes evidence for the first person's next move. This circularity is why repeating the same argument can feel maddening. Each person believes they are responding reasonably to what just happened, while missing how their response sets up the next turn.

The earliest cue is often a shift in meaning. The words are still practical, but the emotional translation has changed. "Did you send the email?" becomes "You think I am irresponsible." "Can we talk tonight?" becomes "You are going to corner me." "You are quiet" becomes "You are leaving me." "Let me help" becomes "You do not trust me to do it." Once the translation changes, the body responds to the translated meaning, not the literal sentence. Spotting the loop means noticing when translation has taken over.

A useful question is, "What am I hearing that may not have been said?" The pursuer may be hearing abandonment inside delay. The withdrawer may be hearing attack inside urgency. The defender may be hearing character assassination inside impact. The fixer may be hearing helplessness inside pain. These translations are not foolish. They usually have histories. But they should be checked before they are obeyed. Otherwise the loop is fed by ghosts: old meanings wearing the clothes of current sentences.

Mapping a loop can be done in plain language. "When I feel uncertain, I ask more questions. When I ask more questions, you feel criticised and get short. When you get short, I feel less secure and ask harder. Then you shut down." This map is more useful than "You never reassure me." It shows the sequence, the emotional fuel, and the point where an interruption might be possible. The person who hears it may still feel uncomfortable, but they are being invited into a shared diagram rather than placed in the dock.

The most useful maps include the protective intention behind each move. Pursuit is often an attempt to reconnect. Withdrawal is often an attempt to prevent escalation. Criticism is often an attempt to make a problem visible. Defence is often an attempt to preserve dignity. Fixing is often an attempt to reduce distress. Avoidance is often an attempt to regain inner space. These intentions do not erase impact. They explain why the loop is so persistent. Each move solves something for the person doing it, while creating a new problem for the other.

This is why simply telling someone to stop their move rarely works. "Stop withdrawing" may not work if withdrawal is how the person avoids saying something cruel. "Stop pursuing" may not work if pursuit is how the person prevents abandonment panic. "Stop fixing" may not work if fixing is how the person manages helplessness. The loop must be interrupted at the level of need, not only behaviour. The withdrawing person may need a safe way to ask for space with a return. The pursuing person may need a small reassurance before waiting. The fixer may need to hear that listening is the action required. The avoider may need a defined entry point rather than an open-ended emotional flood.

The train track returns because loops feel inevitable once they are underway. But tracks have switches. The switch is often an early cue named without blame. "I think I am starting to chase." "I am hearing this as criticism and getting defensive." "I am trying to fix before I have heard you." "I want to disappear, which probably means I need to name a pause." These sentences are small acts of pattern recognition. They do not solve the conflict. They slow the train enough that a different route becomes possible.

The forward test is whether the next familiar fight can be recognised as a sequence before it becomes a verdict. When the calendar question sounds like mistrust, when the practical reminder sounds like control, when the silence sounds like abandonment, can either person ask what track they are on? The subject may still matter. Tickets may still need booking, bills may still need paying, messages may still need answering. But the deeper repair begins when two people can see the loop moving beneath the subject and name it early enough to choose the next step rather than perform the old one.

Choosing One Pattern Break

In 1999, psychologist Peter Gollwitzer published influential work on implementation intentions, showing the power of linking a recognised situation with a pre-chosen response. The research belongs to motivation science rather than couple repair, but its lesson travels cleanly into conflict: people are more likely to act differently when the alternative has been prepared before the pressure arrives. A vague wish says, "I will not get pulled into that argument again." A pattern break says, "When I hear myself starting to defend, I will ask one question before explaining."

Repeat fights do not usually give people enough time to become wise from scratch. The old sequence begins too quickly. A reminder lands as criticism. Silence lands as abandonment. Advice lands as control. The body recognises the pattern and reaches for its familiar tool before the reflective mind has opened the drawer. That is why new skills are rarely invented mid-argument. They are rehearsed beforehand, then retrieved under pressure. The train is already moving. The switch has to be close at hand.

A pattern break is one small interruption placed at the earliest reliable cue in the loop. It does not solve the whole conflict, reveal every hidden need, or prove who is right. Its purpose is narrower and more disciplined: stop escalation before the old choreography takes the room. One person slows the pace. One asks a genuine question. One names a timed pause. One changes posture, lowers volume, or reflects the impact before arguing the facts. The action is deliberately modest because modest actions are more likely to survive the heat. A pattern break that cannot be used while irritated is only a theory.

The strongest pattern break is chosen according to the loop, not according to personality ideals. In a pursue-withdraw loop, the pursuing partner may need a move that slows pursuit without abandoning the need for contact: "I am getting urgent, and I do not want to chase. Can you tell me when you can come back to this?" The withdrawing partner may need a move that creates space without disappearing: "I need a pause, and I will come back after I have calmed down." In a criticise-defend loop, the critic may need to name impact before accusation; the defender may need to reflect one sentence before correcting the record. The break must interrupt the actual rail the argument runs on.

Slowing down is often the simplest break because speed feeds almost every loop. When people accelerate, they interrupt more, hear less, and mistake volume for clarity. A slowed sentence can change the atmosphere without sounding like a formal technique. "I am going too fast." "Let me slow this down." "I want to answer, but not from defence." These lines do not concede the argument. They interrupt the machinery. The visible effect may be small: a longer pause, less overlap, a shift from accusation to impact. Small is enough if it changes direction.

Asking one question is another powerful break, but only if the question is genuine. A question used as a weapon is not a break; it is escalation in polite clothing. "Why do you always do this?" is a charge with a question mark attached. "What did that land like for you?" does different work. "Are you asking for reassurance or a decision?" may prevent a logistics argument from becoming a character trial. "What are you hearing me say?" can reveal that the fight has moved from the actual sentence to the meaning attached to it. One honest question can slow the old track because it invites information where the loop expects accusation.

A timed pause is the right break when continuing would only feed the pattern. The timing matters. "I am done" often sounds like abandonment or punishment. "I need fifteen minutes, and I will come back" is a different act. It contains distance and connection at once. It tells the other person that the pause is meant to protect the repair, not escape it. The pause must be believable, and the return must be kept. Otherwise the pattern break becomes a new injury. A timed pause is not a disappearing act. It is a held boundary with a door in it.

The work of John Gottman and colleagues on couple interaction gives useful language to this principle through the idea of repair attempts: small moves that reduce tension and alter the course of conflict. Such moves are not valuable because they are elegant. They are valuable because they change what happens next. A clumsy but sincere "I am getting defensive" may be more useful than a beautifully argued explanation. A brief "Can we restart that sentence?" may prevent an hour of escalation. Repair attempts live or die by whether they interrupt momentum. The pattern break is one repair attempt chosen in advance and practised until it can be found under stress.

Rehearsal can feel artificial to intelligent adults, especially those who value spontaneity. They may resist the idea of practising a sentence for conflict because it sounds mechanical or theatrical. Yet people already rehearse conflict unconsciously. They rehearse grievances in the shower, defences while driving, speeches after the room has gone quiet. The question is not whether rehearsal will occur. The question is whether rehearsal will prepare the old fight or a new move. A neutral sentence practised in calm is less artificial than a cutting sentence delivered from panic.

The pattern-break sentence should be neutral and clear. Neutral means it does not accuse. Clear means it identifies the process without hiding in vagueness. "We are doing it again" may be too loaded if "it" sounds like blame. "I think we are in the old pursue-withdraw pattern" may work if both people know the phrase and neither uses it as a weapon. "I am starting to defend instead of listening" is clean because it owns the speaker's part. "Can we slow down before we lose the point?" names the danger without naming a villain. The sentence should be short enough to remember when the nervous system is not feeling literary.

The train track motif matters because a pattern break is not a new destination; it is a switch. The argument may still need to go somewhere. The tickets may still need booking. The money still needs discussing. The family boundary still needs setting. The switch simply prevents the conversation from travelling to the old station of contempt, withdrawal, pressure, or despair. This distinction protects the break from being misunderstood as avoidance. The aim is not to stop the issue. The aim is to stop the escalation that makes the issue harder to solve.

A short example shows the difference. One person asks, "Have you dealt with the insurance form?" The other hears judgement and replies, "I said I would." The first hears evasion and says, "I cannot keep carrying everything." The second feels accused and starts listing tasks they completed. The train is moving. A pattern break might be, "I think this is turning into the reliability fight. What I need is reassurance that it is handled, not a debate about everything we both do." That sentence changes the level of the conversation. The issue remains practical, but the hidden bid is named: reassurance, not prosecution.

A different break could come from the other side: "I am hearing this as criticism and getting defensive. The form is not done yet; I will do it tonight and show you when it is sent." Here the person does not argue their worth. They name the defensive cue, answer the practical question, and offer a visible next step. The fight loses some of its fuel because the old role is not performed in the usual way. The break is not dramatic. It is just precise enough to keep the loop from completing itself.

There is a credible limitation. One person cannot reliably interrupt a destructive pattern alone if the other is committed to escalation, contempt, intimidation, or refusal. A pattern break is not a magic phrase that makes unsafe behaviour safe. It cannot turn mockery into respect or coercion into collaboration. When harm is severe or one-sided, the necessary interruption may not be a conversational sentence but a firmer boundary, distance, or outside support. The language of mutual loops must never be used to make a vulnerable person responsible for managing another person's cruelty.

The reconciliation is to choose a pattern break for repairable loops, not for situations where basic dignity is absent. In ordinary repeat conflicts, one changed move can alter the sequence because the loop depends on both people playing familiar parts. In harmful dynamics, the task may be protection rather than pattern interruption. Discernment matters. A neutral sentence can help when both people are caught. It is inadequate when one person is being used. The pattern break belongs where good-faith repair remains possible.

Choosing only one break is important because overloading the repair plan weakens retrieval. People often leave a calm conversation with five new promises: speak softly, ask questions, avoid old examples, pause sooner, validate first, use a code word, avoid sarcasm, return within an agreed period. All of those may be sensible. In the heat of conflict, they may become impossible to remember. One break gives the mind a handle. "Ask one question before defending." "Name the loop." "Take a timed pause." "Reflect impact before intent." The simpler the cue-action pair, the more likely it is to appear when needed.

The work of psychologist Albert Bandura on self-efficacy is relevant here because people are more likely to attempt behaviours they believe they can perform. A pattern break that feels too ambitious will be abandoned under threat. Someone who freezes in conflict may not be able to deliver a beautifully balanced reflection of impact and intent. They may be able to say, "I need a minute, and I am coming back." Someone who floods with words may not be able to become instantly spacious and calm. They may be able to say, "I am talking too much; I am going to ask one question." Confidence grows through usable moves, not impossible standards.

The pattern break should be rehearsed in the actual language a person would use. If the sentence sounds borrowed, stiff, or morally superior, it will not survive the room. "I notice we are entering a maladaptive interactional sequence" may be accurate and useless. "We are on the old track" may work for one couple and irritate another. "I am starting to defend" may be perfect for someone who respects plainness. "Can we pause the spiral?" may suit another. The sentence should sound like the speaker on a more disciplined day, not like a therapist hidden under the table.

Rehearsal does not require ceremony. It can be as simple as saying the sentence aloud once when calm, agreeing what it means, and deciding how the other person will respond if they can. The response matters because a pattern break can fail if the other person treats it as manipulation. If one says, "I am starting to defend," and the other replies, "Of course you are," the break collapses. A shared repair culture gives the break a fair hearing. The other person might answer, "All right, let us slow down," or "I can say the impact again without attacking." The break works better when both know it is meant to protect the conversation.

A pattern break should interrupt escalation, not win the point. This is a crucial distinction. "I am noticing your tone" may be true, but it often functions as a move to regain advantage. "I want to slow down because we are losing the issue" is less adversarial. The speaker must examine their motive. Are they using the break to stop harm, or to stop the other person from saying something inconvenient? Are they pausing to regulate, or pausing to avoid accountability? Are they asking a question to understand, or to expose inconsistency? The same technique can serve repair or self-protection. Motive shapes impact.

The best breaks often include self-location. "I am getting urgent." "I am starting to shut down." "I am moving into fixing." "I am hearing blame and want to defend." These sentences reduce blame because they begin with the speaker's own pattern rather than diagnosing the other person. They also model the kind of responsibility the loop needs. Instead of "You are withdrawing," the sentence becomes, "I feel myself chasing because I am scared we will not come back to this." The first version pins the other person. The second reveals the cue and creates a chance for a different response.

The break may also be a physical action paired with language. Sitting down rather than standing over someone. Putting the phone face down. Moving from text to voice. Taking one step back from the doorway. These actions matter because loops are embodied. A person who follows another from room to room may intensify pursuit without intending to. A person who keeps typing may feed a digital escalation that would soften in voice. A person who remains turned away may communicate withdrawal even while claiming to listen. A pattern break can change posture, setting, or medium before changing content.

There is another limitation: a break can become stale if used mechanically. If someone says the same phrase in every conflict without genuine intention, the other person may hear it as a tactic. "We are in the old loop" can begin to mean "Stop being upset." "I need a pause" can begin to mean "I do not want accountability." To prevent this, the break must be followed by the promised repair behaviour. The pause returns. The question is answered. The slower pace continues. The phrase is only the switch. The train still has to change track.

A useful pattern break also leaves room for the other person's correction. If someone says, "We are in the criticise-defend loop," the other might respond, "Maybe, but I also need you to hear that the impact is real." The break should not be used to erase content. The pattern and the issue both matter. The old track may be active, and the practical concern may still be valid. Repair requires holding both truths: "Yes, the form still needs doing, and we are turning the form into the reliability fight." This prevents pattern language from becoming a clever way to avoid the actual task.

The more serious the repeat pattern, the earlier the break must occur. Once contempt, repeated interruption, or threats of leaving enter the conversation, a subtle question may be too late. The break may need to be a complete pause. If the loop is mild, slowing down may be enough. If the loop is moderate, a named pattern and one clarifying question may work. If the loop is hot, the safest interruption may be, "We are too escalated. I want to stop and return at a clear time." The choice of break must match the temperature, not the ideal image of mature conversation.

The forward test is whether one small rehearsed move can be found before the loop gathers speed. When the old argument begins, will the person reach for victory, evidence, withdrawal, fixing, or pursuit? Or will they reach for the switch: slow down, ask one honest question, name the pattern, or take a timed pause? The aim is not to win the fight by sounding calm. The aim is to keep the fight from becoming the same fight, with the same roles, the same injuries, and the same tired ending. The next repeat will offer the track. The repair depends on whether the switch has been practised enough to appear.

Repairing After a Repeat

In 1972, NASA launched Apollo 16 from Kennedy Space Center in Florida, less than two years after the near-disaster of Apollo 13. The agency did not treat one failure as proof that spaceflight itself was hopeless, nor did it pretend the earlier rupture had been a passing inconvenience. The work was more exacting than either despair or denial: study what failed, revise what could be revised, and return with better safeguards. The repeat risk did not vanish. It became information.

A relationship faces its own smaller version of that test when the same argument happens again. The door closes too firmly. The same message goes unanswered. The same family visit creates the same split. The same practical question becomes the same accusation. Two people stand in the familiar wreckage and feel a particular kind of exhaustion: not only hurt, but the humiliation of having been here before. Here we are again.

That sentence can become poison if it is allowed to mean, "Nothing changes." It can also become useful if it means, "The pattern is still active, and we need better data." The difference is not cosmetic. Despair treats the repeat as a verdict on character, compatibility, or love. Repair treats the repeat as evidence that the previous agreement did not yet reach the true trigger, did not have enough support, or was not practised under the conditions in which the pattern actually returns. The repeat hurts. It also teaches.

The first task after a repeat is to acknowledge it without making it hopeless. This requires language with a narrow spine. "We are in the same pattern again, and I do not want to pretend that does not matter." That sentence does not minimise the disappointment. It also does not collapse into fatalism. It keeps the repeat visible without letting it become the whole future. A more damaging version would be, "You never change," or "We are always going to be like this." Those sentences may express real grief, but they close the door on learning before the evidence has been examined.

A repeat is not the same as a failure to care. This distinction is essential. People often repeat patterns they sincerely dislike because the trigger arrives faster than the new behaviour. The old response has years of rehearsal behind it; the new repair move may have only a conversation, an agreement, and a hopeful intention. When pressure rises, the mind goes to the practised route. The train track reappears beneath the wheels. The question is not whether disappointment is justified. It often is. The better question is what the repeat reveals about the cue, the capacity, the agreement, and the support needed next time.

The trigger may have been earlier than anyone realised. A couple may think the conflict begins when one person raises their voice, but the real trigger may be the first clipped reply. They may think the pattern begins when one person leaves the room, but the real trigger may be the third repeated question. A team may think the problem is missed deadlines, when the conflict actually begins when risk is raised too late for anyone to respond without embarrassment. Repairing after a repeat means moving upstream. What looked like the start may have been the middle.

This is where the repeat becomes data. Not cold data, stripped of feeling, but relational data: the moment the old pattern caught, the cue that went unnoticed, the support that was missing, the agreement that proved too vague or too ambitious. "We missed the cue when I started correcting details." "The pause failed because I did not give a return time." "The no-text agreement broke because we had no plan for urgent logistics." "The family boundary failed because we agreed privately but did not decide what to say publicly." Each sentence turns disappointment into a map.

The work of Chris Argyris on organisational learning is useful here because he distinguished between simply correcting an error and examining the thinking that produced the error. In relationships, a repeat fight often invites a superficial correction: "We need to try harder." Trying harder may help for a day. It rarely changes a loop on its own. A deeper review asks why the previous attempt did not hold. Was the cue too late? Was the action too complicated? Was the agreement one-sided? Was someone agreeing from guilt rather than willingness? Was the emotional need misidentified? The point is not to analyse forever. It is to correct the actual failure.

A repeat can reveal that the repair action did not match the impact. Someone apologised for sounding sharp, but the real injury was that they did not return after taking space. Someone agreed to "be more present", but the real injury was the phone during the first minutes after work. Someone promised not to "bring family into it", but the real injury was allowing a third party to influence shared decisions before the couple had spoken. When the repeat returns, it may be exposing a mismatch. The apology addressed one layer; the pattern lived in another.

There is also the possibility that the agreement was realistic in language but unsupported in practice. A person may agree not to argue by text, then receive a provocative message during a workday and have no prepared response. A couple may agree to pause when heated, but neither has practised the sentence that makes the pause feel safe. A colleague may agree to let others finish speaking, but the meeting structure still rewards speed and dominance. Behaviour does not change in a vacuum. Support is not indulgence. It is the design that makes the chosen behaviour easier to retrieve under pressure.

The train track motif returns because repeat patterns do not ask permission before reappearing. They wait in familiar settings: the late evening, the doorway, the family gathering, the meeting under deadline, the text thread with too much subtext and too little tone. A person who expects themselves to improvise maturity at full speed is setting themselves up for another derailment. The repair after a repeat asks where the switch was missed. Was there a moment when the route could have changed? Was the switch too subtle? Was it placed after the train had already gathered speed?

A short example makes the process visible. Two partners have agreed that when one needs space during conflict, they will name a return time. The next argument comes, pressure rises, and one leaves the room saying, "I cannot do this." The other feels abandoned and sends several sharp messages. The old loop returns. A despairing repair says, "You did it again. You clearly do not care." A data-based repair says, "We repeated the pause-without-return pattern. The cue was earlier than the exit; you were already shutting down when I asked the third question, and I started chasing when you got quiet. We need the return-time sentence before either of us reaches that point." The second version still names harm. It also shows where to intervene.

The language after a repeat should acknowledge pain before analysis. If the injured person hears only process language, they may feel the emotional cost is being intellectualised away. "This hurt because it was the same pattern" may need to come before "What cue did we miss?" Recognition keeps the data from becoming sterile. The repeat matters precisely because it carries history. The person who says,

"We need to learn from this," without also saying, "I understand why it hurt more because it happened again," may sound more interested in improvement than in impact.

Repair after a repeat therefore has a particular order: name the repeat, recognise the added sting, identify the missed cue, and choose the next support. This order prevents two common failures. One failure is despair, where the repeat becomes proof that nothing will ever change. The other is premature problem-solving, where the pain is skipped in favour of a new technique. The middle path is sturdier: "This was the same loop, and I know that makes it harder to trust the apology. Let us look at where the pattern caught so the next support is more specific."

There is a credible limitation. Repetition is not always neutral data. If the same harmful behaviour continues after clear impact, agreed boundaries, and realistic supports, the repeat may indicate unwillingness, contempt, or a deeper problem than this repair method can address. Treating every repeat as a learning opportunity can become dangerous if it excuses chronic harm. A person should not be asked to endlessly refine a plan for someone who repeatedly violates it without meaningful ownership. Data can reveal a design flaw. It can also reveal a refusal.

The reconciliation lies in looking at response after the repeat. Does the person who repeated the harm show precise ownership, curiosity about the trigger, and willingness to adjust conduct? Or do they minimise, blame, collapse, evade, or ask for indefinite patience? Does the pattern become more understood over time, or merely more politely described? Repair remains credible when repetition leads to sharper accountability and better support. It loses credibility when repetition becomes a ritual: harm, apology, promise, repeat, with no increasing specificity.

The work of psychologist Carol Dweck on mindset, especially her 2006 book *Mindset*, offers a useful but limited frame. A learning posture can help people treat difficulty as information rather than proof of fixed inability. Applied to repair, this means a repeat can be met with, "What did this show us?" rather than, "This proves we are broken." But the idea should not be stretched into naive optimism.

Some patterns require firmer boundaries. Some require outside help. A learning posture is not a permission slip for endless injury. It is a way of keeping honest effort from being suffocated by shame.

The phrase "what support is needed?" is often more useful than "why did you do it again?" The why question may matter, but it can also invite self-defence. Support asks about conditions. Does the person need an earlier cue? A shorter phrase? A visible reminder? A timed pause? A less demanding agreement? A shared signal? A boundary around text? A clearer division of responsibility before family visits? Support does not mean the injured person becomes the caretaker of the change. It means the repair plan is designed for the conditions that actually exist, not the ideal selves people imagine during calm.

Support must be specific enough to be tested. "I need you to support me in communicating better" is too vague. "When I say I need a pause, I will also say when I am coming back; if I forget, you can ask 'return time?' once, and I will answer before leaving" is clearer. "We need to stop fighting about logistics" is broad. "Before asking about a task, we will say whether we are asking for information or reassurance" is more useful. The support should reduce the likelihood of the same route, not decorate the apology with hopeful language.

Repairing after a repeat also requires care with shame. The person who repeated the pattern may feel exposed and discouraged. Shame can make them defend or collapse. The injured person may feel bitter, as though compassion is being demanded from the person hurt. A responsible repair does not ask the injured person to soothe the shame. It asks the responsible person to stay steady enough to learn. "I hate that I repeated this, and I do not want you to have to reassure me. I want to look at the cue I missed." That sentence keeps shame from becoming the centre.

The injured person also needs language that does not convert disappointment into a life sentence. "This is the same hurt, and it makes me less trusting right now" is different from "You will never change." The first sentence is severe and honest. The second may feel true in the moment, but it pushes the other person towards hopelessness or defence. Strong language is sometimes necessary; global condemnation is rarely useful if repair is still possible. The aim is not to protect the responsible person from discomfort. It is to keep the conversation in a form where change can still be discussed.

A professional repeat offers another example. A team agrees that no major revisions will be circulated without section-owner review. Under deadline pressure, the same thing happens again. The injured colleague feels overridden and embarrassed. A blame spiral says, "You clearly do not respect my work." A repair after the repeat says, "This is the same review failure, and it affects trust because we had named it. The missed trigger was deadline pressure; the agreement did not specify what happens when time is short. We need a fast-track version of the review rule." The accountability remains. The plan becomes more intelligent.

The repeated rupture may also reveal a hidden disagreement about the agreement itself. Someone may have said yes to avoid conflict, not because they believed the plan was fair or workable. Then the agreement fails, and the other person feels betrayed. Repair requires naming the false agreement: "I agreed too quickly because I wanted the argument to end. I did not actually think I could do that every evening. That was unfair, because it made you trust a plan I had not fully accepted." This is uncomfortable, but it is better than continuing to repair a promise that was never real.

Sometimes the repeat shows that the emotional need was misnamed. A person may think they need constant updates, when what they actually need is reassurance that the other will return. Another may think they need fewer questions, when what they actually need is to hear that questions are not accusations. A couple may think they need a strict schedule, when what they need is a softer transition into logistics. Repeats refine diagnosis. They reveal whether the agreed behaviour touches the actual wound or only its surface.

The data approach keeps problem-solving alive, but it must not become bloodless. The repeat hurts because history has entered the room. The person who was harmed may need to say, "This is why I get scared that the agreement will not matter." The responsible person may need to hear that without rushing to design. Then, when the hurt has been recognised, the data can be used. This sequencing prevents the language of learning from becoming another way to avoid feeling the cost of repetition.

A good repair after a repeat might sound like this in essence: "We repeated the same loop. I know that makes my apology harder to trust. I can see that the trigger was earlier than I noticed: when you asked the second time, I heard criticism and started defending. The support I need is to say, 'I am hearing this as criticism; can you tell me what you need?' before I explain." The sentence does not guarantee transformation. It gives the next attempt a sharper switch.

The next step should be modest. After a repeat, people often overcorrect. They create stricter rules, longer talks, heavier promises, or sweeping declarations. This may be understandable, but it can overload the repair. A better response is often a more precise version of the previous agreement. Move the cue earlier. Make the sentence shorter. Add a return time. Name the exception. Clarify who carries which part. The goal is not to punish the pattern with complexity. The goal is to interrupt it with better placement.

The forward test is whether a repeat can be faced without becoming a verdict. What hurt more because it happened again? What cue was missed? What support was absent? What part of the agreement was unrealistic, unclear, or not truly accepted? The old train track may still be there, and the next argument may find it faster than either person wishes. Repair after a repeat asks whether the pair can study the switch without denying the damage, and whether disappointment can become sharper design rather than another reason to stop trying.

Chapter 10
Reconnecting After Tension

The repair has happened, at least in the formal sense. The sharp sentence has been named. The apology was cleaner this time. Someone took responsibility without collapsing, and the practical agreement is no longer floating in the air. Yet the room still feels uncertain. One person reaches for a mug, the other folds a tea towel, and both are suddenly aware of the strange awkwardness that follows a difficult truth. The fight is over, but closeness has not quite remembered how to return.

A gentle joke comes to mind and is abandoned before it is spoken. A hand hovers near a shoulder and withdraws. One person wants warmth to prove the repair worked; the other needs a little more space before their body believes it. Nothing is obviously wrong, and that is part of the discomfort. After tension, even ordinary gestures can feel charged. A touch can be tenderness or pressure. Silence can be peace or avoidance. A smile can be ease or an attempt to hurry the other person past the hurt.

Reconnection is the tender stage of repair because it asks two people to rebuild ordinary ease without pretending the rupture did not matter. This is more delicate than it sounds. Some people rush warmth because they fear distance. Some withhold warmth because they fear being made foolish for softening too soon. Some perform cheerfulness to prove that everything is fine. Others remain stiff because returning to kindness feels like surrender. The relationship may have been repaired in language, but it still has to be repaired in the body: the next look, the next shared task, the next small decision not to punish.

The central tension is between closeness and consent. After a bad moment, the person who caused impact may long for reassurance that the bond is intact. The injured person may long for care but not yet want touch, humour, or normal conversation. Neither need should automatically govern the room. Warmth is most trustworthy when it is offered, not imposed. A quiet "Would a hug help, or would space feel better?" can be more loving than assuming closeness is owed because an apology has been made. The question protects tenderness from becoming another demand.

The stakes are immediate because the minutes after repair often decide whether the body records safety or pressure. If reconnection comes too fast, the injured person may feel rushed into absolution. If it never comes, both may drift into a chilly politeness that makes the repair feel unfinished. The signs are visible: a laugh that does not reach the eyes, a shoulder that stiffens under touch, a task completed side by side with no warmth, a goodnight said carefully rather than freely. These details may seem small, but relationships are rebuilt in exactly such small evidence.

The stakes also accumulate because trust is rarely restored by one excellent conversation. It is restored by ordinary proof repeated without ceremony. Someone shows up when they said they would. Someone remembers the agreement without being prompted. Someone notices effort without turning it into a scorecard. Someone chooses a gentler tone in the place where the old pattern usually entered. These are quiet acts, almost too plain to praise, yet they teach the relationship that repair was not merely spoken. The new evidence has begun to arrive.

The work now shifts from mending the rupture to living after the mending. Warmth has to return in ways that respect the pace of both people: a shared cup of tea, a task done together, a brief check-in, a lightness that does not mock the hurt, a touch asked for rather than assumed. Then trust has to be strengthened in the uneventful places where nobody is making a speech: punctuality, follow-through, remembered boundaries, the small acknowledgement that says, "I saw you trying." Reconnection is not a reward for repair. It is the atmosphere in which repair becomes believable.

A lamp is the right image here. After tension, the relationship does not need floodlights. It needs a small lamp switched on carefully enough not to startle the room. Too much brightness can feel like performance; too little leaves everyone feeling their way around the furniture. A quiet reconnection move says, "There is still warmth here, and it will not be forced." Daily follow-through keeps the lamp lit: not dramatically, not perfectly, but often enough for the room to feel inhabitable again.

The unresolved question is how to come close without using closeness to erase what happened. Can warmth return without becoming pressure? Can progress be noticed without becoming a ledger? Can one consistent behaviour calm an old fear more effectively than another long conversation? The next test will not always look like conflict. It may look like an ordinary evening, a kept promise, a softened greeting, a hand offered rather than taken, and the quiet decision to let repair become visible in daily life.

Restoring Warmth Safely

In 1951, Carl Rogers published *Client-Centred Therapy* in the United States and gave unusually serious attention to the conditions under which a person can become open again after feeling threatened: accurate understanding, acceptance, and a kind of human presence that does not push. Rogers was not writing about the quiet after a domestic argument, the awkwardness after an apology, or the strange difficulty of touching someone kindly after hurting them. Yet the principle is close to the bone. Warmth cannot be forced into a room simply because the correct words have been spoken.

After repair, the room may still feel altered. A person has apologised. The impact has been named. Perhaps a small agreement has been made. But the body is slower than language. One person may feel ready to move close again while the other is still checking whether closeness is safe. A hand reaches towards a shoulder and pauses. Someone tries a light comment, then hears how fragile it sounds. The kettle clicks off. The ordinary world resumes, but not quite as before.

This is the delicate interval many people mishandle. They assume that because an apology has been accepted, ease should return immediately. Or they assume that because ease has not returned, the repair must have failed. Neither conclusion is reliable. A repaired rupture often leaves behind a small awkwardness, not because the repair was false, but because closeness is re-entering the room carefully. The lamp comes on slowly.

Warmth after tension has to be restored without becoming pressure. That is the first discipline. A hug can be a gesture of care, or it can be a request for absolution made through the body. A joke can soften the atmosphere, or it can hurry the injured person past the wound. A shared task can rebuild ease, or it can become a way to avoid the remaining truth. The gesture itself is not the whole meaning. Timing, consent, tone, and accountability decide whether it heals or crowds.

This is why consent for closeness matters after conflict. Consent is not only a principle for dramatic boundaries; it belongs in ordinary tenderness too. "Would a hug help, or would space feel better?" may sound almost too simple, but it protects both people from guessing. It allows the person who caused impact to offer warmth without demanding it be received. It allows the injured person to accept care without feeling trapped by it. The question says, "I still want connection, and I will not take it from you by assumption." That is warmth with dignity.

The work of John Bowlby on attachment, developed from the mid-twentieth century onwards, offers one useful frame for why this stage is so charged. When a significant bond feels threatened, people often become alert to signals of availability, rejection, pursuit, or withdrawal. After a conflict, the nervous system may keep asking quiet questions: Are you safe? Are you still here? Will you rush me? Will you punish me? Will I be foolish if I soften? Reconnection moves answer those questions not through grand declarations, but through small evidence: a softened face, a respectful distance, a hand offered rather than taken, a calm return to an agreed task.

Touch can restore warmth when it is invited rather than assumed. In many close relationships, touch is part of the ordinary language of repair: a hand on the back, a brief embrace, knees touching under the table, fingers brushed while passing a cup. After tension, however, touch should be treated as an offer. The injured person may want it. They may also need time before their body can receive what their mind has agreed to. A person who insists, "Come here, we are fine," may be trying to repair, but the insistence can feel like being overruled. A better gesture leaves room for no.

A shared task can be safer than direct closeness when the emotional air is still tender. Two people make tea, fold washing, walk the dog, clear the table, or sit near each other while doing something simple. The point is not to avoid the repair; the repair has already been addressed enough to permit a softer form of contact. The task gives the relationship a low-pressure way to remember cooperation. It says, "We can be side by side again," without requiring immediate intensity. This kind of warmth is quiet, and its quietness is its strength.

A gentle joke can help, but only when it does not mock the wound, the injured person, or the repair itself. Humour is powerful because it can return proportion to a room that has become too solemn. It can also become evasion. The difference is usually obvious in the other person's face. A joke that invites shared humanity may loosen the air. A joke that implies "surely we can stop being serious now" will tighten it. Humour after repair should be light enough to refuse domination and respectful enough not to step on the bruise.

A quiet check-in is often the most reliable reconnection move. It does not reopen the whole fight. It does not demand a verdict on the relationship. It simply asks whether the present moment is bearable. "How are we doing now?" "Do you want closeness or a little space?" "Would it help to sit together for a while?" The value of such questions lies in their modesty. They are not attempts to extract forgiveness. They are attempts to locate the other person accurately. Accuracy is warm when it is offered without pressure.

There is a credible limitation. Reconnection can be misused to bypass accountability. Some people reach for affection too quickly because they want the emotional discomfort to end. They offer a hug before naming the action. They make a joke before acknowledging the impact. They start a shared task because practical normality feels easier than the exposed work of apology. In these cases, warmth becomes a sedative. It reduces tension without repairing trust. That kind of reconnection may feel peaceful for an hour and costly later.

The reconciliation is sequence. Accountability must not be skipped, but warmth must not be exiled. A relationship cannot live permanently inside repair language. Once the harm has been recognised, responsibility taken, and the next step named, closeness needs a way back into ordinary life. The question is not whether warmth should return. It is whether warmth returns as a continuation of repair or as a substitute for it. If the touch, joke, task, or check in honours what has been learned, it can help. If it tries to erase what happened, it will likely deepen distrust.

The lamp motif matters because safe reconnection is rarely a flood of brightness. Some people want to turn every light on at once after conflict: affection, reassurance, sex, humour, ordinary conversation, plans, productivity, proof that the relationship is intact. The injured person may need a smaller light. A cup placed nearby. A softened "I am here." A quiet evening without forced analysis. A hand offered with an easy withdrawal if it is not wanted. Warmth becomes trustworthy when it can be gentle without being fragile.

Restoring warmth also asks the person who caused impact to tolerate delayed relief. This is hard. After apologising, a person may want some sign that they are forgiven, still loved, still acceptable. That desire is human, but if it becomes urgent, it burdens the injured person. "Are we okay?" can be tender, but it can also ask the other to reassure before they are ready. A steadier version might be, "I know you may still feel tender. I am here, and I will not push you to be fine." That sentence offers connection without demanding emotional paperwork.

The injured person faces a different difficulty: allowing warmth without feeling that they have surrendered the seriousness of the impact. Some people stay cold because softening feels like losing the case. They fear that if they laugh, accept a hug, or sit close, the other person will think the harm no longer matters. That fear is understandable when repair has been rushed before. Safe reconnection solves it by making warmth and accountability compatible. A person can say, "I want to sit with you, and I still want us to keep the agreement we made." Closeness does not cancel the record.

In close relationships, the return of ease often happens through ordinary gestures that would look insignificant to an outsider. Someone asks whether the other wants tea. Someone saves the better seat. Someone sends the message they said they would send. Someone comes back into the room without performance. These gestures are not grand enough for cinema, which is why they are useful in life. They let repair become embodied without requiring a dramatic scene. The relationship starts to feel inhabitable again because care has resumed in visible, unforced ways.

A workplace version is more restrained but no less real. After a tense exchange, a manager who has apologised for cutting someone off may restore warmth not through personal intensity but through professional ease: inviting the colleague to finish the point at the next meeting, greeting them without awkward overcompensation, giving credit where it is due, and checking privately whether the repaired process is working. The warmth here is respect made visible. It is not sentimental. It is the steady restoration of working trust.

The work of Erving Goffman, especially *Interaction Ritual* published in 1967, offers a useful social lens. Goffman examined how people manage face, embarrassment, and the small rituals that preserve ordinary social life. After conflict, both people are often managing face: the injured person does not want to seem needy or unforgiving; the responsible person does not want to seem careless or morally reduced. Safe reconnection allows both to retain dignity. It does not expose one person's need for closeness or the other's need for time as weakness. It gives the social fabric a way to be rewoven without spectacle.

Awkwardness should therefore be expected rather than feared. The first few moments after repair may not feel natural. Someone may overthink where to sit. A joke may fail softly. A hug may be declined kindly. A check-in may receive only a short answer. This does not automatically mean the repair failed. It may mean the relationship is re-entering contact at a humane pace. The lamp is still small. The important question is whether the awkwardness is treated with respect or forced to disappear.

A small reconnection move works best when it leaves the other person more free, not less. "Would you like me to stay nearby or give you a little space?" gives freedom. "Please do not be distant now" reduces it. "Can I hold your hand?" gives freedom. Taking the hand because closeness feels overdue may reduce it. "Do you want to reset and make dinner together?" gives freedom. Starting cheerful conversation as though the repair has been completed by decree may reduce it. The test is whether the gesture invites or corners.

There is also a difference between warmth and performance. Performance asks to be noticed as proof: "Look how loving I am being now." Warmth simply offers itself. Performance may become elaborate: excessive affection, exaggerated helpfulness, a sudden flood of compliments, a grand gesture out of proportion to the rupture. These may seem generous, but they can make the injured person feel managed. Safe warmth is more ordinary. It does not try to overwhelm the residue of hurt. It respects that trust is rebuilt by repeated evidence, not emotional display.

The question of physical closeness deserves particular care. Some people experience touch as the fastest route back to safety; others experience it as pressure when conflict is still fresh. Neither response is superior. The repair culture between two people should make room for both. A question before touch is not cold. It is precise. "Would it feel good if I sat closer?" can carry more tenderness than an assumed embrace because it shows attention to the other person's state, not only to one's own wish to reconnect.

In some moments, the safest reconnection is parallel rather than face-to-face. Sitting in the same room, walking side by side, cooking together, or driving without forcing conversation can reduce intensity while preserving nearness. Face-to-face repair is useful when something needs to be named clearly. After naming, side-by-side contact may help the body settle. People are not only minds exchanging statements. They are nervous systems learning whether contact is safe again.

The next day matters as much as the immediate aftermath. If warmth returns briefly and the agreement is forgotten, the reconnection may begin to feel hollow. If the agreed change appears in ordinary life, warmth becomes more believable. The person who asked for space receives the promised return. The person who felt ignored sees the phone placed down at the vulnerable moment. The person who felt exposed notices that the private detail is not repeated. These acts are not dramatic, but they turn the lamp from a brief glow into a reliable light.

The forward test is whether closeness can be offered without being used to hurry the repair. Can the person who caused hurt tolerate a slower return of warmth? Can the injured person accept a small gesture without feeling they have surrendered accountability? Can both treat awkwardness not as failure, but as the tender sound of the relationship finding its footing again? After tension, the next move may be a touch, a task, a joke, a check-in, or simply the respectful space in which warmth is allowed to return at the speed of trust.

Repairing Trust in Daily Moments

In 1958, social psychologist Fritz Heider published *The Psychology of Interpersonal Relations*, a work that helped shape how later thinkers understood attribution: the way people explain behaviour, decide what it means, and draw conclusions about character. The principle belongs to social psychology, but it becomes deeply personal after conflict. A person does not rebuild trust by hearing one impressive declaration. They rebuild it by collecting repeated evidence that a painful meaning may no longer be true.

After a rupture, daily life becomes a field of small tests. The person who felt abandoned watches whether the other returns when they said they would. The person who felt dismissed notices whether their sentence is allowed to finish. The person who felt exposed listens for whether the private detail is kept private. These tests are not always conscious. Nobody may be keeping a notebook. Still, the body is measuring. It watches the doorway, the phone, the clock, the tone at the vulnerable moment. Trust returns through the ordinary.

Micro-follow-through is the unglamorous centre of repair. It means doing the small thing that proves the repair was not confined to the repair conversation. Showing up on time after lateness hurt. Sending the brief update after silence caused worry. Remembering the no-phone agreement after distraction became a wound. Asking before giving advice when advice has often landed as control. These acts are small enough to look almost trivial from the outside. Inside a relationship, they may carry immense meaning because they answer an old fear with present evidence.

This is why consistency calms more deeply than intensity. Intensity says, "Please believe how much I mean this." Consistency says, "You do not have to rely only on belief." A dramatic apology may move someone for an evening; a repeated kept return time may change what their body expects over weeks. A long conversation about caring may matter; putting the phone face down at the vulnerable moment may matter more. The lamp does not need to blaze. It needs to keep coming on.

The research tradition associated with John Gottman and colleagues is useful here because it draws attention to the importance of small bids, responses, and repair attempts in intimate life. Relationships are not only made in major declarations. They are made in repeated moments of turning towards or away: answering, noticing, softening, returning, pausing, remembering. The language may be academic, but the behaviour is plain. Someone asks for attention, and attention is given. Someone signals effort, and it is noticed. Someone makes a small repair, and the other allows it to count without pretending the whole history has vanished.

Trust is often misunderstood as a feeling that must return before ordinary life can resume. More often, trust is rebuilt by ordinary life resuming differently enough that the feeling gradually follows. The person who fears being forgotten does not become calm because they are told, "You matter." They become calmer when the other remembers the agreement in the moment where forgetting used to happen. The person who fears being controlled does not become freer because of one speech about respect. They become freer when decisions that affect them are brought to them before they are final. The feeling follows the evidence.

A brief example shows the scale. One partner has long feared that taking space means being abandoned. In past conflicts, the other would leave the room, become quiet for hours, and return only when the subject had gone cold. After repair, they agree on a simple behaviour: when space is needed, a return time is named. The first few times, the injured partner still feels anxious. They hear the old story begin. But the return happens. Then it happens again. The body begins to revise its forecast. The fear is not argued out of existence; it is contradicted by repeated ordinary evidence.

The work of philosopher Annette Baier, especially her writing on trust in the 1980s and 1990s, offers a careful reminder that trust always contains vulnerability. To trust someone is not merely to predict them. It is to allow something one values to be affected by their conduct. This is why small follow-through matters so much after conflict. A person who has been hurt is not asking only whether the other can perform a task. They are asking whether it is safe to place some part of their emotional life back into that person's hands. A kept promise is therefore not just efficient. It is protective.

Noticing effort is part of this rebuilding, but it has to be done without keeping score. "I saw you pause before answering; that helped" is different from "Well, you finally listened for once." The first sentence marks progress and makes repetition more likely. The second turns progress into a fresh humiliation. Acknowledgement should not flatter falsely or reward minimal decency as though it were heroism. It should simply name the evidence that repair is becoming visible. "Thank you for coming back when you said you would." "I noticed you checked before making the plan." "That felt different."

The difficulty is that noticing progress can feel risky to the injured person. If they acknowledge the effort, they may fear the other will assume everything is fixed. They may worry that gratitude will be used as a receipt: "You said I was trying, so why are you still upset?" That fear is not irrational if repair has been rushed before. Progress must be allowed to count without being used to close the matter prematurely. A person can say, "That helped, and I still need us to keep practising it." Warmth and caution can stand in the same room.

The responsible person, meanwhile, must resist treating effort as entitlement. "I did the thing; why are you not over it?" is one of the fastest ways to damage new trust. Micro-follow-through is evidence, not a demand for immediate restoration. It may take repeated consistency before the injured person's body believes the pattern has changed. This delay can feel unfair to the person trying, especially when the effort is sincere. But trust is not a switch controlled by the apologiser's intention. It is a gradual adjustment to what reliably happens next.

There is a credible limitation. Daily follow-through cannot repair serious or ongoing harm by itself. A pattern of contempt, intimidation, secrecy, coercion, or repeated boundary violations cannot be healed by punctuality, small kindnesses, or carefully remembered agreements at the edges. Ordinary evidence matters where both people are participating in good faith and where the harm is repairable through changed conduct. Where safety or dignity is repeatedly compromised, larger decisions, firmer boundaries, or outside support may be necessary. Small evidence is powerful; it is not a substitute for basic safety.

The reconciliation lies in matching the evidence to the wound. If the wound is unreliability, punctuality and clear updates matter. If the wound is dismissal, listening without interruption matters. If the wound is exposure, privacy matters. If the wound is abandonment after conflict, returning matters. If the wound is control, checking before deciding matters. Trust is rebuilt when the evidence answers the specific fear. Generic niceness can feel pleasant and still miss the injury. A bouquet after a broken return promise may be kind; a kept return promise is the real repair.

The lamp motif belongs here because trust is often restored by low, steady light. Not spectacle. Not a floodlit performance of devotion. The person who wants to repair may prefer a grand gesture because it feels decisive, but grand gestures can vanish quickly if daily conduct remains unchanged. The lamp is smaller. It is the message sent when promised. The gentler start after work. The avoided joke. The remembered boundary. The apology followed by altered timing. Each act makes the room a little more inhabitable.

Daily trust also depends on remembering agreements without making the injured person supervise them. If one person must always remind the other not to interrupt, not to disappear, not to share private information, not to begin serious arguments by text, then the labour of repair has been returned to the person harmed. Remembering is therefore part of accountability. It says, "I carried this too." The injured person may still name the pattern when needed, but they should not become the keeper of every guardrail.

There is a quiet dignity in progress that does not announce itself. A person who used to defend immediately now pauses and reflects impact. They do not ask to be praised. A person who used to withdraw after conflict sends the promised message. They do not demand gratitude. A person who used to make unilateral plans says, "Let me check before I answer." They do not turn the check into a performance of sacrifice. Such restraint matters. Repair becomes more trustworthy when the new behaviour is offered as responsibility, not as a bid for applause.

At the same time, unacknowledged effort can wither. People need some evidence that change is landing. Not constant praise, not emotional payment, but occasional recognition of the specific behaviour that helped. "When you came back at the time you said, I felt less anxious." That sentence gives useful information. It teaches the responsible person which action soothed which fear. It also lets the injured person participate in rebuilding trust without erasing the wound. The acknowledgement is not a score. It is a signal.

Micro-follow-through is especially important when the old fear is longstanding. A person who has spent years expecting disappointment will not be reassured by one kept promise. Their caution may outlast the apologiser's patience. This is where maturity is required. The responsible person must understand that repeated injury creates repeated checking. The injured person must also remain open, where it is safe to do so, to evidence that the old story may be changing. Trust rebuilds between these two disciplines: reliable conduct and the willingness to let reliable conduct matter.

The danger of scorekeeping appears on both sides. The responsible person may count their efforts and expect a proportional reward. The injured person may count failures and overlook improvement. Neither form of accounting restores warmth. Scorekeeping turns repair into a ledger where each act is weighed for advantage. Noticing is different. Noticing says, "That behaviour helped." Scorekeeping says, "You owe me now," or "This still does not erase what you did." The past may indeed not be erased. But if every new act is swallowed by the old ledger, trust has no place to grow.

A useful way to acknowledge progress is to name the behaviour and the effect, then stop. "You remembered the agreement about the first minutes after work, and I felt more welcomed." "You told me when you needed space, and that made it easier not to chase." "You checked before sharing that story, and I felt respected." These sentences do not overstate. They do not declare the wound healed. They give the new evidence a place in the relationship's memory. That memory matters because repeated repair needs to be remembered too, not only repeated injury.

The same principle applies in professional life. A colleague who previously circulated changes without review begins sending the relevant section back before distribution. A manager who previously cut people off now pauses and invites the unfinished point. A team member who missed deadlines now flags delay early rather than letting others discover it late. Trust in work settings is also rebuilt through micro-follow-through: not grand speeches about collaboration, but repeated behaviours that reduce uncertainty, protect contribution, and make promises easier to believe.

The ordinary nature of this work should not be mistaken for small emotional significance. Showing up on time after repeated lateness may calm the fear of not mattering. Remembering a boundary may calm the fear of being exposed. Asking before advising may calm the fear of being managed. Returning after a pause may calm the fear of abandonment. These acts are small only in appearance. In context, they speak directly to the place where trust was injured.

The forward test is whether repair can become visible when nobody is making a speech. Will the agreement be remembered at the doorway, in the text thread, before the family commitment, after the pause, during the meeting, at the moment when the old pattern usually begins? Can progress be noticed without turning into a ledger? Can one consistent behaviour, repeated without drama, teach an old fear that the future may not have to resemble the past? Trust is rebuilt not by insisting the lamp is bright enough, but by keeping it lit in the ordinary rooms where people actually live.

Chapter 11
Repair Across Different Styles

One person wants to talk while the hurt is still warm. They stand in the kitchen with their hands on the counter, trying to keep their voice level, needing words because silence feels like a door closing. The other person is still, too still, eyes lowered towards the floor, not because they do not care, but because every sentence now feels like a trap. One reaches. One retreats. The disagreement is no longer only about what happened. It has become a disagreement about how repair is supposed to happen.

This is where many couples misread style as character. The person who needs words is called intense, dramatic, relentless, impossible to satisfy. The person who needs space is called cold, avoidant, withholding, emotionally unavailable. Each label contains a little pain and very little wisdom. Underneath the clash, both may be trying to protect the same thing: the possibility of returning safely. One seeks safety through contact. The other seeks safety through room to think. The trouble begins when each person's method feels like danger to the other.

The central tension is not whether words or space are better. Neither is morally superior. Words can repair, and words can flood. Space can regulate, and space can abandon. A long conversation can become a courtroom; a quiet pause can become a locked door. The question is whether each style can be made relational enough to protect both autonomy and connection. A person who needs words must not use urgency to corner. A person who needs space must not use distance to disappear.

The stakes are immediate because process fights quickly eclipse the original injury. A sharp comment, a missed message, or a tense exchange may begin the rupture, but soon the real argument becomes: "Why will you not talk to me?" "Why will you not give me room?" "Why are you pushing?" "Why are you shutting down?" The repair itself becomes the battlefield. The visible signs are familiar: repeated messages, unanswered calls, clipped replies, a person followed from room to room, a person retreating behind a screen, both feeling increasingly wronged by the other's way of coping.

The stakes deepen when these styles become a fixed story. The word-needing person starts to expect abandonment before space is even requested. The space-needing person starts to expect pressure before a conversation has begun. Each enters the next rupture prepared for the old injury, and preparation often creates what it fears. The one who fears silence pushes harder; the one who fears pressure withdraws faster. Style becomes loop. The bridge between them narrows.

Repair across different styles requires a shared language for process before the next conflict begins. The person who needs words may need a brief reassurance that the relationship is not being abandoned, paired with a limit that keeps the conversation from flooding. The person who needs space may need a clean way to pause, with a return time and a commitment that the issue will not be buried. Between them lies a protocol that is neither pursuit nor disappearance: brief connection, timed space where needed, then a return to impact and agreement. Digital messages add another layer, because the same sentence can harden on a screen, stripped of tone and saved like evidence for a future trial.

A bridge is the right image for this work. It does not require both people to live on the same side of the river. It gives them a crossing that can hold weight. The person who needs words does not have to pretend silence feels easy. The person who needs space does not have to perform instant emotional availability. But the bridge must be built from visible commitments: a short reassurance, a named pause, a return time, a message that reduces ambiguity rather than adds heat.

This chapter's deeper movement is towards process safety. Repair fails when people argue only about content while the method of repair keeps injuring them. A couple may understand impact, clarify intent, apologise well, and still fracture if one person experiences every pause as abandonment and the other experiences every request to talk as control. The task is to stop treating style difference as a defect and start treating it as design information. What kind of repair structure lets both nervous systems stay human?

The next rupture will ask the question in practical terms. When one person needs words and the other needs space, whose need sets the pace? If the answer is always the louder need, repair becomes coercive. If the answer is always the more withdrawn need, repair becomes evasive. The bridge has to hold both. It begins at the tense moment when silence feels like rejection, conversation feels like pressure, and both people must decide whether their style will protect the repair or become the next wound.

When One Needs Words

In 1988, psychologist Sue Johnson and psychiatrist Leslie Greenberg published early work on emotionally focused therapy, giving language to a pattern many couples already knew by feel: when connection seems threatened, one person may reach harder while the other steps back. The reaching person is not always trying to control the conversation. Often, they are trying to locate the bond. Silence does not arrive as neutral space; it arrives as a closed door.

The scene is painfully ordinary. A sharp exchange happens after dinner. One person says, "Can we talk about what just happened?" The other, still tight with defensiveness, says, "I cannot do this right now," and turns towards the sink. The first person hears the water running and feels the old alarm rise. They ask again, then ask differently, then ask with more urgency. The second person feels pursued and becomes harder to reach. The problem is no longer only the bad moment. The repair style has become the new rupture.

For people who repair through talking, words provide orientation. They need to hear that the relationship is still intact, that the issue has not been buried, that silence is not punishment, that the person stepping away intends to return. Without language, the mind begins to fill the gap. A pause becomes abandonment. A blank face becomes indifference. A closed door becomes evidence. This is not immaturity in its simplest form. It is the nervous system asking whether it is safe to wait.

The difficulty is that the need for words can easily flood the conversation. A person who feels abandoned may ask for reassurance, then ask for it again because the first answer did not fully settle the body. They may want to process every angle immediately: what happened, what was meant, whether it will happen again, whether the other still cares, why the tone changed, what the silence means. The need is understandable. The volume can become impossible. Words meant to restore safety may create pressure so intense that the other person retreats further.

The repair task, then, is to offer enough verbal reassurance to keep connection alive without turning the moment into an endless debate. This requires a particular kind of sentence: brief, emotionally present, and bounded. "I care about this, and I am not leaving the conversation. I need a short pause so I can come back properly." The sentence is not a full repair. It is a bridge. It tells the word-needing person that silence is not abandonment, while also protecting the space-needing person from being pulled into a conversation they cannot yet hold well.

The bridge matters because reassurance and debate are often confused. Reassurance answers the attachment question underneath the conflict: "Are we still connected enough to repair?" Debate answers the argumentative question: "Who is right, and what exactly happened?" When one person needs words, the temptation is to keep debating until safety appears. But safety rarely appears through more argument once both people are activated. A few carefully chosen words may do more than a long exchange. "I hear that you felt dismissed. I want to understand it. I need a few minutes before I can listen well." This gives contact without surrendering to escalation.

The work of John Bowlby on attachment, developed across the mid-twentieth century, helps explain why verbal reassurance can be so powerful. Human beings monitor significant bonds for signs of availability and response. In adult repair, the words "I am coming back" can matter because they answer the fear that distance means disconnection. They do not solve the whole issue. They keep the attachment system from having to shout. A person who knows the other will return may be able to wait. A person who does not know may experience waiting as emotional freefall.

Still, the person who needs words has a responsibility not to make reassurance impossible to provide. If every pause is challenged, every short answer cross-examined, and every boundary treated as rejection, the conversation becomes flooded. Flooding is not simply "too much emotion", it is too much input for either person to process constructively. The visible signs are familiar: repeated questions, overlapping speech, rising speed, exhausted faces, a partner saying the same reassurance in different words while sounding less reassuring each time. The more words are demanded, the less emotionally present they become.

A boundary around length can protect both people. "I can give this ten careful minutes now, then I need a pause and a return time." "I can answer one thing before we stop for a while." "I want to stay emotionally present, and I cannot do that if we keep going in circles." Such boundaries do not reject the need for words. They shape it. The aim is to prevent repair from becoming an endurance test where the person who lasts longest decides the pace of closeness. Length is not the same as depth. Sometimes the shorter conversation is the more truthful one.

The person offering reassurance should avoid making the boundary sound like punishment. "You are too much; I am done" will confirm the fear of abandonment. "I want to repair this, and I am getting overwhelmed. I can stay for a few minutes, then I need a break and I will come back" sends a different signal. The distinction is not cosmetic. One sentence shames the need. The other respects the need while naming capacity. The bridge holds because it has both railings: care and limit.

The person receiving the boundary also has work to do. They may need to tolerate partial reassurance without forcing it to become total reassurance. "I am here and I will come back" may not feel as satisfying as a full emotional conversation, but it is not nothing. It is a marker of connection. If the word-needing person rejects every marker because it does not resolve the whole fear, the repair process may become unworkable. Waiting becomes possible when the smaller assurance is allowed to count.

A short example shows the difference. After a tense exchange about plans, one partner says, "You just shut me out whenever I say something difficult." The other feels the urge to defend: "No, I do not; I just need time." If they stop there, the first person may feel dismissed again. A more useful response might be, "I understand that my silence feels like shutting you out. I am not trying to leave this. I need twenty minutes to calm down, and I will come back to talk about the impact." The sentence offers words, but not unlimited words. It gives the waiting person something to hold.

The word-needing person may then answer with a boundaried need of their own: "I can wait if I know you will return. Please do not let it disappear." This is different from pursuing. It names the fear without turning it into accusation. It also gives the space-needing person a clear obligation. The repair style gap narrows because both people are speaking process rather than fighting about character. One says, "I need words to wait safely." The other says, "I need space to speak safely." The bridge begins there.

There is a credible limitation. Some people use the language of needing words to demand immediate access to another person's attention, body, or emotional labour. They may call it repair when it is really pressure. They may insist that love requires staying in a conversation long after it has become harmful. This is not a healthy need for reassurance; it is urgency without respect for the other person's limits. A need is real, but it does not automatically authorise unlimited pursuit. Repair requires consent to the process as well as care for the outcome.

There is also an opposite limitation. Some people use the fear of being flooded as a reason to provide almost no reassurance. They offer silence, vagueness, or disappearance, then accuse the other person of being needy for becoming alarmed. This, too, distorts repair. If one person repeatedly leaves without words, the other's urgency may be a predictable response to uncertainty. Space becomes safer when it is framed. Silence becomes less frightening when it carries a return. The person who needs fewer words still has to provide enough language to prevent the gap from becoming abandonment.

The reconciliation lies in proportional reassurance. The word-needing person does not require a full debate in order to receive connection. The space-needing person does not get to disappear in order to feel regulated. A few sentences can meet the human need beneath the process clash. "I care." "I heard the impact." "I am not leaving it." "I need a pause." "I will return at this time." These sentences are modest, but they change the meaning of silence. The bridge does not need to be ornate. It needs to be strong enough to cross.

Tone matters as much as wording. "I said I am coming back" can sound like a slammed door. "I am coming back; I know waiting is hard for you" sounds like care. The second sentence does not require endless discussion. It recognises the other person's style without mocking it. When verbal reassurance is delivered with irritation, the reassurance often fails. The words say connection; the tone says burden. People hear both. A short sentence with genuine warmth can calm more than a long explanation delivered in resentment.

The word-needing person can help by asking for the smallest useful reassurance rather than the largest possible conversation. "Can you tell me you are coming back?" may work better than "Talk to me until I feel better." "Can you say you understand why that hurt?" may work better than asking for a complete analysis while both are still activated. This does not mean shrinking the injury. It means identifying the immediate verbal signal that would make waiting possible. The deeper conversation can still come later.

The person offering words can also be specific about what kind of conversation is available. "I can reassure you now, but I cannot problem-solve yet." "I can hear the impact, but I cannot do a long back-and-forth while I am this heated." "I can stay for a short check-in, then I need to pause." These distinctions prevent misunderstanding. The word-needing person is not left guessing why the conversation is being limited. The boundary becomes part of repair rather than a refusal of it.

Digital messages complicate this style difference. A person who needs words may send several messages when anxious, hoping the next one will create contact. The person who needs space may feel invaded and stop replying, which intensifies the first person's alarm. A brief message can interrupt the spiral: "I see this matters. I cannot text well right now. I will call after dinner." This is not a complete repair. It is verbal reassurance in a form that prevents the silence from becoming a story. It also sets a boundary around the medium.

The person who needs words must be careful not to confuse more words with better repair. There is a point at which conversation becomes repetition, and repetition becomes pressure. The same question asked five ways does not necessarily produce more security; it may produce exhaustion. A useful sign is whether new information is still emerging. If the conversation is only circling the same fear, a pause with reassurance may be more effective than another round. Words should serve repair, not become a ritual of anxious checking.

A verbal reassurance can be simple enough to remember under stress. "I am here." "I care about this." "I need space, not distance from you." "I will come back." "This matters, and I am not dropping it." Such sentences may sound too small when calm, but in the charged interval after hurt they can be powerful. They answer the specific fear that silence has awakened. They give the waiting person a thread. A thread is not the whole cloth, but it can keep the tear from widening.

The lamp motif from the previous chapter still applies, but here the light is verbal. Some people need the lamp switched on with words before they can sit in the room without panic. They do not need floodlights. They need enough light to know the room is still inhabited. Too many words can glare. Too few can leave the other person feeling alone in the dark. The art is to offer a small, steady light and then honour the promise it makes.

A professional example makes the same dynamic less intimate but equally recognisable. A colleague raises concern after feeling dismissed in a meeting. One person wants to discuss it immediately; the other has another call and cannot engage fully. A poor response is, "I cannot get into this now." A better response is, "I hear that the meeting landed badly, and I do want to address it. I cannot do it properly before this call, but I will come back at three and make space for it." The verbal reassurance is not lengthy. It prevents the gap from being interpreted as avoidance.

A family example may be sharper because old roles are easily triggered. An adult child says, "You never listen when I tell you something matters." A parent, overwhelmed, wants to withdraw. If the parent says nothing, the old abandonment may deepen. If they stay and argue, the exchange may explode. A bounded verbal response offers a third path: "I hear that you feel dismissed. I want to respond properly, and I need to slow down. I will sit with you after I have had a few minutes." The words do not solve a lifetime. They prevent the current moment from becoming another exhibit in the same case.

The forward test is whether words can be used as connection rather than ammunition. When silence feels like abandonment, can the need be named without flooding the other person? When conversation feels too much, can reassurance be offered without disappearing? The next rupture may turn not on who has the better argument, but on whether one person can say, "I need words to wait," and the other can answer, "I will give you enough words to know I am still here, and enough boundary to make sure I can truly return."

When One Needs Space

In 1998, psychologist John Gottman published *The Seven Principles for Making Marriage Work*, drawing on years of observational work with couples and describing how physiological overwhelm can make constructive conversation far harder. The language of research is careful; the lived moment is unmistakable. Someone asks for a conversation after a hurt, and the other person feels the room narrow. Words begin to sound like demands. Questions begin to feel like corners. The need is not indifference. It is air.

The person who needs space may not know how to ask for it cleanly. They may simply go quiet, turn away, pick up a task, leave the room, or answer with a flat "not now". To them, the pause may feel like restraint: a way to avoid saying something sharp, a way to think, a way to return with less heat. To the other person, the same pause may land as abandonment, punishment, or proof that the hurt is inconvenient. Space becomes frightening when it has no shape.

A need for distance is not a failure of care. Some people think by speaking; others think by stepping back. Some can find their truth only when the immediate pressure drops. If they are pushed to talk before they are ready, they may defend, freeze, appease, or become cruel. Pressure to speak can feel less like intimacy and more like control: the other person's urgency setting the terms of their nervous system. Yet space, if taken without reassurance, can injure the bond it is meant to protect. The skill is to make distance relational.

A clean request for space has two commitments inside it. It names the need for distance, and it names the intention to return. "I need time to think" is incomplete if the other person has learned that thinking often means disappearing. "I need a break, and I will come back after I have calmed down" is stronger. "I care about repairing this, but I cannot do it well while I feel cornered" is stronger still. These sentences do not ask the other person to like waiting. They make waiting safer by giving it a boundary.

The bridge between autonomy and connection is a clear return time. Without it, the person left behind must guess whether the pause is regulation, avoidance, punishment, or the beginning of a longer withdrawal. Guessing is rarely neutral after hurt. It pulls old stories towards the present: "They never come back," "My feelings are too much," "I have to chase or the issue will vanish." A return time does not solve the conflict, but it prevents the break from becoming another rupture. It says, "I am stepping back from the heat, not from the repair."

The return time must be realistic. If someone says they will come back shortly but knows they need longer, the promise may soothe the moment and damage trust later. If they set the return so far away that the other person is left holding the wound alone, the pause may feel like exile. The exact length matters less than the reliability of the commitment. A shorter check-in followed by a fuller conversation may sometimes work better than pretending a complete repair will be possible immediately. The point is not perfect timing. The point is not to leave the other person in fog.

Space also needs a clear emotional message. "I need to be alone" may be true, but after conflict it can sound like rejection. A safer version carries reassurance: "I need to be alone so I do not react badly, and I do want to come back to you." This matters because the person who needs words may not be afraid of the pause itself; they may be afraid of what the pause means. If the meaning is clarified, the waiting becomes less hostile. The door is closed, but not locked.

What happens during the break determines whether space helps or hardens. A useful pause reduces heat, widens perspective, and prepares the person to return with greater honesty. It is not an interval for rehearsing a closing argument. It is not a chance to collect evidence, text an ally for confirmation, scroll until the issue feels distant, or write a speech that makes the other person unreasonable. A break used for prosecution may lower volume while preserving combat. The person returns calmer in tone and more fixed in judgement. That is not regulation. It is defence with better posture.

During a helpful pause, the person asks different questions. What did I hear as threat? What part of the impact can I acknowledge? What am I not yet ready to agree with? What would help me return without attacking or disappearing? The questions are plain, but they change the use of solitude. Space becomes a workshop rather than a bunker. The person is not hiding from the relationship; they are preparing to re-enter it with fewer weapons.

The work of James Gross on emotion regulation, particularly research from the 1990s onwards at Stanford University, offers a useful distinction between suppressing expression and changing one's relationship to the emotion. Suppression can make someone appear calmer while the internal argument continues at full volume. Reappraisal, by contrast, can alter the meaning of the moment: from "I am being attacked" to "They are hurt and I need to respond carefully"; from "I must defend myself now" to "I can acknowledge impact before clarifying intent." In repair, space is useful when it supports that kind of shift. It is less useful when it simply hides the heat.

The person taking space should also avoid self-righteous solitude. It is tempting to use distance to become more certain of one's innocence. Alone, a person can edit the exchange in their favour, emphasise the other person's tone, minimise their own contribution, and return with a case rather than an open mind. This is how space hardens. The break becomes a private courtroom. The other person is not present to complicate the story, so the story becomes cleaner and less true. A pause that begins as self-protection can end as self-deception.

A better pause includes one small act of preparation. It may be writing down the impact as the other person described it, not as the speaker prefers to remember it. It may be naming one's own part in a sentence. It may be deciding on the first line of return: "I can see that my silence made you feel abandoned." It may be noticing the difference between needing space and wanting to avoid shame. The act should be small because the pause is not meant to become a full private analysis. It is meant to make return possible.

There is a credible limitation. Some people ask for space because they genuinely need to regulate; others use space to control the conversation, escape accountability, or punish the other person with absence. The same words can hide different motives. "I need space" can mean "I want to think clearly." It can also mean "I refuse to deal with your hurt." The difference appears in behaviour. Does the person return when promised? Do they engage the impact when they return? Do they use the break to become more open or more armoured? Space earns trust through follow-through.

There is also a limitation on the other side. The person who fears abandonment may treat every request for space as betrayal, even when continuing would plainly make the conversation worse. They may follow, text repeatedly, stand in doorways, demand immediate reassurance, or keep speaking after the other has said they are too activated. This pressure may come from fear, but it can still feel controlling. The need for closeness does not erase the other person's need for autonomy. Repair requires both to be taken seriously.

The reconciliation is a structured pause: reassurance, boundary, return. Reassurance says the relationship still matters. Boundary says the conversation cannot continue well at this intensity. Return says the issue will not be buried. "I care about this. I am too flooded to talk well. I will come back after I have had time to settle." The exact words may differ, but the architecture matters. Without reassurance, the pause feels cold. Without boundary, the person needing space may feel trapped. Without return, distance becomes abandonment.

A short example shows the difference. After a tense conversation about money, one partner says, "You always make me feel like a child." The other feels accused and wants to leave the room. A damaging exit would be, "I cannot deal with this," followed by silence. A cleaner request would be, "I hear that you felt talked down to. I am getting defensive, and I do not want to argue from that place. I need a pause, and I will come back after I have thought about what you said." The repair is not complete, but the bridge remains in place.

When the person returns, the first sentence should prove the break was not avoidance. It should not begin with a counterattack, a corrected detail, or a complaint about the other person's intensity. It should begin close to the impact: "I have thought about it, and I can see how my tone made you feel managed." Or, "I still see the decision differently, but I understand that my leaving without a return time made you feel alone." Return is where space becomes trustworthy. Without return, the pause is only absence.

Digital space requires particular care. A person who needs distance may stop replying to messages, believing silence is the only way to avoid escalation. The person waiting may reread the last line, watch for typing bubbles, and build a harsher story with every minute. A short message can protect both: "I cannot text about this well. I want to repair it. I will call later." The message should reduce ambiguity, not invite debate. Long written explanations often become evidence in a trial. A short return commitment keeps the channel from turning into a battlefield.

The person needing space should not outsource repair to time. Time can lower intensity, but it does not automatically create understanding. People often say, "Let us just sleep on it," when what they mean is, "Let the discomfort fade until neither of us has the energy to reopen it." That kind of space hardens quietly. The issue becomes less discussable, not more resolved. A useful pause carries a return plan precisely because time alone is unreliable. Calm without return can become avoidance with a softer face.

The bridge motif clarifies the ethical demand. A bridge allows distance without severance. It recognises that two people may not be able to stand in the same emotional place at the same moment. One may need language; the other may need quiet. One may need immediate reassurance; the other may need lower pressure before reassurance can be sincere. The bridge is made from promises that can be seen: I am not leaving the repair. I am taking space to return better. I will tell you when that return will happen.

Space also protects the quality of apology. A rushed apology from someone who feels cornered may sound compliant rather than accountable. It may later become resentment: "I only said sorry because you would not let me breathe." A pause can prevent false repair by giving the person time to distinguish what they can honestly own from what they do not yet understand. This protects trust more than forced agreement. An apology that arrives later with clarity may be more useful than an immediate sentence spoken under pressure to make the conversation stop.

The break should not become too private. If one person repeatedly takes space but refuses to share what happened inside that space when they return, the other may feel shut out of the repair process. The return does not need to include every thought, but it should include the relevant movement: "I realised I heard criticism where you were asking for reassurance," or "I noticed I was more ashamed than angry," or "I still need to understand part of it, but I can own my tone." This helps the waiting person see that the pause was active, not empty.

A person who needs space may also need to set a boundary around being pursued during the break. That boundary should be calm and specific. "Please do not follow me from room to room. I will come back at the time I said." This is different from "Leave me alone," which may land as contempt or rejection. The first protects the break and repeats the return. The second may intensify fear. A boundary that includes the bridge is easier to respect because it does not ask the other person to wait in total uncertainty.

The person waiting can help by agreeing to one form of contact if needed, rather than repeatedly seeking reassurance. For example, if anxiety rises during the pause, one agreed message might be allowed: "Still coming back?" The person taking space can answer briefly: "Yes." This is not ideal for every pair, but the principle matters. The waiting person should not be left without any reassurance if waiting is hard, and the person needing space should not be drawn into a full exchange before they can return well. The bridge must hold weight from both sides.

There are cases where the need for space is actually the need for safety from one's own reaction. A person may know that if they continue, they will become sarcastic, cruel, or contemptuous. Naming this honestly can be an act of care. "I am too angry to speak respectfully right now, and I do not want to hurt you." This is not noble if it becomes a repeated excuse never to learn restraint, but in the moment it may prevent damage. The return later must include accountability for the emotion and a plan for recognising it earlier next time.

The forward test is whether space can be requested without becoming disappearance. Can the person who needs distance name care, set a limit, and keep a return? Can the person who fears silence allow a structured pause without turning the pursuit into another injury? The next rupture may not be solved by more words or more distance alone. It may require the harder skill: stepping back with a bridge still visible, using the break to soften rather than harden, and returning with enough intention that autonomy and connection do not have to compete for the same breath.

Bridging the Style Gap

In 1988, Sue Johnson and Leslie Greenberg's early work on emotionally focused therapy helped make one relational truth harder to ignore: the argument people appear to be having is often not the argument that is running the relationship. A couple may seem to be fighting about tone, timing, chores, messages, or money, while underneath they are fighting about process itself. One person reaches for words to feel safe. The other reaches for space to stay regulated. Each method is an attempt at protection. Each method can feel like threat.

The familiar scene has a cruel efficiency. A hurt is named. One person says, "Can we talk now?" because waiting feels like being left alone with the wound. The other says, "I need space," because immediate conversation feels like being trapped inside accusation. The first hears abandonment and pushes for reassurance. The second hears pressure and retreats further. Soon the original rupture has been joined by a second one: the clash over how repair is meant to happen. The bridge is needed before either person can cross.

A shared repair protocol is not a bureaucratic answer to human pain. It is a small structure built for a predictable weather pattern. Without it, every rupture requires the couple to negotiate the process while already activated. That is asking too much of people whose bodies have begun to defend. The person who needs words cannot be expected to wait indefinitely on faith. The person who needs space cannot be expected to produce tenderness under pressure. A protocol gives both needs a legitimate place before either becomes desperate.

The sequence is simple because repair under stress cannot rely on complexity: brief connection, timed space if needed, then a return to impact and agreement. Brief connection answers the fear that the bond has been dropped. Timed space answers the need to think without being cornered. Return answers the moral requirement that distance must not become disappearance. Impact and agreement ensure that the process does not soothe the moment while leaving the injury untouched. The bridge has more than one plank. Remove one, and the crossing becomes unsafe.

The brief connection matters most for the person who needs words, but it helps both. It might sound like, "I care about this, and I am not leaving it." Or, "I hear that this hurt, and I want to repair it."

The sentence does not open the entire discussion. It simply prevents silence from becoming a story of abandonment. John Bowlby's attachment work, developed across the mid-twentieth century, helps explain why this matters: when a significant bond feels threatened, people look for signs of availability. A short sentence can be a sign. It gives the waiting person a thread to hold without requiring the space-needing person to stay beyond capacity.

Timed space matters most for the person who needs distance, but it also protects the person who needs words. Space without a return time often leaves the other person in a field of guesses. Space with a return time changes the meaning of the pause. It says, "I am stepping away from escalation, not away from you." The difference is visible in conduct. A person who walks out with no return leaves the other listening to silence. A person who says, "I need half an hour, and I will come back after dinner," gives the silence a boundary. The pause becomes a bridge rather than a cliff.

The return is where the protocol earns trust. Many couples can agree on space; fewer keep the return. Yet the return is the evidence that the pause was not avoidance. It begins close to impact, not with a prepared defence. "I understand that when I went quiet, you felt abandoned." "I can see that my push to talk felt controlling." "I still need to explain my intent, but I want to start with how it landed for you." These sentences bring the couple back from process into repair. They stop the discussion from becoming only a negotiation about timing and return it to the injury that needs attention.

The final movement is a small agreement, because style differences need practical protection. If one person needs words, the agreement may be that a pause always begins with reassurance. If one person needs space, the agreement may be that a hard conversation can be paused with a return time before it escalates. If text messages intensify the process clash, the agreement may be that one line confirms the return and then the conversation stops until voice or in-person repair is possible. A protocol is not a personality cure. It is a shared guardrail at a known bend.

A short example shows the bridge at work. After a tense exchange about a family visit, one partner wants to talk immediately; the other looks overwhelmed. The old pattern would begin with pursuit and retreat. The new protocol begins with brief connection: "I know this hurt, and I want to repair it." Then timed space: "I need time to think so I do not get defensive." Then one text line if they are not in the same room: "I am still coming back at eight." The message does not reopen the argument. It reduces ambiguity. At eight, the return begins with impact, not litigation: "I can see that when I agreed to the visit before checking with you, you felt left out." Only then does the agreement emerge: future plans affecting both people are not confirmed outside the relationship before both have spoken.

The bridge works because it honours both nervous systems without letting either one rule the relationship. If the person who needs words always sets the pace, repair can become coercive: talk now, answer now, reassure until the fear quiets. If the person who needs space always sets the pace, repair can become evasive: wait, wait longer, accept distance as the price of staying connected. A shared protocol refuses both extremes. It gives words at the beginning, space in the middle if needed, and return at the end. It keeps autonomy and connection in the same design.

The work of John Gottman and colleagues on couple interaction offers another useful anchor, particularly around repair attempts and the importance of recognising small moves that redirect conflict. A shared protocol is essentially a rehearsed repair attempt. Its power lies not in elegance, but in recognisability. When both people know what the sequence means, the words do not have to be perfect. "Connection, space, return?" may become enough to interrupt the old process fight. The sentence is small, but it carries an agreement: neither of us will use our style to injure the other.

There is a credible limitation. A protocol cannot compensate for contempt, intimidation, chronic dishonesty, coercion, or repeated refusal to return. Process agreements require good faith. If one person uses timed space to disappear, the protocol becomes a polished form of avoidance. If one person uses the need for words to prevent the other from ever leaving a heated exchange, the protocol becomes a cage. The structure is only as trustworthy as the conduct that follows it. A bridge that is never crossed becomes scenery.

The reconciliation is to treat the protocol as evidence-based, not sacred. If the brief connection feels too thin, it may need a clearer reassurance. If the timed space is too long, it may need a shorter check-in followed by a fuller return. If the return keeps collapsing into defence, the first sentence may need to be agreed in advance. The couple is not trying to create the perfect repair ritual. They are trying to reduce predictable harm. The protocol should evolve when real use reveals where it fails.

Digital communication deserves special caution because it can intensify style differences. The word-needing person may send more messages to reduce anxiety. The space-needing person may stop replying to reduce pressure. The screen then becomes the worst possible bridge: too much access for one person, too little reassurance for the other. A one-line return confirmation can help because it gives information without inviting a written trial. "I am still coming back at eight." "I need space and I will call after work." "I care about this; I cannot text it well." These lines should be plain, unsarcastic, and brief. Their purpose is not persuasion. Their purpose is containment.

The protocol also reduces shame because it normalises difference without excusing harm. The person who needs words is not "too much"; they need enough connection to wait. The person who needs space is not "cold"; they need enough room to return well. Once both styles have a legitimate place, the couple can stop arguing about whose nervous system is morally correct. The question becomes more practical and more compassionate: what sequence protects us from turning our coping styles into weapons?

The bridge is strongest when each person carries the part that stretches them. The word-needing person practises receiving brief reassurance without forcing a full conversation before the other is ready. The space-needing person practises giving clear reassurance and a reliable return rather than vanishing into silence. Each gives something. Each receives something. That reciprocity prevents the protocol from becoming a demand issued by the more distressed person or an escape route controlled by the more avoidant one.

A shared repair protocol will still feel awkward at first. The first attempts may sound stiff. Someone may forget the return line. Someone may ask for too many words or take too much space. This does not mean the bridge has failed. It means the old route is well worn and the new one still needs footfall. The test is not whether the sequence feels natural immediately. The test is whether it reduces the secondary fight about the process itself. Less chasing. Less vanishing. Less arguing about arguing. More return.

The forward test is whether the next rupture can begin with a bridge rather than a battle over repair style. Can one person say, "I need words," without flooding? Can the other say, "I need space," without disappearing? Can a single text line hold the return time without becoming evidence in another argument? The original hurt will still need attention, but the couple will have stopped losing precious energy to the question of how to begin. Repair becomes more possible when the crossing is already there.

Repairing in Texts and Messages

On 19 September 1982, at Carnegie Mellon University in Pittsburgh, computer scientist Scott Fahlman suggested using the character sequence :-) to mark jokes in online bulletin-board messages and :-(for messages that were not jokes. The proposal was modest, almost playful, but the problem underneath it was serious enough to endure: typed words travel without the full human body. No face. No timing of breath. No softening glance. A sentence meant lightly can arrive like a blade.

The same problem now sits in the palm of the hand. A conflict begins with one line: "Fine." Or, "Do whatever you want." Or, "Interesting that you only mention this now." The message is short, but the meaning expands inside the reader. Is it irritation, resignation, contempt, tiredness, fear, sarcasm, or a badly chosen word sent between tasks? The screen does not say. The body fills in the missing parts, often from old injury rather than present evidence. The thumb hovers. The next reply is already hotter.

Digital repair is difficult because messages create the illusion of control while stripping away much of the information that makes repair humane. A person can edit, delete, rewrite, and choose punctuation with surgical care, but the receiver still reads through mood, history, timing, and expectation. A full stop may feel cold. A delayed reply may feel punitive. A long paragraph may feel like prosecution. A short reply may feel like dismissal. The text is fixed; the interpretation is alive. That mismatch is where escalation breeds.

The first rule of repair by message is to know when the medium has become too thin for the weight of the subject. Text can carry a brief acknowledgement, a return time, a small apology, or a clarification of intent. It is poor at carrying tone-sensitive repair, layered hurt, repeated patterns, shame, fear, or anything that requires immediate correction of misunderstanding. The more emotional density the conflict carries, the more dangerous the screen becomes. A message can hold a thread. It should not be asked to hold the whole bridge.

Communication theorists Richard Daft and Robert Lengel introduced media richness theory in 1986, arguing that different communication channels vary in their ability to handle ambiguity, feedback, tone, and complexity. The theory belongs to organisational communication, not intimate repair, but its basic insight travels well. A typed message is lean compared with voice or face-to-face conversation. It can be efficient when the meaning is clear. It can be hazardous when the meaning is disputed. Repair usually requires richness: timing, warmth, pauses, correction, and the chance to hear how a sentence lands before it hardens.

The moment to stop typing often arrives before people want to stop. One sign is speed: replies are coming faster than thought can examine them. Another is quotation: one person begins copying phrases back as evidence. Another is sarcasm, especially the kind that looks clever on the screen and cruel in the body. Another is widening scope: the message that began about a missed call now contains last month, last year, family history, and a full account of who always cares more. When the thread becomes a trial, the repair has already left the medium.

Screenshots are the emblem of that trial. Once people begin imagining how the exchange would look if shown to a friend, a sibling, a therapist, or a future version of the argument, the conversation has become performative. The words are no longer only addressed to the person in the thread; they are being preserved as exhibits. This does not mean written records are always wrong or that serious matters should never be documented. It means that intimate repair suffers when each person starts writing for the archive rather than the relationship. The aim changes from understanding to evidentiary advantage.

A short repair message should reduce ambiguity, not win the point. "I can see that landed badly. I do not want to repair this by text. Can we speak later?" is useful because it recognises impact, names the limit of the medium, and creates a path back. "I am getting defensive and I do not want to type something careless" does the same work from the inside. "I care about this. I need a pause, and I will call after dinner" gives reassurance and a return. None of these messages settles the conflict. That is their strength. They keep the bridge visible without pretending the bridge is the whole road.

The worst repair messages often contain sarcasm disguised as restraint. "Well, I am sorry I am such a terrible person." "Thanks for making that clear." "Good to know." "I guess I will just never speak again." These lines may feel satisfying to send because they compress hurt into style. But style becomes poison quickly in text. Without face, voice, or immediate repair, sarcasm expands. The receiver is left with the sharpest possible reading, and the sender can later claim they were "just saying". Text preserves plausible deniability while deepening injury. Avoiding sarcasm is not politeness. It is damage control.

Kristin Byron's 2008 review on emotion in email communication is useful here because it examined how people often misinterpret emotional tone in lean digital channels, especially when cues are absent and receivers rely on their own expectations. The relevance to repair is plain. A person may believe their message is measured, but the other reads coldness. A person may intend brevity as containment, but the other reads indifference. A person may intend a delayed reply as carefulness, but the other reads punishment. Digital repair requires humility about how easily tone is lost.

One clean rule is to use text for logistics around repair, not for the full repair when the subject is hot. Logistics means: naming a pause, confirming a return, asking whether voice is possible, giving a brief acknowledgement, or clarifying that silence is not abandonment. "I am not ignoring you. I am too activated to text well. I will call at seven." "I hear that this hurt. I want to speak, not type, because I do not want to misread you." "I need space, and I am coming back." These messages are small. They are also protective. They stop the screen from becoming the room where everything must be solved.

There is a credible limitation. Text can be safer or more accessible for some people in some circumstances. A person may need time to choose words, may become overwhelmed in live conversation, may use written language to avoid interruption, or may need a written record for clarity. Voice or in-person repair is not automatically superior in every case. The issue is not that text is morally inferior. The issue is whether the medium supports the kind of repair required. A brief written impact statement may help. A spiralling exchange of accusations at midnight usually will not.

The reconciliation is to match the medium to the repair task. Use text when the task is simple, bounded, and low in ambiguity. Move to voice or in-person when tone, intent, impact, pattern, apology, or agreement needs careful handling. If the relationship has a history of text escalation, the boundary should be set before the next rupture: once either person says the thread is heating, the conversation pauses and moves to a richer medium. The rule is not an escape hatch. It is a guardrail. The issue will still be addressed; it will not be fed to the least forgiving channel.

Short repair messages work best when they carry four quiet elements: acknowledgement, care, limit, return. "I see that my reply sounded dismissive. I care about this. I cannot repair it properly while typing between meetings. I will call after work." The order matters because it prevents the limit from sounding like rejection. A limit without care can feel cold. Care without a return can feel vague. A return without acknowledgement can feel procedural. The message should be plain enough that it cannot easily be mistaken for a tactic.

Timing matters as much as wording. A repair message sent too soon may be defensive. A message sent too late may leave the other person alone with a story that hardens. The useful window is often after enough regulation to avoid a careless reply, but before silence becomes its own injury. This does not require an immediate full answer. It may require a holding line: "I have seen this. I want to answer carefully, and I will come back to it tonight." Such a message gives the waiting person something better than a blank screen. It also gives the sender time not to react from threat.

The person receiving a holding message must also respect the boundary if it has been offered in good faith. Sending seven more messages after someone has said they cannot text well turns the thread into pursuit. The anxiety may be understandable, but the effect is pressure. If reassurance is needed, the agreement can include one brief confirmation: "Still coming back later?" The reply can be equally brief: "Yes." Beyond that, the repair waits. A boundary only works if both people honour the fact that waiting is part of the repair, not a failure of it.

Digital repair is especially vulnerable to the false clarity of written words. Because the message is visible, people assume the meaning is obvious. "Read what you wrote." "That is exactly what you said." But written words do not contain all of their context. The sender's tone may be missing; the receiver's history may be active; the timing may have changed the message. This does not excuse harmful writing. It simply means that repair should avoid treating the screen as a perfect witness. The message is evidence of wording, not full evidence of intention, impact, or emotional state.

A practical example shows the safer route. One person texts, "You forgot again." The other reads accusation and wants to reply, "Maybe because I am doing everything else." The old thread would escalate. A repair-oriented reply might say, "I hear that you feel let down. I am getting defensive, and text will make this worse. I will call after I finish work." If a practical commitment is needed, it can be added without argument: "I will also send the form before then."

The message acknowledges impact, prevents the counterattack, and moves the repair to a better channel.

Another example belongs to delayed replies. One person writes something vulnerable and receives no answer for hours. By the time the reply comes, the silence has become part of the injury. A cleaner habit is a brief holding message: "I want to answer this properly. I cannot do it while I am with people, but I will reply when I am home." This small act prevents absence from being interpreted as indifference. It does not require constant availability. It requires respect for the meaning silence can acquire after hurt.

Long messages deserve suspicion when the body is activated. They often feel productive to the sender because they organise the case. To the receiver, they may feel like being cornered by paragraphs. The longer the message, the more likely it contains mixed material: apology, defence, accusation, history, interpretation, correction, and demand. A good digital repair often becomes shorter as it becomes cleaner. "I am sorry I wrote that sharply. I want to speak when we can both do this better." This may repair more than a thousand-word defence with an apology hidden near the end.

There are times when writing can help if it is used before, not during, the exchange. A person may draft what they want to say and then choose what should actually be sent. The draft can hold the heat; the sent message should carry only what helps repair. This distinction is important. The phone may be used as a notebook without becoming a weapon. Write the full argument elsewhere if needed. Send the bridge. Not every true sentence deserves transmission while the relationship is flammable.

The digital bridge should avoid ambiguity where ambiguity is likely to injure. "Later" may be too vague. "I will call after dinner" is better. "I need space" may be too open-ended. "I need space and I will text at nine to set a time to talk" is clearer. "We need to talk" may sound ominous. "I want to repair what happened earlier" is more grounded. Specificity reduces the amount of meaning the other person has to invent. After conflict, invention tends towards fear.

Sarcasm should be treated as a stop sign. If the next message would be sarcastic, stop typing. If the message includes "fine" when fine is not meant, stop typing. If the point of the message is to make the other person feel guilty for not already understanding, stop typing. If the message is being shaped for how it will look in a screenshot, stop typing. These are not rules of etiquette. They are signs that the medium has become part of the escalation.

A short repair message can also acknowledge a misread without surrendering every point. "I think my last message sounded colder than I meant. I was trying to pause, not dismiss you." This gives intent as context without arguing the other person out of impact. "I can see how 'whatever' sounded dismissive. I should not have sent it that way." This names the behaviour. "I am too upset to keep texting respectfully, and I do not want to make this worse" sets a boundary without contempt. Each message reduces harm by removing ambiguity and refusing the pleasures of the sharp reply.

The bridge motif becomes literal in digital repair. A message should help people cross from heat to conversation, not become the place where they set up camp and throw stones. A bridge has direction. It gets you somewhere else: to a call, a calmer hour, an in-person conversation, a return to impact and agreement. If the text thread is not moving towards repair, it is probably moving towards evidence. That is the moment to leave the bridge before it turns into a courtroom.

The person who dislikes texting should not weaponise that preference by ignoring messages. A dislike of digital conflict is legitimate. Silence without explanation is still costly. "I do not want to do this by text" becomes repair only when paired with a return: "I will call later." The person who prefers texting should not weaponise the written word by sending long arguments the other cannot process well. "I need to write to think" becomes repair only when the writing is used to clarify, not overwhelm. Each style needs a boundary.

Professional relationships carry the same risks. An email reply written in haste can sound dismissive for days because it sits in the inbox unchanged. A chat thread can escalate because each person responds between meetings and misreads brevity as contempt. A clean professional repair might say, "My last message was too abrupt. I was trying to flag the deadline, not dismiss your concern. Let us speak before this becomes a longer thread." The principle is the same: use the message to reduce ambiguity and move to a richer exchange when needed.

The forward test is whether the next tense message can remain a bridge rather than becoming an exhibit. Does it acknowledge impact without sarcasm? Does it name a limit without disappearing? Does it set a return rather than leaving silence to harden? Does it move the repair towards voice or presence when the subject has become too heavy for text? The screen will always invite speed, certainty, and the small cruelty of the perfectly typed line. Repair asks for a slower courage: send the sentence that keeps the connection possible, then stop typing before the thread becomes the trial.

Chapter 12
Keeping Repair as a Habit

The argument is small enough to dismiss. A clipped answer while shoes are being put away. A message read and left unanswered. A sigh at the wrong moment. Neither person wants to make a ceremony of it, and both are tired of treating ordinary friction as if it were a crisis. So the moment is passed over. Dinner is made, the bin is taken out, the evening moves on. Yet somewhere under the surface, a tiny entry has been made in the private ledger.

By morning, the household may look peaceful. The sentence has not been repeated. Nobody has raised their voice. The practical day resumes with all its familiar evidence of cooperation. But a small residue remains: a little less softness in the greeting, a little more caution before asking for help, a little more readiness to hear criticism where none was intended. Minor ruptures rarely announce themselves as important. They become important when they are allowed to collect.

Repair becomes a habit when it stops depending on drama. If repair is reserved only for the obvious explosion, then the quiet injuries keep finding storage. A habit does not mean turning every irritation into a formal conversation. It means creating a light, recognisable way to check the small places where warmth has snagged. The act should be ordinary enough to use often and respectful enough not to feel trivial. A relationship that knows how to repair small friction does not have to wait for resentment to become articulate.

The central tension is that repair must become normal without becoming heavy. Too little attention, and hurts are stockpiled until the next conflict arrives carrying old material. Too much attention, and the relationship begins to feel over-managed, as if every awkward tone requires inspection. The art is proportion. A brief ritual after friction can lower dread because both people know what happens next: the moment is named, the impact is checked, the next small adjustment is made, and ordinary life is allowed to continue without pretending nothing happened.

The stakes are immediate because predictable repair changes the meaning of conflict. When people do not know whether a hurt will be acknowledged, they often become louder, colder, or more guarded. When they know there is a simple route back, they do not have to make the injury larger in order to be taken seriously. The visible evidence is plain: fewer trailing silences, fewer sarcastic aftershocks, fewer old grievances smuggled into new conversations. Repair as a habit gives the relationship a broom for the daily crumbs, not only a rescue team for the fire.

The stakes deepen because no one repairs perfectly. A person will still interrupt after promising not to. Someone will still pause badly, forget the return time, send the sharp message, over-explain intent, or apologise with more self-protection than they intended. If every missed repair becomes proof of failure, shame takes over and the old pattern hardens. A sustainable repair habit needs a way back from the botched attempt itself: name the miss, return to the impact, remake the agreement. Direction matters more than purity. The relationship is not kept alive by flawless conduct, but by recoverable conduct.

The work ahead is to make repair predictable, resilient, and honest about its limits. A lightweight ritual turns small friction into a normal check rather than a dreaded confrontation. Setbacks are treated as part of learning the skill, not as evidence that the skill is impossible. And some patterns must be recognised as needing more support than quick repair can provide: repeated contempt, fear, an inability to pause safely, or a rupture that keeps returning with greater force. Seeking help, in that context, is not a verdict of failure. It is a refusal to let the relationship keep injuring itself without better tools.

A small broom is the right image for this final movement. It is not dramatic. It does not rebuild the house. It does not prove that dust will never return. It is simply kept within reach because life creates mess, and leaving every small spill unattended eventually changes the room. Repair as a habit works in the same humble way. It asks people to sweep before the floor becomes dangerous, to notice before resentment thickens, to return before distance starts to feel normal.

The unresolved question is whether repair can become part of the relationship's ordinary maintenance rather than an emergency measure used only when pain becomes impossible to ignore. Can two people make it normal to say, "That landed badly," without fear of starting a war? Can they restart after a clumsy repair without sinking into blame? Can they recognise when the broom is no longer enough and bring in stronger support without shame? The final test of repair is not whether conflict disappears. It is whether the relationship has learned what to do next when friction inevitably appears.

Building a Repair Ritual

In 1906, William James published *The Energies of Men* after decades of work at Harvard on habit, attention, and the practical architecture of human conduct. James was not writing about couples repairing after a clipped answer in the kitchen, yet his larger insight remains bracing: what people repeat becomes easier to repeat. Character is not built only by grand decisions. It is shaped by small acts made familiar. Small frictions gather in silence.

A relationship without a repair ritual often waits too long. Someone sighs in a way that lands badly. Someone answers a message with unnecessary sharpness. Someone turns away when a gentler response was possible. Neither wants to start a serious conversation, so the moment is folded away. The day continues, but the atmosphere is fractionally altered. The next request is made with less ease. The next silence is interpreted less generously. The issue was minor; the storage was not.

A repair ritual makes repair normal rather than exceptional. It does not mean dragging every irritation into a heavy emotional summit. It means giving small ruptures a known route back into connection before they become private evidence. The routine should be light enough to use often: notice the snag, name it without drama, check the impact, make one small adjustment, and return to ordinary life. The value lies not in ceremony but in predictability. When people know what happens after friction, dread has less room to invent a catastrophe.

The word ritual can sound too formal, but the best repair rituals are almost domestic in scale. A couple might have a phrase that means, "Something landed badly; let us check it before it grows." A family might use a short evening pause to clear small misunderstandings before they harden overnight. Colleagues might end a tense meeting by asking whether anything needs cleaning up before the next decision. The ritual is not a performance of emotional sophistication. It is a broom kept within reach. Nobody praises the broom for existing. They simply use it before the floor becomes unsafe.

The work of John Gottman and his colleagues on couple interaction is useful here because it gives serious attention to small repair attempts: gestures, phrases, humour, softening, and acknowledgements that change the direction of conflict. The important point is not that every pair must adopt research vocabulary. It is that repair often succeeds through modest, recognisable moves made at the right time. "That came out sharper than I meant." "Can I redo that?" "I think I missed you just now." These sentences are short because the ritual is meant to interrupt accumulation, not open a trial.

A ritual reduces dread because it removes some uncertainty from the aftermath of friction. Without a routine, the injured person may wonder whether naming a small hurt will create defensiveness, distance, mockery, or a long evening of analysis. The person who caused the impact may wonder whether any acknowledgement will become an endless prosecution. Predictability changes the emotional cost. If both people understand that a small check-in is brief, bounded, and practical, the threshold for repair drops. A hurt can be named while it is still small enough to handle cleanly.

The check-in should begin with the moment, not the whole relationship. "When I answered quickly just then, did that land badly?" is easier to receive than "Are we okay?" and far easier than "You always take things the wrong way." The first sentence points to a specific exchange. It gives the other person permission to say, "Yes, it felt dismissive," without having to produce a full case. A ritual works because it keeps the unit of repair small. The smaller the unit, the less threatening the repair.

Impact then needs a brief place to stand. The person affected may say, "It felt like you were irritated with me," or "I felt brushed off," or "I was trying to tell you something and lost the thread." This is not the moment to prove intent at length. It is a moment to let the effect be known. The responsible person may answer, "I can see that. I was rushed, and I spoke too sharply." If more is needed, more can be scheduled. But many small ruptures are repaired by accurate recognition before they require larger treatment.

The ritual should include one practical adjustment. Without adjustment, repair becomes emotional housekeeping with no behavioural consequence. The adjustment might be a redo: "Ask me again; I will answer properly." It might be a small pause: "Let me put the phone down before you continue." It might be a boundary: "Let us not start this while one of us is halfway out of the door." The action should match the scale of the moment. A small spill does not require rebuilding the kitchen. It does require wiping the surface before someone leans on it.

The work of Peter Gollwitzer on implementation intentions, especially research from the 1990s, offers a useful frame for making such rituals reliable. When people connect a cue with a response, they are more likely to act when the cue appears. In repair, the cue might be a changed face, a clipped tone, a familiar silence, or the sentence, "That landed badly." The response is pre-decided: pause, check impact, own the part that is clear, and make one adjustment. The ritual works because it is not invented from scratch while both people are already activated.

There is a credible limitation. Some relationships can over-ritualise repair until every ordinary misattunement feels monitored. If a person must account for every sigh, every pause, every imperfect tone, the relationship may become anxious rather than safe. A repair ritual should lower pressure, not turn daily life into a performance review. Not every awkward moment needs analysis. Some need generosity. Some need sleep. Some need the humility to let ordinary human imperfection pass without making it part of a pattern.

The reconciliation lies in proportion. A repair ritual is most useful when a moment has left a noticeable residue: a face has changed, warmth has dropped, someone has gone quiet, a sentence keeps echoing, or the same small injury has appeared before. The ritual should be brief enough that it does not punish honesty and specific enough that it does not become vague emotional checking. Its purpose is not to eliminate friction. Its purpose is to keep friction from becoming a hidden account.

Stockpiling grievances is one of the quietest ways relationships become heavy. No single item seems worth naming, so each is stored privately. The late reply, the distracted nod, the interrupted sentence, the joke that stung, the forgotten return after space: all of it goes into the ledger. Later, when a larger conflict appears, the ledger opens. The current disagreement is suddenly crowded with old entries. The other person feels ambushed. The injured person feels forced to prove that the present hurt has a history. A repair ritual prevents some of this by giving small hurts a short shelf life.

The broom motif matters because daily repair is humble work. It is not glamorous to say, "I think I was brusque just now." It is not dramatic to ask, "Do we need to clean that up?" Yet these small acts preserve the floor on which larger trust stands. A relationship that never sweeps must eventually explain why the room feels unliveable. A relationship that sweeps constantly, anxiously, and ceremonially may exhaust itself. The skill is keeping the broom near without making everyone stare at it.

A brief ritual also protects against the fantasy that good relationships should not need repair. This fantasy is destructive because it turns every rupture into evidence of inadequacy. Mature connection is not the absence of misattunement. It is the ability to notice misattunement early and respond without panic. A couple who can say, "That was off; let us reset," is not less stable than a couple who never names anything. They may be more stable because their bond does not depend on pretending friction has not occurred.

The ritual should be easy to begin. If starting repair requires perfect language, people will avoid it. A simple opener is enough: "Can we clean that up?" "I think I missed you there." "That sounded sharper than I wanted." "Did that land badly?" These are not magic phrases; they are doors. Their power lies in how quickly they move the moment from private interpretation into shared attention. Once the door opens, the exchange can remain small.

It should also be easy to end. Repair rituals fail when they have no exit. If every check-in becomes a long examination of motives, childhood, fairness, history, and emotional availability, people will avoid the ritual to preserve their evening. A clean ending might sound like, "All right, that helps," or "Thank you for naming it," or "Let us try that again." Ending does not mean the issue was trivial. It means the repair matched the scale of the rupture. Larger patterns can still be addressed elsewhere. The ritual is for small friction before it grows teeth.

A domestic example shows the ritual at work. One person asks a practical question about tomorrow morning, and the other answers with irritation because they are tired. The first person goes quiet. In an unrepaired pattern, the silence might last through dinner and appear later as resentment. In a ritualised repair, the person who snapped notices the shift and says, "That came out sharp. Did it feel like I was annoyed with you?" The answer comes: "Yes, a bit. I was only trying to check the plan." The repair is simple: "You were right to ask. Let me answer properly." The whole exchange may take less than a minute. Its effect may last far longer.

A professional version is equally useful. After a tense exchange in a meeting, a colleague might say, "I cut across you when you were explaining the risk. Before we move on, I want to make sure your point is heard." That small ritual prevents the colleague from having to decide later whether to raise the slight, let it go, or quietly disengage. It also signals to the group that repair is normal, not humiliating. In teams as in households, dread decreases when people know small ruptures can be cleaned up without theatre.

The ritual must remain voluntary enough to be sincere. If one person uses it as a demand -- "Now do the repair phrase" -- it may become another form of control. The point is to create a shared habit, not a compulsory script. Scripts can help early on, but they should eventually become natural language. A repair ritual is alive when people can adapt it to the moment and still preserve the essentials: notice, name, hear, adjust, return.

Handling resistance is part of building the habit. Some people feel embarrassed by quick repair because it exposes vulnerability in real time. Some fear that naming a small impact will make them seem fragile. Others fear that acknowledging a small mistake will invite more criticism. The ritual must therefore prove itself through gentleness. If small repair is met with sarcasm, punishment, or a lecture, it will not survive. If it is met with proportion, gratitude, and brevity, it becomes easier to use again.

A repair ritual also requires remembering that not every check-in must be symmetrical. Sometimes one person caused the small impact and the other received it. Sometimes both contributed. Sometimes the best repair is one person saying, "That was mine." Forcing equality into every minor rupture can become evasive. The ritual should honour proportion. If the harm was one-sided, the repair should not be diluted into "we both did things." If both were sharp, both can own a part. Precision keeps the ritual trustworthy.

Over time, the ritual changes the emotional meaning of friction. A bad tone no longer automatically predicts a cold evening. A missed cue no longer becomes proof of indifference. A small silence no longer has to gather allies in memory. The relationship begins to know that small repair is available. This knowledge does not remove pain; it reduces panic. It allows people to speak earlier, soften faster, and treat mistakes as workable rather than ominous.

The forward test is whether repair can become ordinary without becoming trivial. Can a small hurt be named before it joins the ledger? Can a sharp tone be corrected before it becomes the evening's weather? Can two people use the broom without turning every crumb into a crisis? A repair ritual earns its place when it makes the next act of honesty less frightening: not because conflict has disappeared, but because everyone knows what happens after friction, and the way back is no longer hidden.

Handling Setbacks Without Shame

In 2006, psychologist Carol Dweck published *Mindset*, bringing wider attention to a distinction that had already shaped her research:

people respond differently to mistakes depending on whether they treat ability as fixed or developable. The idea has often been oversimplified, but its central usefulness remains. A mistake can become a verdict, or it can become information. In repair, that difference is not academic. It can decide whether a botched apology becomes another wound or the beginning of a better return.

The setback usually arrives with a wince. Someone had meant to repair cleanly, then defended. Someone had promised to pause, then interrupted. Someone had agreed to return after taking space, then let the evening disappear. Someone had tried to apologise, but added a "but" that turned the apology into a fresh argument. The room feels heavier because the failure is no longer only the original rupture. It is the disappointment of having tried to do better and missing the mark. That second pain is sharp.

Shame enters quickly here because repair carries moral weight. People do not merely think, "I used the wrong sentence." They think, "I am hopeless at this," or "They will never trust me now," or "We are back where we started." The injured person may feel the same collapse from the other side: "This proves nothing changes." These reactions are understandable, but they are dangerous if they become the story. Shame turns a missed repair into an identity. Once identity takes over, the practical question disappears: what exactly went wrong, and what is the next responsible move?

Handling a setback without shame begins by naming the miss plainly. Not theatrically. Not evasively. Plainly. "I tried to explain my intent before I acknowledged the impact." "I said I needed space, but I did not give you a return time." "I apologised, then I defended myself." "I used the old tone." The sentence should be narrow enough to be useful. "I ruined everything" is not useful. It is a fog. "I interrupted you when you were telling me how it landed" is useful because it identifies the repairable action. The broom returns to the actual spill.

The first discipline is resisting collapse. Collapse can look like remorse, but it often pulls attention away from the harm. "I am terrible at this. I do not know why you bother" asks the injured person to become a comforter before their impact has been met.

The more useful sentence is steadier: "I missed that. I want to come back to what you were saying." It accepts responsibility without making self-punishment the centre. The injured person does not need the responsible person to suffer grandly. They need them to become available again.

The second discipline is resisting blame. When a repair attempt goes badly, the mind searches for an exit. "Well, you kept pushing." "You did not give me time." "You said it in a way that made me defensive." There may be pieces of truth there, but if they arrive first, they repeat the same injury. Blame turns the failed repair into a trial over why the failure was understandable. A better sequence is to own the miss before examining the conditions that made it harder. "I did get defensive. Later, I want to talk about how we can slow down sooner, but I need to return to your impact first."

Returning to impact is what rescues the repair from becoming a conversation about repair performance. The injured person did not begin with a request for the other person to execute a technique perfectly. They named a hurt. If the repair was botched, the path back is not to analyse the botched repair at length while the original hurt waits unattended. The path is to say, "Let me go back. When I left without telling you when I would return, you felt alone and unsure whether I cared enough to come back." The original wound is brought back into view. The repair regains its subject.

The work of June Price Tangney and colleagues on shame and guilt is useful here because it helps separate a global attack on the self from responsibility for behaviour. Guilt can guide repair because it says, "I did something wrong." Shame can derail repair because it says, "I am wrong." A person who is trapped in shame may defend, disappear, or collapse. A person who can bear guilt without becoming swallowed by it can act. In practical terms, the useful question is not "What does this mistake prove about me?" but "What conduct needs correcting now?"

A setback often reveals that the agreement was too vague, too ambitious, or missing a recovery step. If someone promised not to interrupt and then interrupted, the next agreement may not be "I will never interrupt again." It may be, "If I interrupt, I will stop myself and ask you to finish." If someone promised to come back after space and failed, the agreement may need a visible return point: "Before I take space, I will name when I am coming back, and if I cannot meet that time, I will send a short update." Repair improves when a miss becomes design information rather than proof of moral failure.

This is where direction matters more than perfection. Perfection says the only acceptable repair is the flawless one: the right words, the right timing, the right tone, the right response from the other person. Direction asks whether the next movement is closer to accountability, clarity, and care than the old movement was. A person may still stumble while learning to pause before defending. The question is whether they notice sooner, return faster, and repair the secondary injury with less self-protection. Progress often looks like a shorter distance between miss and return.

The repair after a setback can be compact. "I missed that. I defended instead of listening. Let me try again: you felt dismissed when I moved on before you finished, and I am sorry." This sentence does not perform despair. It does not demand applause for trying again. It simply restores the direction of travel. If the injured person is still upset, that does not mean the restart failed. They may need time to believe the correction. A restart is an opening, not an entitlement to immediate warmth.

There is a credible limitation. Not every repeated "setback" deserves endless patience. If someone keeps naming the miss but does not change the behaviour, the language of learning can become another form of avoidance. "I am working on it" may be sincere at first and empty later if no visible adjustment follows. Handling setbacks without shame does not mean lowering the standard until harm becomes routine. It means addressing failure without humiliation so that actual change remains possible. If the same miss keeps returning, the repair must become more specific, not merely more forgiving.

The reconciliation lies in evidence. A trustworthy restart does not only say, "I botched that." It changes the next step. It returns to impact, remakes the agreement, and follows through in a visible way.

If the person who failed to return after space now gives a clear return time and keeps it, the setback has produced learning. If the person who over-explained intent now reflects impact before adding context, the setback has changed the sequence. Evidence protects the process from becoming either shame theatre or hollow optimism.

The injured person also needs a way to respond to a repair setback without turning disappointment into a life sentence. "You did it again; nothing ever changes" may express a real fear, especially after repeated harm, but if used in a repairable situation it can freeze the very movement that needs to continue. A sharper and more workable sentence is, "When the repair turned defensive, it made me less hopeful. I need you to go back to the impact before explaining." That statement is not soft. It names the cost and the next necessary action. It keeps the door open without pretending the setback did not matter.

This does not mean the injured person must become endlessly generous. They may need to say, "I cannot do another round right now," or "I need to see this change, not just hear it named." Those boundaries can be part of repair. What matters is that the boundary describes what is needed rather than becoming a verdict on the other person's entire capacity to change. "I need a pause because this repeat is too much right now" leaves a path. "You are hopeless" burns the path and then mourns the smoke.

A practical example shows the sequence. During a conversation about a missed promise, one partner says, "When you did not come back after saying you needed space, I felt abandoned." The other replies too quickly: "I was exhausted, and you know I cannot talk when you push me." The room tightens. The repair has gone wrong. A shame spiral would say, "Forget it, I am useless at this." A blame spiral would say, "You made me defensive." A restart says, "I just defended. Let me come back. I left you without a return time, and that made the space feel like abandonment. I am sorry. Next time I need space, I will give a return time before I leave."

The difference is not style alone. The restart repairs two layers: the original miss and the botched repair. It does not erase the injured person's frustration. It does not require instant trust. But it gives the conversation a direction again. The broom has not been used to pretend there was no mess. It has been used to stop the mess from spreading into the rest of the house.

The work of James Clear and others in popular habit writing is often invoked around tiny changes, but the deeper idea is older and broader: repeated behaviour becomes easier when the system supports it. In repair, the system must include recovery. If a person only has a plan for perfect execution, the first failure becomes catastrophic. If the plan includes a recovery phrase, a return to impact, and a remade agreement, failure becomes uncomfortable but usable. The skill is not merely "do not miss." The skill is "when you miss, repair the miss."

Setbacks are also easier to handle when the pair distinguishes between a slip and a pattern. A slip is a single missed move in a context where effort and follow-through are otherwise visible. A pattern is a repeated miss that remains unchanged despite recognition. Slips call for quick repair and adjustment. Patterns call for deeper accountability and perhaps more support. Confusing the two causes trouble. Treating every slip as a pattern creates despair. Treating every pattern as a slip creates denial.

A setback may expose that one person agreed to something they did not actually believe they could do. This is not a minor discovery. A false agreement creates false hope. If someone promised, "I will always talk before bed," but they shut down when exhausted, the repair may need honesty: "I agreed because I wanted to reassure you, but I do not think I can do a full conversation late at night. I can do a brief acknowledgement and set a time for the morning." This is not backing out of care. It is replacing an unsustainable promise with a more reliable one.

Another common setback is the apology that becomes self-punishment. The person begins well, then says, "I am such a failure; I always hurt you." The repair derails because the injured person is pulled into managing shame. The restart might sound like, "I am making this about my shame. That is not fair. The impact is that you felt dismissed when I joked about it. I want to stay with that." This is difficult because it requires the person to notice not only the original harm, but the way shame has taken over the repair. That noticing is a sign of maturity.

There is also the setback of premature closure. Someone apologises and then quickly tries to restore normality: a joke, a hug, a change of subject, a practical task. The injured person stiffens. The responsible person may feel rejected. A restart could say, "I think I rushed us into being fine. You may still need more time. I do not want to use warmth to skip the impact." This kind of correction is subtle but important. It teaches the relationship that even reconnection can be adjusted when it has moved too quickly.

Handling setbacks without shame requires a different relationship with the phrase "again." "Again" can be a hammer: "You did this again." It can also be a marker: "This is the point where the pattern appeared again." The first may be necessary when harm is repeated without accountability, but in ordinary repair learning the second is often more useful. It points to the recurring cue. It asks what support was missing. It allows the conversation to move from accusation to design. "Again" becomes a signal to look more closely, not automatically a sentence of doom.

The practical restart has three movements: name the miss, return to impact, remake the agreement. "I interrupted. You were trying to explain why it hurt, and I cut you off. I will listen until you finish, then I will ask one question before I respond." This is enough. It does not need an essay. It does not need a defence of how tired or stressed the speaker was, unless that context later helps prevent the repeat. The restart is clean because it gives the injured person evidence that the direction has changed.

In professional settings, the same principle applies. A manager apologises for cutting someone off, then does it again in the next meeting. Shame might produce an embarrassed silence. Defensiveness might produce a justification about time pressure. A repair restart says, "I cut across you again when you were making the risk point. I said I would make space for it, and I missed that. Please finish now, and I will hold my response until you are done." The correction is immediate, behavioural, and public enough to match the public impact. It restores direction.

The emotional posture is steady humility. Humility says, "I can be wrong and still remain responsible." Shame says, "If I am wrong, I am unbearable." Pride says, "If I am wrong, I must defend." Only humility can restart repair without turning it into another contest. It allows a person to be corrected without disappearing, to feel remorse without demanding comfort, and to adjust without requiring the other person to pretend the miss did not hurt.

The broom motif returns because setbacks are part of maintenance. A broom does not prevent dust. It gives the household a way to respond when dust appears. Repair skills do not prevent every defensive sentence, every sharp tone, every missed return, every awkward reconnection. They give the relationship a way to recover with less damage. The goal is not to keep the floor immaculate. The goal is to keep it from becoming neglected.

The forward test is whether a botched repair can become the next repair, rather than the end of hope. Can the miss be named without collapse? Can the impact be brought back into view without another defence? Can the agreement be remade in a form that is smaller, clearer, and more likely to hold? Perfection is too brittle for real relationships. Direction is sturdier. When repair goes wrong, the decisive question is not whether shame can be avoided entirely, but whether shame will be allowed to take the wheel, or whether the relationship can turn back towards impact, accountability, and the next honest step.

Knowing When More Help Is Needed

In 2014, the National Institute for Health and Care Excellence in England issued guidance on domestic violence and abuse that treated safety, fear, and coercive control as matters requiring more than ordinary communication skill. The context was public health and safeguarding, not the small repair attempts of daily partnership. Still, the distinction is vital. Some relational patterns can be improved by better timing, clearer impact statements, and more accountable apologies. Others are too entrenched, too frightening, or too unequal to be solved by a quick repair conversation at the kitchen table.

The difference is not always obvious from the outside. A couple may look as if they are merely arguing again, when one person is actually monitoring the other's mood before speaking. A family may describe a "communication problem" when the real pattern is contempt that has become routine. Two colleagues may call a conflict "personality clash" when one person is too intimidated to challenge repeated humiliation. The language of repair is useful only when it protects truth. When it is used to make serious harm sound like ordinary friction, it becomes part of the problem.

A repair habit has limits. That sentence is not a defeat; it is a guardrail. The tools in this book are designed for moments where people can still act in good faith, recognise impact, pause without punishment, and return with enough honesty to change the next step. When those conditions are absent, the task changes. The question is no longer simply, "How do we repair this moment?" It becomes, "Do we have enough safety, willingness, and structure to repair this without more support?" That question deserves to be asked plainly.

Repeated contempt is one cue. Contempt is not ordinary irritation. It shows itself in sneering, mocking, eye-rolling, disgusted tone, cruel imitation, public belittling, or language that treats the other person as beneath respect. A single contemptuous moment may be repairable if it is named, owned, and changed. A pattern of contempt is different. It does not merely wound; it changes the room in which repair is attempted. The person on the receiving end begins to speak defensively, cautiously, or not at all. Apology becomes difficult because dignity has already been made unstable.

Fear is another cue, and it should be taken seriously even when no one has raised their voice. If a person edits normal requests because they are afraid of the reaction, avoids certain subjects to prevent punishment, feels unable to disagree, or worries about what will happen if they ask for space, the relationship is no longer operating within ordinary repair conditions. Fear narrows choice. It turns communication into risk management. A person cannot practise healthy repair while also calculating how to avoid the other person's anger, withdrawal, retaliation, or ridicule.

An inability to pause safely is a quieter but important signal. Repair depends on the possibility of stopping before harm escalates. If one person follows the other from room to room, blocks a pause, floods the phone with messages after a boundary has been named, or uses a pause to disappear for long periods without return, the repair process itself has become unsafe. Space must not become abandonment, and closeness must not become pursuit without consent. When neither person can create a pause that protects both autonomy and connection, outside structure may be needed.

Another cue is the repeated failure of agreements that have been clearly made. If a person repeatedly promises to return after space and does not, repeatedly agrees not to share private details and does, repeatedly apologises for contempt and then repeats it, or repeatedly says they will stop escalating by text and continues, the issue is no longer only wording. The pattern is showing that ordinary repair is not changing conduct. That does not automatically mean the relationship is hopeless. It does mean the repair method being used is insufficient for the weight it is being asked to carry.

The work of John Gottman and colleagues on couple interaction is often associated with the corrosive role of contempt in relationship conflict. The point here is not to reduce intimate life to a checklist, but to respect what repeated contempt reveals: a relationship cannot be repaired only by better phrasing if one person's basic regard for the other keeps collapsing. Repair needs a minimum moral climate. Without that, even good techniques become brittle. "I hear your impact" means little if the next exchange returns to humiliation.

Outside help should therefore be framed not as a verdict of failure, but as a commitment to better conditions. A couple may need a skilled third party because their conversations escalate too quickly for either to interrupt alone. A family may need support because old roles take over before current reality can be heard. An individual may need private support because their threat response is so strong that they cannot stay present without collapsing, defending, or attacking.

Seeking help can be an act of loyalty to the relationship's future, provided the help chosen is safe, appropriate, and honest about the pattern.

This framing matters because shame often delays support. People tell themselves that needing help means they are weak, broken, immature, or incompatible. They compare their private difficulty with the polished surfaces of other people's lives and decide they should be able to solve it alone. That pride can be costly. A skilled outside perspective may see the loop sooner, slow the pace, protect the quieter person's voice, challenge the person who dominates the room, and distinguish mutual misunderstanding from harm that requires firmer boundaries. Support is not magic. It is structure.

There is a credible limitation. Outside help is not automatically helpful merely because it is outside. Poorly chosen support can deepen problems, especially if it minimises fear, treats coercive behaviour as equal "communication difficulty", or encourages premature reconciliation where safety has not been established. Informal support can also distort the picture if friends or relatives hear only one side and become an audience for grievance rather than a source of clarity. The question is not simply whether help is external. The question is whether it increases truth, safety, accountability, and the capacity to choose.

The reconciliation is discernment. More help is needed when the repair system cannot protect people from the pattern it is trying to address. If the same conversation repeatedly ends in contempt, fear, intimidation, disappearance, or emotional collapse, the solution is not just a better sentence. If one person cannot speak honestly without consequence, the issue is not just timing. If attempts to pause make the conflict more dangerous, the issue is not just regulation. Quick repair belongs to relationships where the basic conditions of respect remain reachable. When those conditions are not reachable, the repair must become more supported, more structured, and sometimes more protective.

The small broom motif returns here with humility. A broom is useful for daily dust, crumbs, and ordinary spills. It is not enough when the ceiling leaks or the floorboards are unsafe. To keep sweeping while the structure fails is not diligence; it is denial. In the same way, a repair ritual can clear minor friction, reset after clumsy words, and prevent grievances from gathering. It cannot carry the full burden of fear, contempt, coercion, or repeated betrayal without stronger intervention.

Sometimes the cue for more help is not dramatic harm, but exhaustion. Two people may still care, still try, still apologise, and still find themselves unable to move the pattern. They know the words. They understand the loop. They can identify the trigger afterwards. Yet in the moment, the old sequence wins. This kind of stuckness deserves respect. It does not mean the effort has been false. It means the pattern has more force than the current tools. A new structure may be needed so the repair can happen earlier, slower, and with less threat.

The language used to propose help matters. "We need counselling because you are impossible" will likely deepen shame or defence. "I think we need support because our repairs keep turning into the same fight" is cleaner. "I want us to get help with this pattern before we do more damage" frames support as protection rather than prosecution. The wording should avoid making outside help a punishment. It should also avoid making it a vague gesture with no accountability. The aim is not to outsource the relationship, but to strengthen the conditions under which both people can take responsibility.

The person who is more eager for help should also beware of using outside support as a way to win. If the hidden hope is, "A professional will finally prove that I am right," the process begins with a trial mentality. The better hope is, "We need a safer place to see the pattern clearly and practise a different response." That distinction changes the whole posture. Support is most useful when it is not recruited as a judge, but engaged as a structure for truth and repair.

There are moments when the need for help belongs first to one person rather than the pair. Someone may recognise that their anger escalates too quickly, that shame makes them disappear, that fear makes them pursue, that old experiences are flooding current conflict, or that they cannot hear impact without becoming defensive. Individual work can be an act of accountability when it is used to change conduct, not to produce better explanations for it. "I need help learning to stay present without attacking" is a serious repair sentence. It points towards skill rather than excuse.

The injured person may also need support to trust their own perception. If repeated minimising has made them doubt whether contempt is really contempt, whether fear is really fear, whether a boundary is reasonable, or whether every injury is somehow their fault, outside perspective can restore moral clarity. Repair requires a person to know what has happened to them. If the relationship has trained them to mistrust their own reading of impact, private support may be necessary before shared repair can even be honest.

A professional or structured setting can also help protect against the familiar problem of unequal pace. One person talks quickly and persuasively. The other needs time and loses access to words under pressure. In ordinary conflict, the faster speaker may control the story without intending to. A skilled facilitator can slow the exchange, make room for the quieter person, and prevent eloquence from being mistaken for accuracy. This is one reason more help may be needed even when neither person is malicious. The pattern may be unfair because the process favours one style.

Still, outside help should not be romanticised. It does not remove the need for daily follow-through. A person can attend sessions, learn concepts, understand their childhood, map their loop, and still fail to return after a pause. Insight without conduct becomes another form of eloquence. The real test remains ordinary: Does contempt reduce? Does fear lessen? Are pauses safer? Are agreements remembered? Are apologies cleaner? Does the person who was harmed feel more able to speak truth without bracing for punishment? Support is valuable when it helps these daily behaviours change.

The final reminder is simple and demanding: repair is a skill. Skills are learned through attention, repetition, feedback, and adjustment. Nobody becomes fluent by wanting fluency. Nobody repairs well by merely hating conflict or longing for closeness. Skill means recognising impact, regulating before speaking, clarifying intent without defence, apologising with content, making small agreements, interrupting loops, bridging style differences, and returning after mistakes. Some people learn these skills in ordinary life with practice. Some need more support because the pattern is older, hotter, or heavier than quick repair can hold.

Knowing when more help is needed is itself part of the skill. It requires the humility to admit that care alone may not be enough, the honesty to distinguish repairable friction from unsafe patterns, and the courage to seek structure before damage becomes normal. The forward test is not whether a relationship can avoid ever needing help. It is whether the people inside it can recognise the moment when the broom is no longer enough, and choose something stronger not because the relationship has failed, but because it still matters enough to protect.

About the Author

Kaia Solander writes about the small, human moments that decide whether relationships harden or heal. Her work is grounded in the belief that connection is not sustained by grand gestures, but by the ordinary courage to return, name what happened, and try again with clearer care. She is drawn to practical language: the exact sentence that prevents a spiral, the short question that turns a fight into an agreement, the follow-through that makes an apology believable.

Her perspective is shaped by lived experience of close relationships under everyday pressure - busy households, mixed communication styles, and the particular ache of a misunderstanding that could have been repaired in five minutes but instead lasted for days. She writes for readers who want to be accountable without being crushed by guilt, and honest without being harsh.

Kaia's approach carries a quiet historical thread: the long tradition of reconciliation through deliberate words, from handwritten notes that bridged family rifts to the post-war emphasis on rebuilding trust one neighbourly act at a time. She brings that same spirit into modern life, where the speed of communication often outpaces the care of it. Her mission is simple: make repair doable, repeatable, and respectful, so love has a chance to outlast a bad moment.

www.ingramcontent.com/pod-product-compliance
Lightning Source LLC
LaVergne TN
LVHW100726061126
851857LV00011B/418
* 9 7 8 9 3 0 9 3 3 3 5 5 2 *